TOEIC® テスト
新形式問題
やり込みドリル

ヒロ前田／ロス・タロック

はじめに

「新しいTOEICテストの特徴をヒトコトで言うと？」

　ある雑誌のライターから受けた質問です。2016年2月のことでした。新形式による実際のテストが始まる前でしたが、ボクはこう答えました。「単語からストーリーへ」と。2016年4月以前の出題形式に比べると、5月以降は「ストーリーの理解」が成功の鍵を握るという意味です。

　実際、2016年5月以降の公開テストと、韓国で発売されているETS制作の問題集を調べてみると、「ストーリーの理解」を求める設問が明らかに増えています（詳細は省きますが、これは「項目別正答率」にも色濃く表れています）。そこで、次の2つの視点を重視して本書を設計しました。

1. ストーリーの理解が求められる設問をたくさん収録する

　本書には本番と同じ形式の練習問題が249問も収録されており、「意図問題」「文選択問題」「位置選択問題」といった、ストーリーの理解が絶対に必要となる設問が大量に詰まっています。さらに、初級者から上級者まで多くの受験者がミスしがちな「同義語問題」を大量に収録しました。2016年5月以降の公開テストにおいて、Part 7の「同義語問題」が急増したからです。「同義語問題」は、与えられた文脈における単語やフレーズの意味を問う形式ですから、「単語からストーリーへ」という新傾向に見事に合致します。

2. 受験者が苦手意識を持つ問題タイプを徹底的に扱う

　ボクはセミナーを開催するたびに、参加者が抱える不安に耳を傾けてきました。その結果、Part 3、Part 4、Part 7に出題される「意図問題」が圧倒的No. 1であることが分かりました。分かった以上、何もしないわけにはいきませんでした。本書には、本編とは別に「3文トレーニング」（P. 65参照）が用意されています。それにより、本書に収録された「意図問題」の総計は、実に105問に及び、実際のテストに換算すると15回分になります。本書でしっかり鍛えれば、近い将来、あなたは「意図問題は楽勝」と感じるようになるでしょう。

　本編と「3文トレーニング」を合わせた、練習問題の総計は321問です。ぜひ、徹底的にやり込んでください。あなたの目標スコア達成を願っています。

第211回TOEIC公開テスト　結果発表の日に
著者代表　ヒロ前田

もくじ

はじめに ……………………………………… 003
TOEIC® テスト はこうなった ……………… 006
付属CDについて ……………………………… 008
ダウンロード特典のご案内 …………………… 010

各パートは「まとめ」「ドリル」「解答・解説」（パートによっては「トレーニング」も）で構成されてます。

Part 3

Part 3のまとめ ……………………………… 012

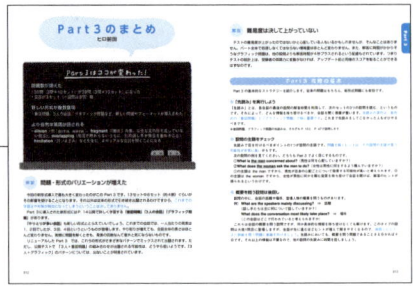

「まとめ」
「アナリスト」を自認するヒロ前田が、独自の切り口で新形式を分析し、基本的な対策を解説します。

①意図問題
「意図問題」はこんな問題！ ………………… 014
ドリル ………………………………………… 016
ドリルの解答・解説 ………………………… 020

②3人の会話
「3人の会話」はこんな形式！ ……………… 032
ドリル ………………………………………… 034
ドリルの解答・解説 ………………………… 036

「ドリル」
出題ページです。同カテゴリーの問題を集中的に解くことにより、形式に慣れて、ストラテジーの実践練習も豊富に行うことができます。

③グラフィック問題
「グラフィック問題」はこんな問題！ ……… 046
ドリル ………………………………………… 048
ドリルの解答・解説 ………………………… 053

3文トレーニングのススメ ………………… 065

3文トレーニング [Part 3編] ……………… 066

「解答・解説」
解答プロセスが見えてくる分かりやすい解説です。復習に欠かせない、英文スクリプト、日本語訳、語注も付いています。

Part 4

Part 4のまとめ ……………………………… 074
ドリル ………………………………………… 076

ドリルの解答・解説 ……………………………… 080
3文トレーニング［Part 4編］ …………………… 092

「3文トレーニング」
意図問題が出題されるPart 3、4、7には、文脈(ストーリー)を把握する力を鍛える特別メニューがあります。

Part 6

Part 6 のまとめ …………………………………… 100
ドリル …………………………………………… 102
ドリルの解答・解説 …………………………… 112

Part 7

Part 7 のまとめ …………………………………… 132

①位置選択問題
「位置選択問題」はこんな問題！ ……………… 134
ドリル …………………………………………… 136
ドリルの解答・解説 …………………………… 144

②チャット系
「チャット系」はこんな形式！ ………………… 154
ドリル …………………………………………… 156
ドリルの解答・解説 …………………………… 164

3文トレーニング［Part 7編］ …………………… 180

③トリプルパッセージ
「トリプルパッセージ」はこんな形式！ ……… 188
ドリル …………………………………………… 190
ドリルの解答・解説 …………………………… 208

解答用紙 …………………………………………… 245

TOEIC® テストはこうなった

TOEIC® Listening & Reading Testは、米国の非営利テスト開発機関 ETS (Educational Testing Service) によって制作されているテストで、英語によるコミュニケーションの能力を測定します。

2015年11月、ETS は10年ぶりとなる出題形式の変更を発表しました。その新形式は、公開テストでは2016年5月29日実施の第210回から導入されました。(IP テストは2017年4月から導入の予定)。試験の実施スケジュール、申し込み方法など最新の情報は、TOEIC(R) テストの公式サイトで確認することができます。

※「TOEIC® テスト」は、2016年8月5日より、「TOEIC Listening & Reading Test」(略称：TOEIC L&R) に名称変更されました。

公式サイト
http:// www.toeic.or.jp/

●変更前との比較

テスト全体の構成を、変更前と変更後で比較してみましょう。

リスニングセクション（100問／約45分間）⇒合計問題数、試験時間は変更なし

変更前

パート	パート名	問題数
Part 1	写真描写問題 Photographs	10問
Part 2	応答問題 Question-Response	30問
Part 3	会話問題 Conversations	30問
Part 4	説明文問題 Talks	30問

変更後（2016年5月以降）

パート名	問題数
写真描写問題 Photographs	6問（−4問）
応答問題 Question-Response	25問（−5問）
会話問題 Conversations (with and without a visual image)	39問（＋9問）
説明文問題 Talks (with and without a visual image)	30問

リーディングセクション（100問／約75分間）⇒合計問題数、試験時間は変更なし

変更前

パート	パート名	問題数
Part 5	短文穴埋め問題 Incomplete Sentences	40問
Part 6	長文穴埋め問題 Text Completion	12問
Part 7	1つの文書 Single passages	28問
Part 7	2つの文書 Double passages	20問

変更後（2016年5月以降）

パート名	問題数
短文穴埋め問題 Incomplete Sentences	30問（−10問）
長文穴埋め問題 Text Completion	16問（＋4問）
1つの文書 Single passages	29問（＋1問）
複数の文書 Multiple passages	25問（＋5問）

●各パートの概要

パートごとに、変更の概要を見ていきましょう。

【Part 1　写真描写問題】
出題数が10問から6問に減った。
出題形式は変更なし。難易度や写真の構成（「人物（1人）」「人物（複数）」「風景（無人）」など、タイプ別に占める割合）に特に変化は見られない。

【Part 2　応答問題】
出題数が30問から25問に減った。
問題タイプ（「Yes/No 疑問文」「WH 疑問文」「付加疑問文」など）の割合に大きな変化は見られない。5問減った分は、各問題タイプからまんべんなく減らされていると見ていい。
言いよどみのような、自然な音声が聞かれるようになったのも、「よりオーセンティックなコミュニケーション」というテーマを反映してのことと思われる。

【Part 3　会話問題】
出題数が30問から39問に増えた（3セット増）。
「意図問題」「3人の会話」「グラフィック問題」など、新しい設問や形式も導入され、最も大きな変更があったパート。言いよどみ、オーバーラッピングなどを含んだ、よりリアルな会話が増える。
★P. 12-15、32-33、46-47に関連記事あり

【Part 4　説明文問題】
出題数は変更なし。
Part 3に導入された「意図問題」「グラフィック問題」が Part 4にも新しく登場する。従来の問題も引き続き出題される。
★P. 74-75に関連記事あり

【Part 5　短文穴埋め問題】
出題数が40問から30問に減った。
全体に占める問題タイプ（「語彙問題」「品詞問題」「動詞問題」など）別の割合に大きな変化はなさそうだ。

【Part 6　長文穴埋め問題】
1セット当たりの設問が3問から4問に増え、パート全体では4問増。
4つある設問のうちの1つは、従来の単語やフレーズではなく、空所に入れるべき「文」を選ぶ問題。
★P. 100-101に関連記事あり

【Part 7　読解問題】
「シングルパッセージ（1つの文書問題）」は文書の数が9から10に増え、設問も28から1問増え29問になった。
設問の数は2つから4つまで。設問が5つ付いたセットは、シングルパッセージからは消滅した。
従来の「ダブルパッセージ（2つの文書問題）」が「マルチプルパッセージ（複数の文書問題）」に変更。2つの文書問題は4セットから2セットに減るものの、引き続き出題される。新たに「トリプルパッセージ（3つの文書問題）」が登場。3セット出題される。
★P. 132-135、154-155、188-189に関連記事あり

Part 3、4、6、7に的を絞った本書では、各パートの新形式問題を集中的に解くことができます。本番の試験で実力が発揮できるよう、たくさん問題を解いて形式に慣れてください。また各セクションの冒頭では、著者・ヒロ前田が独自の切り口で新形式を分析しています。攻略のヒントも示されているので、ぜひ参考にしてください。

付属CDについて

付属CDには、本書の学習に必要なPart 3、4「ドリル」の音声が収録されています。
※「3文トレーニング」の復習用音声はダウンロード特典です（ダウンロード方法はP.10をご覧ください）

本文では次のような表示によって、該当トラックが示されています。「ドリル」ページで実際に問題を解く際は、1つのカテゴリーを通して再生／解答することを推奨しています。「解答・解説」ページでは、復習しやすいよう、単独のトラック番号を掲載しています。

例）

 CDのトラック01〜12を通して再生することが推奨される場合

 CDのトラック01を単独で再生する場合

各トラックの収録内容は下の表の通りです。

トラック番号	パート	問題番号	トラック番号	パート	問題番号
1	Part 3　①意図問題	Q. 1-3	11	〃	Q. 31-33
2	〃	Q. 4-6	12	〃	Q. 34-36
3	〃	Q. 7-9	13	Part 3　②3人の会話	Q. 37-39
4	〃	Q. 10-12	14	〃	Q. 40-42
5	〃	Q. 13-15	15	〃	Q. 43-45
6	〃	Q. 16-18	16	〃	Q. 46-48
7	〃	Q. 19-21	17	〃	Q. 49-51
8	〃	Q. 22-24	18	〃	Q. 52-54
9	〃	Q. 25-27	19	〃	Q. 55-57
10	〃	Q. 28-30	20	〃	Q. 58-60

21	Part 3 ③グラフィック問題	Q. 61-63	31	Part 4	Q. 1-3
22	〃	Q. 64-66	32	〃	Q. 4-6
23	〃	Q. 67-69	33	〃	Q. 7-9
24	〃	Q. 70-72	34	〃	Q. 10-12
25	〃	Q. 73-75	35	〃	Q. 13-15
26	〃	Q. 76-78	36	〃	Q. 16-18
27	〃	Q. 79-81	37	〃	Q. 19-21
28	〃	Q. 82-84	38	〃	Q. 22-24
29	〃	Q. 85-87	39	〃	Q. 25-27
30	〃	Q. 88-90	40	〃	Q. 28-30

ナレーションは実際のテストで耳にするバリエーションに対応し、米・英・カナダ・豪のナレーターを採用しています。

US（米）……… Josh Keller ／ Chris Koprowski
UK（英）……… Guy Perryman ／ Nadia McKechnie
CA（カナダ）‥ Edith Kayumi
AU（豪）……… Sara Greeves

- 弊社制作の音声CDは、CDプレーヤーでの再生を保証する規格品です。
- パソコンでご使用になる場合、CD-ROMドライブとの相性により、ディスクを再生できない場合がございます。ご了承ください。
- パソコンでタイトル・トラック情報を表示させたい場合は、iTunesをご利用ください。iTunesでは、弊社がCDのタイトル・トラック情報を登録しているGracenote社のCDDB（データベース）からインターネットを介してトラック情報を取得することができます。
- CDとして正常に音声が再生できるディスクからパソコンやmp3プレーヤー等への取り込み時にトラブルが生じた際は、まず、そのアプリケーション（ソフト）、プレーヤーの製作元へご相談ください。

ダウンロード特典のご案内

以下の①〜③の特典を、弊社ダウンロードセンターよりダウンロードしていただくことができます（要ご登録）。

① 「3文トレーニング」復習用音声（データ形式：MP3）
② 付属CDと同じ内容の音声（データ形式：MP3）
③ 本書P. 245-246掲載の解答用紙（データ形式：PDFデータ）

特典のダウンロードはこちらから

ALC DOWNLOAD CENTER
ダウンロードセンター
http://www.alc.co.jp/dl/

ダウンロードで本書を探す際には、本書固有の商品コード「7016038」をご利用いただくと便利です。
スマートフォンで利用できるアプリ「語学のオトモ ALCO」もご紹介しています。ぜひご利用ください。
※本サービスの内容は、予告なく変更する場合がございます。あらかじめご了承ください。

Part 3 のまとめ
ヒロ前田

Part 3 はココが変わった！

問題数が増えた
- 30問（3問×10セット）が39問（3問×13セット）になった
- 会話が3セット（＝設問は9問）増

新しい形式が複数登場
- 意図問題、3人の会話、グラフィック問題など、新しい問題やフォーマットが導入された

より自然な英語が話される
- **elision**（例：gonna、wanna）、**fragment**（「断片」の意。完全な文の形を成していない発言）、**overlapping**（発言が終わらないうちに、別の話し手が発言を重ねること）、**hesitation**（言いよどみ）などを含む、よりリアルな会話を聞くことになる

解説 問題・形式のバリエーションが増えた

　今回の新形式導入で最も大きく変わったのがこのPart 3です。13セット中6セット（約4割）ぐらいがその影響を受けることになります。それ以外は従来の形式で引き続き出題されるわけですから、これまでの学習法や対策が無効になってしまうということは決してありません。

　Part 3に導入された新形式にはP. 14以降で詳しく学習する「意図問題」「3人の会話」「グラフィック問題」があります。

　「やりとりが多い会話」も新しい形式ととらえていいでしょう。これまでの会話では、一人当たりの発言は1、2回でしたが、3回、4回というものが登場します。やりとりが増えても、会話全体の長さはほとんど変わりません。実際に問題を解くときも、発言の回数なんて意外と気にならないものです。

　リニューアルしたPart 3では、これらの形式がさまざまなパターンでミックスされて出題されます。ただし、「3人＋グラフィック」のパターンについては、出ないことが明言されています。

解説　難易度は決して上がっていない

　テストの難易度が上がったのではないかと心配している人もいるかもしれませんが、そんなことはありません。パート全体で処理しなくてはならない情報量はほとんど変わりません。また、解答に時間がかかりそうなグラフィック問題は、他の設問よりも解答時間が4秒プラスされるという配慮もされています。つまりテストの設計上は、受験者の英語力に変動がなければ、アップデート前と同様のスコアを取ることができるはずなのです。

Part 3 攻略の基本

　Part 3 の基本的なストラテジーを紹介します。従来の問題はもちろん、新形式問題にも有効です。

●「先読み」を実行しよう

　「先読み」とは、各会話の最後の設問の解答時間を利用して、次のセットの3つの設問を読む、というものです。それによって、どんな情報を待ち受けるべきか、会話を聞く準備が整います。先読みの実行は、新形式の「意図問題」と「グラフィック問題」で特に重要です。これまで先読みをしてこなかった人もぜひやるべきです。

※意図問題、グラフィック問題の先読みは、それぞれ P.15 と P.47 で説明します

● 設問の主語をチェック

　先読みで目を付けるべきポイントの1つが設問の主語です。問題を解くヒントは、その設問の主語が言う可能性が非常に高いからです。
　次の設問の例を見てください。どちらも Part 3 でよく目にするものです。
①**What is the man concerned about?**（男性は何を心配していますか？）
②**What does the woman ask the man to do?**（女性は男性に何をするよう頼んでいますか？）
　①の主語は the man ですから、男性が自身の心配ごとについて発言する可能性が高いと考えられます。②の主語は the woman ですから、女性が男性に何かを頼む発言を待ち受けて会話を聞けば、解答のヒントが得られるというわけです。

● 概要を問う設問は後回し

　設問の中に、会話の話題や場所、登場人物の職業を問うものがあります。
　例）**What are the speakers mainly discussing?**　⇒　話題
　　　（話し手たちは主に何について話していますか？）
　　　Where does the conversation most likely take place?　⇒　場所
　　　（この会話はどこで行われていると考えられますか）
　これらは会話の概要を問う設問ですが、何か具体的な情報を待ち受けなくても解けます。このタイプの設問は大抵1問目に登場しますが、会話が先に進むほどヒントが増え解きやすくなるので、後回しにして、より詳細を問う問題に意識を向けましょう。先読みにおいても、概要を問う問題であることさえ分かれば十分です。それ以上の情報は不要なので、他の設問の先読みに時間を回しましょう。

「意図問題」はこんな問題！

1回のテストで2、3問出題される
- グラフィック問題と合わせて5問になる計算
- 出題位置は特に定まっていない

発言の意図を問う問題である
- 話し手の発言の意図・動機を問う問題
- 会話の文脈を把握しているかどうかが試される

設問の形が独特
- 設問に会話中のセリフがそのままの形で引用されている（設問の形にはバリエーションあり）
- 選択肢は文も語句もある。文の場合は非常に長くなることがある

解説　画期的な新形式！

典型的な意図問題の設問に次のような形があります。

What does the man mean when he says, "xxxxxxxxxxxx"?

（男性は"xxxxxxxxxxxx"と言う際、何を意図していますか？）

""の中には、会話で聞こえてくるセリフがそのままの形で印刷されています。会話を聞く前に、会話の一部が情報として与えられるなんて、画期的ではありませんか。本書ではこの""内の文をと呼ぶことにします。

設問に mean という言葉が使われていますが、これはターゲット文の「意味」を尋ねているわけではありません。意図問題はターゲット文を発言する「意図」や「動機」を問う問題です。

次の例を見てください。

What does the man mean when he says, "たまらん"?

(A) 彼はもう耐えられない。
(B) 彼はもっと水がほしい。
(C) 彼は味を気に入っている。
(D) 彼は貯金に失敗している。

意図問題とはこういうことです。「たまらん」という表現の意味そのものは、あまり重要ではありません。与えられた文脈の中で、男性がなぜこんな発言をするのかを把握することが、正解を選ぶ上で大切です。

「意図問題」攻略の基本

● 「先読み」は必須

意図問題の先読みで最も重要な情報は" "内のターゲット文です。それを誰が言うのかも確認しましょう。誰が言うのかは、従来の問題と同様（→ P.13）、設問の主語で確認することができます。

● 選択肢の真偽を見極める

意図問題は4択ですが、多くの場合、会話を聞かずに2択に絞り込めます。「正解候補」と「ニセモノ」が混ざっているからです。先ほどの「たまらん」の例で言えば、(A)と(C)は正解候補です。何らかの苦痛を感じている男性が「たまらん」と言っていれば、(A)が正解。その男性が出張先で名物を食べながら「たまらん」と言ったら、正解は(C)です。この2つの選択肢に優劣はありませんし、文字を見るだけではどちらも除外できません。正解の可能性があるということです。

では、(B)と(D)はどうでしょうか。(B)は「水が溜まらない」、(D)は「お金が貯まらない」という状況でのボヤキかもしれませんが、そのようなときに私たちは「たまらん」とは言わないですよね。これらは問題作成者が頑張って作った「ニセモノ」なのです。ニセモノは(B)や(D)のように強い違和感を放っているため、先読みをしておけば、会話を聞かなくても消去しやすいです。これは実際のテストでも同じです。

● ヒントはサンドイッチ状に存在する

意図問題のヒントは、ターゲット文の直前と直後に存在する場合が非常に多いです。つまり、ターゲット文という具を2つのヒントが前と後ろからサンドイッチのように挟んでいるという構図です。大抵は、どちらか1つのヒントがより重要ではありますが、ヒントを2つ得ることで、正解を選びやすくなります。

それでは、次頁から始まるドリルで、早速「意図問題」を解いてみましょう。
全12セット、なるべく一気に解いてください。

＊解答には P.245～ のマークシートを使うことをお勧めします
＊設問の先読みをする人は、まず20秒程度、最初のセットの設問を先読みし、それから音声をスタートさせてください

Part 3 ①意図問題 | ドリル

 会話を聞き、各設問の解答として最も適切なものを選ぼう。問題の先読み（→P.15）を実践しよう。

1. What does the woman want to do?
   (A) Talk about a marketing plan
   (B) Write a sales report
   (C) Practice a presentation
   (D) Submit an order form

2. Where does the man say he will go?
   (A) To a sporting event
   (B) To a workshop
   (C) To a production facility
   (D) To a client's office

3. What does the man mean when he says, "You've got it"?
   (A) He is impressed with a performance.
   (B) He can see that the woman understands.
   (C) He agrees with a request.
   (D) He will cancel an appointment.

4. Where most likely does the man work?
   (A) At a bus company
   (B) At a cleaning business
   (C) At a manufacturing plant
   (D) At a government department

5. Why does the man say, "If you like"?
   (A) He wonders if a product is satisfactory.
   (B) He would like to suggest a different option.
   (C) He does not mind a change of schedule.
   (D) He will provide a different service.

6. What does the woman offer to do?
   (A) Give a presentation
   (B) Provide accommodation
   (C) Reduce a price
   (D) Help pay for a meal

7. Where most likely does the conversation take place?
   (A) In a home improvement store
   (B) In a printing company
   (C) In a supermarket
   (D) In a park

8. Why does the woman say, "I'm not sure about that"?
   (A) She disagrees.
   (B) She has not decided.
   (C) She is unconfident about her opinion.
   (D) She would like more information.

9. What does the woman suggest?
   (A) Scheduling a cleaning
   (B) Publishing a report
   (C) Conducting a survey
   (D) Building a café

10. What is the purpose of the meeting?
    (A) To arrange a trip
    (B) To introduce a colleague
    (C) To plan a social event
    (D) To discuss an agreement

11. Where most likely does the man work?
    (A) In a college
    (B) In an airport
    (C) In a factory
    (D) In a legal firm

12. What does the woman mean when she says, "I'm getting there"?
    (A) She is almost ready to sign a document.
    (B) She will arrive very soon.
    (C) She is indicating where she would like to go.
    (D) She is going to purchase some land.

13. Who most likely is the woman?
    (A) A trainer
    (B) A driver
    (C) A cook
    (D) A journalist

14. Why does the woman say, "That's the idea"?
    (A) She is choosing a plan.
    (B) She is expressing agreement.
    (C) She has remembered something.
    (D) She has accepted a suggestion.

15. What will the speakers do next?
    (A) Take a trip
    (B) Watch a video
    (C) Look at hotel rooms
    (D) Attend a meeting

16. Who most likely are the speakers?
    (A) Business leaders
    (B) City officials
    (C) Newspaper staff
    (D) Art students

17. What does the woman mean when she says, "Please make the call"?
    (A) She will let another person decide the winner.
    (B) She needs to have something constructed.
    (C) She must have a project completed.
    (D) She would like to be contacted by telephone.

18. How will an announcement most likely be made?
    (A) On the radio
    (B) On television
    (C) On a Web site
    (D) In a newspaper

19. Where is the man?
    (A) In a storeroom
    (B) At an Internet café
    (C) At a stationery store
    (D) In a hardware store

20. Why does the woman say, "forget it"?
    (A) She accepts an apology.
    (B) She has changed her mind.
    (C) She has fixed an error.
    (D) She will pay for a meal.

21. What does the woman ask the man to do?
    (A) Purchase a beverage
    (B) Update a price list
    (C) Return to the office
    (D) Submit a document

22. What have the training staff requested?
    (A) An extension to a deadline
    (B) New equipment
    (C) A larger office
    (D) More staff

23. What does the man mean when he says, "Got it"?
    (A) He has the document the woman needs.
    (B) He has found what he was looking for.
    (C) He understands the woman's position.
    (D) He wants the woman to fetch an item.

24. What does the man say about productivity?
    (A) It is dependent on suppliers.
    (B) It will be evaluated.
    (C) It has improved.
    (D) It is expected to fall.

GO ON TO THE NEXT PAGE

25. What does the man ask the woman about?
    (A) Her preparations for a trip
    (B) The topic of her presentation
    (C) Her opinion about a project
    (D) The location of a new office

26. What does the woman mean when she says, "Something's come up"?
    (A) She has had a new idea.
    (B) Someone has mentioned an important point.
    (C) She has another engagement.
    (D) There has been a rise in some figures.

27. What does the woman say about Mr. Robinson?
    (A) She has asked him about his schedule.
    (B) He has been practicing his presentation.
    (C) He made an improvement to a design.
    (D) She wants him to take her place.

28. What does the woman say she has been doing?
    (A) Viewing an online schedule
    (B) Checking the weather forecast
    (C) Meeting with a client
    (D) Enjoying a meal

29. Why does the woman say, "It's hard to imagine she will"?
    (A) She needs to go somewhere quieter.
    (B) She doubts that Ms. Yang will approve a plan.
    (C) She believes that Ms. Yang will check her e-mail soon.
    (D) She does not expect Ms. Yang to attend a meeting.

30. What will the man offer Ms. Yang?
    (A) A promotion
    (B) An extension to a deadline
    (C) A larger budget
    (D) A ticket to a concert

31. Where most likely is the woman calling?
    (A) A hotel
    (B) A restaurant
    (C) A catering company
    (D) A cake shop

32. What does the man mean when he says, "Let me get this straight"?
    (A) He has to put some items in a line.
    (B) He will adjust the cable of his telephone.
    (C) He will offer some advice.
    (D) He wants to clarify an order.

33. Why does the man say he cannot change the price?
    (A) Package prices are not flexible.
    (B) The request is too late.
    (C) There will be additional costs.
    (D) The client is not a special member.

34. What is the conversation mainly about?
    (A) Hiring new staff members
    (B) Writing an article
    (C) Reviewing a performance
    (D) Choosing a leader

35. What does the woman mean when she says, "It went well"?
    (A) Her work was successful.
    (B) A vehicle ran smoothly.
    (C) She greeted a visitor.
    (D) A device is functioning.

36. How does the woman say she will make a decision?
    (A) By calling references
    (B) By administering a test
    (C) By checking qualifications
    (D) By holding more interviews

Part 3

① 意図問題

Part 3 ①意図問題 | ドリルの解答・解説

 **01** Woman CA Man UK

Questions 1 through 3 refer to the following conversation.
W: ①Colin, we need to start work on the new marketing plan soon. Are you ready to sit down and discuss it?
M: Yes and no. I mean, I was working on it until late, so it's finished. But ②I have to meet with a client at his office in Collingwood this afternoon, and I'm already running late.
W: I see. Well, I'd like to hear about it soon. ③Can you put a copy of the plan on my desk before you leave?
M: You've got it. ④Take a look and we can get together tomorrow to talk about any problems.

問題1-3は次の会話に関するものです。
女性：Colin、新しいマーケティング計画にもうすぐ取り掛かる必要があるわね。それについてじっくり話せる？
男性：「はい」でも「いいえ」でもあります。遅くまで取り組んでいたので、完成はしています。でも、今日の午後はCollingwoodにある先方のオフィスでクライアントに会わなくてはいけなくて、すでに遅れているんです。
女性：なるほど。そうねえ、それについては早く話を聞きたいんだけど。出掛ける前にその計画書のコピーを私の机の上に置いていってくれる？
男性：分かりました。目を通しておいてください。それで問題については明日会って話しましょう。

□**start work on ~**：~に取り掛かる　□**sit down and ~**：じっくり~する、ゆっくり~する　□**take a look**：ざっと目を通す

 会話やトークでより自然な英語が話されるというのも新傾向。男性の発言、Yes and no. の言いよどみがそれ。「準備はできてるけど、今すぐ話せる状況ではない」ということをためらいがちに伝えています。**(R)**

1.
What does the woman want to do?（女性は何がしたいと思っていますか？）
(A) Talk about a marketing plan（マーケティング計画について話す）
(B) Write a sales report（売上報告書を作成する）
(C) Practice a presentation（プレゼンの練習をする）
(D) Submit an order form（注文書を提出する）
正解：(A)　女性はまず①で男性に、「新しいマーケティング計画に取り掛かる必要がある」と切り出し、「それについ

て話せるか」と尋ねている。よって、女性がしたいことは、(A)「マーケティング計画について話をする」である。会話中の discuss が、選択肢では talk about（～について話す）に言い換えられている。

2.
Where does the man say he will go?（男性はどこへ行くと言っていますか？）
(A) To a sporting event（スポーツのイベント）
(B) To a workshop（セミナー）
(C) To a production facility（製造施設）
(D) To a client's office（クライアントのオフィス）
□**workshop**：研修会、セミナー　□**production facility**：製造施設

正解：(D)　設問に the man say とあるので、男性が「どこかへ行く」という発言をすると考えられる。男性は②で「今日の午後は Collingwood にある先方のオフィスでクライアントに会わなくてはいけない」と述べている。よって、正解は (D)。②の直後で聞こえる、I'm already running late の run late は、「遅れる」という意味。

---

3. NEW
What does the man mean when he says, "You've got it"?（男性が "You've got it" と言う際、何を意図していますか？）
(A) He is impressed with a performance.（成績に感心している）
(B) He can see that the woman understands.（女性が理解していることが分かる）
(C) He agrees with a request.（依頼に応じる）
(D) He will cancel an appointment.（約束を取りやめる）
□**be impressed with ~**：~に感心する

正解：(C)　新形式の「意図問題」。「意図問題」は、問われている発言の前後の内容を聞き取り、会話の流れを把握することが正解のカギとなる。設問から、You've got it と言うのは男性だと分かる。男性は、女性の③「コピーを置いておいて」という依頼を受け、You've got it. と言い、④「それに目を通しておいてください」と述べている。つまり、女性の「コピーを置いておいて」という依頼に応じる意味で You've got it と言っているので、正解は (C)。

※リスニングセクションでは、著者のロス・タロックが音声や表現について解説をしています

020

02　Woman AU　Man UK

Questions 4 through 6 refer to the following conversation.
W: Hello, it's Janice Hill from Starfield Tour Company. Um, ①we discussed having the staff from my office come to Dudley Bus Company for a tour of your facilities — um, before our companies start working together.
M: ②Yes, that's tomorrow. I'll be showing you around myself.
W: OK. It's just that we're really busy tomorrow. ③Can we come on Monday instead?
M: If you like. ④We don't have anything big scheduled.
W: Thanks. Everyone's been looking forward to meeting your staff.
M: We feel the same way. ⑤In fact, would you be interested in having lunch together? I'll have some food delivered.
W: ⑥That's a wonderful idea. We'll share the cost, of course.
M: That won't be necessary.

問題4-6は次の会話に関するものです。
女性：もしもし、Starfield Tour Company の Janice Hill です。あの、うちのスタッフが Dudley Bus Company に伺って、御社の施設を見学させていただくというお話をしましたが――その、われわれが一緒に働き始める前にということで。
男性：ええ、明日でしたね。私が自分でご案内するつもりです。
女性：そうですか。実は、明日は非常に忙しい日なんです。代わりに月曜に伺ってもよろしいでしょうか？
男性：その方がよろしければ。こちらは大した予定はありませんので。
女性：ありがとうございます。皆、御社のスタッフにお会いするのを楽しみにしています。
男性：われわれもですよ。でしたら、よろしければ昼食をご一緒しませんか？　食事を届けてもらうことにしましょう。
女性：それは素晴らしい考えですね。代金はもちろんこちらも出します。
男性：その必要はありませんよ。

□ **show ~ around**：~を案内する　□ **in person**：(本人が) 直接

4.
Where most likely does the man work?（男性はどこで働いていると思われますか？）
(A) At a bus company（バス会社で）
(B) At a cleaning business（清掃会社で）
(C) At a manufacturing plant（製造工場で）
(D) At a government department（政府機関で）

正解：(A)　男性が働いている場所を問う問題。①で女性が、「うちのスタッフが Dudley Bus Company に伺って、御社の施設を見学する」と述べている。それに対し、男性は②で「私が案内するつもりだ」と返答しているので、男性は Dudley Bus Company の施設で働いていると判断できる。よって、(A)「バス会社で」が正解。①の直前にある Um などの「言いよどみ」が登場するのも、新形式の特徴である。

5. NEW
Why does the man say, "If you like"?（男性はなぜ "If you like" と言っているのですか？）
(A) He wonders if a product is satisfactory.（製品が満足のいくものかどうか知りたいから）
(B) He would like to suggest a different option.（別の選択肢を提案したいから）
(C) He does not mind a change of schedule.（スケジュールの変更をいとわないから）
(D) He will provide a different service.（別のサービスを提供するから）
□ **satisfactory**：満足のいく

正解：(C)　男性は①で「代わりに月曜に伺ってもいいか」と女性からスケジュール変更を打診される。それに対し、If you like と答え、④「こちらは大した予定はないから」と述べている。よって、男性は「スケジュールを変更しても問題ない」という意味で If you like と言っていることが分かるので、(C) が正解。mind は I don't mind で「気にしない」という意味もあるが、依頼に対しては「それでいい」と許可・同意を伝える応答になる。

6.
What does the woman offer to do?（女性は何をすると申し出ていますか？）
(A) Give a presentation（プレゼンをする）
(B) Provide accommodation（宿を提供する）
(C) Reduce a price（値段を下げる）
(D) Help pay for a meal（食事の支払いを助ける）
□ **accommodation**：宿泊、宿泊施設

正解：(D)　男性が⑤で「昼食を一緒に食べないか」と提案している。⑥で女性はそれに応じ、We'll ~（私たちが~する）という表現で、昼食代を分担して支払うことを申し出ている。よって、彼女が申し出ていることは、(D) である。その他の選択肢は会話に登場していないので不適切。

Part 3　① 意図問題

 03　Man US　Woman UK

Questions 7 through 9 refer to the following conversation.

M: The new ①gardening section has been a great success. It's the source of more than half of our profits now. ②Don't you think we should expand it?
W: I'm not sure about that. ③The customer satisfaction survey showed that people are happy with our range of timber, plants, tools and things like that. ④Rather than expanding ⑤the gardening or hardware sections, I think we should try something new.
M: Do you have anything in mind?
W: Well, ⑥I think a café might be a good idea. Customers often stand at the front of the store chatting. I'm sure they'd prefer to sit down and enjoy a beverage in a nice café while they talk about gardening with their friends.

問題7-9は次の会話に関するものです。
男性：新しいガーデニングコーナーが繁盛してるね。今じゃうちの利益の半分以上の源になってる。拡張すべきだと思わない？
女性：それはどうかしら。顧客満足度調査によれば、お客さまはうちの木材、植物、工具といった品ぞろえに満足しているわ。ガーデニングや工具の売り場を拡張するより、何か新しいことを試すべきだと私は思うけど。
男性：何か考えはあるの？
女性：そうねえ、カフェなんていいアイデアじゃないかしら。よく店の外でお客さんが立ち話をしているでしょ。友達とガーデニングの話をしながら、すてきなカフェで腰掛けて飲み物を楽しむ方がきっといいはずだわ。

□**expand**：～を拡大する　　□**timber**：木材
□**hardware**：工具、金物

7.
Where most likely does the conversation take place?（この会話はどこで行われていると考えられますか？）
(A) In a home improvement store（ホームセンターで）
(B) In a printing company（印刷会社で）
(C) In a supermarket（スーパーマーケットで）
(D) In a park（公園で）
□**home improvement store**：ホームセンター

正解：**(A)**　会話が行われている場所を問う問題。男性は①で「ガーデニングコーナー」と述べている。また、女性は③で「うちの木材、植物、工具」と取扱商品を並べ、さらに⑤で「ガーデニングや工具の売り場」と述べている。これらの発言内容から判断すると、会話が行われている場所としては、(A)「ホームセンター」が最も適切である。

8. NEW
Why does the woman say, "I'm not sure about that"?（女性はなぜ "I'm not sure about that" と言っているのですか？）
(A) She disagrees.（意見が異なるから）
(B) She has not decided.（決心していないから）
(C) She is unconfident about her opinion.（自分の意見に自信がないから）
(D) She would like more information.（もっと情報が欲しいから）
□**unconfident**：自信のない

正解：**(A)**　女性の I'm not sure about that（それはどうかしら）という発言の意図が問われている。thatは、直前の②「ガーデニング売り場を拡張すべきではないか」という男性の意見を指す。それを受け、女性はI'm not sure about that.と言い、その後、③「顧客は現状に満足している」、④の文で「売り場を広げるより、何か新しいことをした方がいい」と述べている。つまり、男性とは異なる意見を述べているので、正解は(A)。

9.
What does the woman suggest?（女性は何を提案していますか？）
(A) Scheduling a cleaning（清掃を計画すること）
(B) Publishing a report（報告書を発行すること）
(C) Conducting a survey（調査を実施すること）
(D) Building a café（カフェを作ること）

正解：**(D)**　女性の提案内容を問う問題。最後の設問なので、後半の女性の発言にヒントがある可能性が高い。④の文で「新しいことを試すべき」と女性が述べ、男性は「何か考えがあるか」と尋ねている。それに対し、女性は⑥でカフェを作ることを提案している。よって、正解は(D)。この会話は③「顧客満足度調査」に基づいて行われているため、(C)「調査を実施すること」は、女性の提案内容としては不適切。

04 Man UK Woman AU

Questions 10 through 12 refer to the following conversation.

M: ①Thanks for coming to our manufacturing facility today for the negotiations. We hope you'll rely on us for all of your clothing lines.
W: I always look forward to my trips to Melbourne. ②Besides, I know how hard it is for you to arrange time away from the factory.
M: You're right about that. Right now, I'm hoping to hire an assistant as soon as possible. ③Anyway, would you like to go over the details once more, or are you ready to sign the contract?
W: I'm getting there. ④I've asked my lawyer to come along today. If she's happy with it, we'll sign before we leave.

問題10-12は次の会話に関するものです。
男性：本日は弊社の製造工場まで交渉にお越しいただきありがとうございます。御社の全ての衣類のラインについて私どもを頼りにしていただければと思っております。
女性：Melbourne に来るのはいつも楽しみなんですよ。それに、工場から離れる予定を組むのが、あなたにとってどんなに大変かは分かっています。
男性：おっしゃる通りです。現在、できるだけ早くアシスタントを採用しようと考えているところです。それはともかく、もう一度詳細をご確認されますか、それとももう契約書に署名をしていただけそうですか？
女性：そろそろその段階に至りそうです。今日は私の弁護士に一緒に来てくれるよう依頼してあります。もし彼女がその内容で満足なら、帰る前に署名をしましょう。

□**manufacturing facility**：製造施設、製造工場
□**besides**：それに、その上

10.
What is the purpose of the meeting?（面会の目的は何ですか？）
(A) To arrange a trip（旅行を手配すること）
(B) To introduce a colleague（同僚を紹介すること）
(C) To plan a social event（社交行事を計画するため）
(D) To discuss an agreement（契約について話し合うため）
□**social event**：社交行事

正解：(D)　面会の目的を問う問題。男性の発言①から、女性は「交渉するため」に製造工場まで来たことが分かる。また、男性は③で「契約書を見直したいか、それとも、もう署名をする準備ができているか」と女性に尋ねている。これらの発言内容から、「契約について話し合うため」に面会が行われていることが分かる。よって、(D) が正解。女性の最初の発言に my trips とあるが、「旅行の手配」についての話はしていないので、(A) は不適切。

11.
Where most likely does the man work?（男性はどこで働いていると考えられますか？）
(A) In a college（大学で）
(B) In an airport（空港で）
(C) In a factory（工場で）
(D) In a legal firm（法律事務所で）
□**legal firm**：法律事務所

正解：(C)　男性が働いている場所を問う問題。女性が②で「工場から離れる予定を組むことが、あなたにとってどんなに大変かは分かっている」と男性に述べている。よって、男性は普段、工場で働いていると判断できるので、正解は (C)「工場で」。④に「弁護士」とあるが、男性のことを指しているわけではないので、(D)「法律事務所で」は不適切。

12. NEW
What does the woman mean when she says, "I'm getting there"?（女性が "I'm getting there" と言う際、何を意図していますか？）
(A) She is almost ready to sign a document.（書類に署名する準備がほぼできている）
(B) She will arrive very soon.（もうすぐ到着する）
(C) She is indicating where she would like to go.（自分がどこへ行きたいかを示している）
(D) She is going to purchase some land.（土地を購入する予定である）

正解：(A)　この会話における、女性の I'm getting there という発言の意図が問われている。③で男性が「契約書に署名ができそうか」と女性に尋ねている。それに対し、女性は I'm getting there と述べ、④「弁護士が内容に満足なら、帰る前に署名をする」と付け加えている。つまり、「女性はもうすぐ契約書に署名をする」ということが分かる。よって、この発言の意図としては (A) が適切である。なお、get there には「そこに着く」という意味があるため、文脈によっては (B) が適切となる。

Part 3　①意図問題

023

05　Woman AU　Man US

Questions 13 through 15 refer to the following conversation.

W: Welcome to the Cicero Hotel. I'm Donna and ①I'll be training you this morning. Are you ready to start?
M: Um, yeah. I was told that I'd be working at the front desk, though.
W: I'll be showing you every aspect of the hotel today. You'll learn about the kitchens, the laundry, the entertainment facilities, housekeeping and even maintenance.
M: ②So that I can better answer customers' questions?
W: That's the idea. ③You never know what you'll be asked. Now, before anything else, ④I'd like to show you the different room types we have on offer. Have you ever stayed at a Cicero Hotel before?
M: No, I've heard the rooms are very nice, though.

問題13-15は次の会話に関するものです。
女性：Cicero Hotel へようこそ。私は Donna といいますが、午前中、あなたの研修を担当します。準備はいいですか？
男性：ええと、はい。ただ、私はフロントで働くことになると聞いていたのですが。
女性：今日はあなたに当ホテルのあらゆる側面をお見せします。厨房、洗濯室、娯楽施設、客室清掃部門、メンテナンス部門についても学んでもらいます。
男性：お客さまからの質問にちゃんと答えられるように、ということですか？
女性：そういうことです。何を尋ねられるか分かりませんからね。では、何はさておき、われわれが提供するさまざまな客室のタイプをお見せしたいと思います。過去に Cicero Hotel に滞在したことはありますか？
男性：いいえ、客室はとても素晴らしいと聞いていますが。

□**aspect**：面、側面　□**housekeeping**：客室清掃
□**before anything else**：何よりも先に、何はさておき
□**have ~ on offer**：~を提供している

13.
Who most likely is the woman?（女性は誰だと考えられますか？）
(A) A trainer（教育係）
(B) A driver（運転手）
(C) A cook（料理人）
(D) A journalist（ジャーナリスト）

□**trainer**：教育係、コーチ

正解：**(A)**　①「あなたの研修を担当する」という発言から、女性は研修を行う立場にいることが分かる。また、2回目の発言では、男性が受ける研修の概要を説明している。よって、彼女は (A)「教育係」だと判断できる。kitchen（キッチン）は会話の中で触れられているが、見学をする場所の1つとして登場しているので、(C)「料理人」は不適切。

14. NEW
Why does the woman say, "That's the idea"?
（女性はなぜ "That's the idea" と言うのですか？）
(A) She is choosing a plan.（プランを選んでいるところだから）
(B) She is expressing agreement.（同意を表明しているから）
(C) She has remembered something.（何かを思い出したから）
(D) She has accepted a suggestion.（提案を受け入れたから）

正解：**(B)**　That's the idea. は「そうだよ」「その調子だよ」と同意や励ましを表す口語表現だが、「意図問題」では問われている表現を知らなくても、会話の流れを理解できれば正解できる。研修でホテルのさまざまな場所を見学する理由を、男性は②「お客さまからの質問に答えられるように」と尋ねている。女性は That's the idea. と返答し、③「何を尋ねられるか分からないから」と述べている。つまり、男性の発言に同意していると判断できるので、(B) が正解。

15.
What will the speakers do next?（話し手たちは次に何をしますか？）
(A) Take a trip（旅行に行く）
(B) Watch a video（ビデオを見る）
(C) Look at hotel rooms（ホテルの部屋を見る）
(D) Attend a meeting（会議に出席する）

正解：**(C)**　話し手たちの次の行動を問う設問。先読み中にこの設問があったら、「会話の後半に予定や願望を表す表現が出てくる」と予想して聞こう。この会話には、女性は ④I'd like to ~（~したい）という表現で、「さまざまな客室タイプを見せたい」と男性に述べている。この発言から、2人はこれから客室を見に行くと判断できる。よって、(C) が正解。

06 　Woman UK　Man US

Questions 16 through 18 refer to the following conversation.

W: All of the entries are in for this year's Baltimore City Art Competition. ①I've had them all displayed in the gallery here at City Hall.
M: ②As leaders of the city's Cultural Development Department, you and I have to choose the winners. So ... do you have any favorites?
W: Yeah, here's a list of the paintings I think could win. The quality is so high — ③I can't choose. Please make the call. ④I'll go along with your decision.
M: How are we going to announce the winners?
W: ⑤I got a call from the *Baltimore Standard* newspaper. They want to cover the story, so let's have them announce the winners.
M: ⑥Good idea.

問題16-18は次の会話に関するものです。
女性：今年のBaltimore City 美術コンテストの応募作品が出そろいました。作品全てこの市役所のギャラリーに展示してもらいました。
男性：市の文化開発部のリーダーとして、あなたと私で受賞者を選ばなくてはなりませんね。それで…気に入った作品はありますか？
女性：ええ、これは私が受賞する可能性があると思う絵画のリストです。質がとても高いんですよ——私には選べなくて。あなたが決めてください。あなたの決定に従います。
男性：受賞者はどのように発表しましょうか？
女性：*Baltimore Standard* 紙から電話がありました。この話を取り上げたいということなので、彼らに受賞者を発表してもらいましょう。
男性：いい考えですね。

□ **city hall**：市役所　□ **call**：決定、選択　□ **cover**：〜を取り上げる、〜を報道する

16.
Who most likely are the speakers?（話し手たちは誰だと考えられますか？）
(A) Business leaders（企業のリーダー）
(B) City officials（市職員）
(C) Newspaper staff（新聞社のスタッフ）
(D) Art students（美術学生）

正解：(B)　話し手たちの職業を問う問題。冒頭①で女性が「この市役所のギャラリー」と述べ、男性が②「市の文化開発部のリーダーとして、あなたと私で」と女性に言っている。よって、2人は市の部署で働いていると判断できるので、その言い換えとしてふさわしい(B)「市の職員」が正解。会話後半で女性は、「*Baltimore Standard* 紙」と述べているが、これは電話をかけてきた相手のことなので、(C)「新聞社のスタッフ」は不適切。

17. NEW
What does the woman mean when she says, "Please make the call"?（女性が"Please make the call"と言う際、何を意図していますか？）

(A) She will let another person decide the winner.（相手に受賞者を決めさせる）
(B) She needs to have something constructed.（何かを組み立ててもらう必要がある）
(C) She must have a project completed.（プロジェクトを完成させなくてはならない）
(D) She would like to be contacted by telephone.（電話で連絡をしてほしい）

正解：(A)　call には「電話」という意味があるので(D)が魅力的だが、make the call で「決断を下す」という意味の定型表現。女性は③で「選べない」と述べた後、男性にPlease make the call.と頼み、④「あなたの決定に従う」と付け加えている。つまり、この発言は「男性に判断を任せる」という意味だ。よって、(A)が正解。意図問題では、発言を文字通りの意味で解釈すると不正解になる可能性があるので、必ず音声を聞き、会話の流れを押さえてから解答しよう。

18.
How will an announcement most likely be made?（発表はどのように行われると考えられますか？）
(A) On the radio（ラジオで）
(B) On television（テレビで）
(C) On a Web site（ウェブサイトで）
(D) In a newspaper（新聞で）

正解：(D)　⑤から、女性は *Baltimore Standard* 紙に受賞者を掲載してもらおうと提案している。その後、男性は⑥「いい考えだ」と述べているので、女性の提案に賛同していることが分かる。よって、発表は(D)「新聞で」行われると判断できる。なお、cover には「〜を覆う」や「（代金など）を含む」など多くの異なる意味がある。

07 　Man US　Woman CA

Questions 19 through 21 refer to the following conversation.

M: ①Hi Juno. I'm at the stationery store, right now. ②I can't find those pens you asked for. I asked the staff, but they don't know anything about them.
W: That's too bad. Uh — forget it. ③I'll get them online, instead.
M: Are you sure? I could drop in at another store on the way back.
W: Never mind the pens. ④I need you back at the office as soon as possible. We have to finish editing this manuscript today.

問題19-21は次の会話に関するものです。
男性：もしもし、Juno。今、文具店にいるよ。君に頼まれたペンが見つからないんだ。店の人にも聞いてみたけど、知らないって。
女性：それは残念。うーん――いいわ。インターネットで買うから。
男性：本当にいいの？　帰りに別の店に寄ることもできるよ。
女性：ペンのことは気にしないで。できるだけ早く会社に戻ってきてほしいのよ。私たち、この原稿の編集を今日中に終わらせなくちゃいけないんだから。

19.
Where is the man?（男性はどこにいますか？）
(A) In a storeroom（倉庫）
(B) At an Internet café（インターネットカフェ）
(C) At a stationery store（文具店）
(D) In a hardware store（ホームセンター）

正解：**(C)**　男性の現在地が問われている。①で「文房具店にいる」と述べていることから、正解は (C)。stationery（文房具）と同様、stapler（ホチキス）や copy machine（コピー機）などの office supplies（事務用品）は TOEIC によく登場する。(A) storeroom（倉庫）の同義語として warehouse も覚えておこう。

20. NEW
Why does the woman say, "forget it"?（女性はなぜ "forget it" と言っているのですか？）
(A) She accepts an apology.（謝罪を受け入れるから）
(B) She has changed her mind.（気が変わったから）
(C) She has fixed an error.（間違いを正したから）
(D) She will pay for a meal.（食事の代金を払うから）

正解：**(B)**　男性の②「頼まれていた商品が見つからない。店員もその商品のことを知らない」という発言を受けて、女性は forget it と述べ、③「インターネットで買うから」と伝えている。つまり、女性はもともと予定していた方法（男性に店舗で買ってきてもらう）ではなく、別の手段で欲しい商品を手に入れようとしていることが分かる。よって、(B) が正解。会話後半で、男性の「別の店舗で購入しようか」という提案を断っていることからも、女性の気が変わったと判断できる。

21.
What does the woman ask the man to do?（女性は男性に何をするよう頼んでいますか？）
(A) Purchase a beverage（飲み物を買う）
(B) Update a price list（価格表を更新する）
(C) Return to the office（会社に戻る）
(D) Submit a document（書類を提出する）

正解：**(C)**　女性が男性に依頼している内容が問われている。女性は④で男性に、「あなたに早く会社に帰ってきてほしい」と述べている。よって、女性が男性に頼んでいる内容は、(C)「会社に戻る」である。女性は男性に stationery（文具）を買ってくるように依頼しているが（②）、beverage（飲み物）については述べていないので、(A)「飲み物を買う」は不適切。

Questions 22 through 24 refer to the following conversation.

M: ①The training center staff have requested an electronic whiteboard to make their presentations more effective.
W: That won't be easy — we have a limited budget this year.
M: There are three classrooms, so I know it won't be cheap.
W: ②Let's just see how much it costs.
M: Got it. ③I've already contacted three suppliers and I'm waiting for them to provide an estimate.
W: Great. I agree that we need to support the training department. They're doing good work.
M: Absolutely. ④Our productivity and service quality have improved enormously since they started their program.
W: Give me that estimate as soon as it comes in.

問題 22-24 は次の会話に関するものです。
男性：研修センターのスタッフから、プレゼンテーションをより効果的にするためにということで、電子ホワイトボードの希望がありました。
女性：それは簡単ではないでしょう――うちは今年、予算が限られているから。
男性：教室は3つあるので、安くないだろうということは分かっています。
女性：いくらするのかだけでも調べてみましょう。
男性：了解です。すでに3社の納入業者に連絡して、見積もりを出してくれるのを待っているところです。
女性：素晴らしいわ。研修部を支援する必要があるという点は同感です。彼らはいい仕事をしているものね。
男性：おっしゃる通りです。わが社の生産性とサービスの質は、彼らがプログラムを始めて以来、格段に向上していますから。
女性：見積もりが届いたらすぐ私に見せてね。

□**electronic whiteboard**：電子ホワイトボード
□**productivity**：生産性　□**enormously**：大いに、格段に

22.
What have the training staff requested?（研修センターの職員は何を頼んでいますか？）
(A) An extension to a deadline（締め切りの延長）
(B) New equipment（新しい備品）
(C) A larger office（もっと広いオフィス）
(D) More staff（増員）
□**extension**：延長

正解：(B)　1問目は研修センターの職員が依頼した内容を問う問題。男性は冒頭①で「研修センターのスタッフから、電子ホワイトボードの依頼があった」述べている。「電子ホワイトボード」の言い換えには、「新しい備品」がふさわしいので、(B) が正解。TOEIC では、computer（コンピューター）、printer（プリンター）、microscope（顕微鏡）など、さまざまな物が equipment に言い換えられる。

23. NEW
What does the man mean when he says, "Got it"?（男性が "Got it" と言う際、何を意図していますか？）
(A) He has the document the woman needs.（女性が必要としている書類を持っている）
(B) He has found what he was looking for.（探していたものが見つかった）
(C) He understands the woman's position.（女性の見解を理解している）
(D) He wants the woman to fetch an item.（女性に品物を持ってきてほしいと思っている）
□**fetch**：〜を持ってくる、〜を取ってくる

正解：(C)　女性が②で「値段だけでも見てみよう」と提案している。それに対し、男性はGot itと述べ、すでに納入業者に見積もり依頼をしたことを伝えている（③）。つまり、「値段だけでも調べよう」という女性の考えに同意していると判断ができる。よって、この発言の意図としてふさわしいのは、(C)「女性の見解を理解している」である。

24.
What does the man say about productivity?（男性は生産性について何と言っていますか？）
(A) It is dependent on suppliers.（納入業者次第である）
(B) It will be evaluated.（評価されるだろう）
(C) It has improved.（改善した）
(D) It is expected to fall.（下がる見通しである）

正解：(C)　男性は、研修センターの仕事ぶりを称賛する女性の発言を受けて、④で「生産性とサービスの質は向上している」と、自社の生産性について触れている。よって、正解は (C)「改善した」である。

🔊 **09** Man US Woman AU

Questions 25 through 27 refer to the following conversation.
M: Hi, Julie. ①Have you booked your ticket for the flight to Arkansas?
W: I did, but I have to cancel it now.
M: What a pity. ②I was really looking forward to attending the sales convention together.
W: Yeah, I'm sorry. Something's come up, and ③I have to meet with some clients on those dates. It was unexpected.
M: Have you chosen someone to take your place, or can I make a suggestion?
W: ④I was going to send Jack Robinson. His performance has been excellent, so we should reward him.
M: Great idea.
W: OK, well, you can give him the good news.

問題25-27は次の会話に関するものです。
男性：やあ、Julie。Arkansas への飛行機のチケットは予約した？
女性：したわよ、でもキャンセルしなくちゃいけないの。
男性：残念だな。販売会議に一緒に出席するのをすごく楽しみにしてたのに。
女性：ええ、残念だわ。用事ができて、その時期にクライアントと会わなくてはいけないの。予想外だったわ。
男性：君の代理を務める人はもう選んだのかな、それとも僕が提案してもいい？
女性：Jack Robinson に行ってもらうつもりだったの。彼の仕事ぶりは優秀だから、ごほうびをあげるべきだわ。
男性：すごくいい考えだよ。
女性：そうだ、じゃあ、あなたが彼に朗報を伝えて。

□**What a pity.**:「残念だ」 □**take *someone's* place**：〜の代わりをする　□**reward**：〜にほうびを与える

 女性が going to を gonna と発音しています。elision（省略）と呼ばれるもので、カジュアルな会話でよく聞かれます。これも新傾向。**(R)**

25.
What does the man ask the woman about?（男性は女性に何を尋ねていますか？）
(A) Her preparations for a trip（出張の準備）
(B) The topic of her presentation（プレゼンテーションの話題）
(C) Her opinion about a project（プロジェクトに関する意見）
(D) The location of a new office（新しいオフィスの場所）

正解：(A)　男性が女性に質問した内容を問う問題。冒頭①で男性は、女性に「Arkansas への飛行機のチケットは予約したか」と尋ねているので、その言い換えとしてふさわしい (A)「出張の準備」が正解。「予約する」という意味の動詞は book の他に reserve を覚えておこう。

26. NEW
What does the woman mean when she says, "Something's come up"?（女性が "Something's come up" と言う際、何を意図していますか？）
(A) She has had a new idea.（新しい考えが浮かんだ）
(B) Someone has mentioned an important point.（誰かが大事なポイントを述べた）
(C) She has another engagement.（彼女には別の約束がある）
(D) There has been a rise in some figures.（いくつかの数字に増加があった）

正解：(C)　男性の発言②から、男性は女性と共に販売会議に参加する予定だったことが分かる。女性は行けなくなったことを謝罪し、Something's come up と述べた後、③で「クライアントと会うことになった」と理由を説明している。よって、「別の約束が入った」という意味で Something's come up と述べたと判断できるので、正解は (C)。

27.
What does the woman say about Mr. Robinson?（女性は Robinson さんについて何と言っていますか？）
(A) She has asked him about his schedule.（彼女は彼に予定について尋ねた）
(B) He has been practicing his presentation.（彼はプレゼンテーションの練習をしている）
(C) He made an improvement to a design.（彼はデザインに改良を加えた）
(D) She wants him to take her place.（彼女は彼に自分の代わりをしてほしいと思っている）

正解：(D)　話し手の男女は1問目に、the man と the woman としてすでに登場している。よって、設問の Mr. Robinson は第3者のことを指し、会話中にその名前が登場すると判断できる。女性は④「Jack Robinson に行ってもらうつもりだった」と言っている。会話前半で、女性は販売会議に出られなくなったと述べている。よって、「自分の代わりとして Robinson 氏に販売会議に参加してもらおう」という内容の発言をしたことになるので、(D) が正解。

10 Woman CA Man US

Questions 28 through 30 refer to the following conversation.
W: ①I've been checking the flight arrival times online. Ms. Yang's flight isn't going to get in on time.
M: ②Is she going to make it to the three o'clock meeting?
W: It's hard to imagine she will. I'll make a summary of the meeting and send it to her by e-mail later.
M: She must be really tired. ③I'll have her submit her travel report tomorrow rather than today. That way, she can take the rest of the day off.

問題28-30は次の会話に関するものです。
女性：インターネットでずっと飛行機の到着時間を確認しているんですが。Yangさんの便は時間通りに着かないようです。
男性：彼女は3時の会議に間に合うだろうか？
女性：それは難しいんじゃないでしょうか。私が会議の概要をまとめて、後から彼女にメールで送ります。
男性：すごく疲れているに違いない。出張報告書は今日じゃなくて明日出してもらうことにするよ。そうすれば、彼女、今日はもう休みにすることができるから。

□ make it to ～：～に間に合う

28.
What does the woman say she has been doing?（女性は何をしていると言っていますか？）
(A) Viewing an online schedule（インターネットで予定を見ている）
(B) Checking the weather forecast（天気予報を確認している）
(C) Meeting with a client（クライアントと面会している）
(D) Enjoying a meal（食事を楽しんでいる）

正解：(A)　女性の行動に関する問題。女性は①で「インターネットで飛行機の到着時刻を見ている」と述べている。その言い換えとしては、(A)「インターネットで予定を見ている」が最も適切である。「会議」の話は登場するが、会議は3時からでまだ行われていないため、(C)は不適切。

29. NEW
Why does the woman say, "It's hard to imagine she will"?（女性はなぜ"It's hard to imagine she will"と言っているのですか？）
(A) She needs to go somewhere quieter.（もっと静かな場所へ行く必要があるから）
(B) She doubts that Ms. Yang will approve a plan.（Yangさんが計画を承認すると思わないから）
(C) She believes that Ms. Yang will check her e-mail soon.（YangさんはすぐにEメールを確認すると思うから）
(D) She does not expect Ms. Yang to attend a meeting.（Yangさんが会議に出席すると思わないから）

正解：(D)　女性は、男性の②「(Yangさん)は3時の会議に間に合うだろうか」と心配する発言を聞いて、It's hard to imagine she willと述べ、「私が会議の概要をまとめて後から彼女にEメールで送る」と申し出ている。つまり、彼女はYangさんが会議に間に合わないと思っているので、「後で概要を送る」と言っていることが分かる。よって、この発言が意図する内容は、(D) である。

30.
What will the man offer Ms. Yang?（男性はYangさんにどんな申し出をしますか？）
(A) A promotion（昇進）
(B) An extension to a deadline（締め切りの延長）
(C) A larger budget（予算の増額）
(D) A ticket to a concert（コンサートのチケット）

正解：(B)　設問から男性がYangさんに何かを申し出ることが分かるので、男性の発言がヒントになる可能性が高い。男性は③で「出張報告書を今日ではなく明日出してもらうことにする」と述べている。つまり、Yangさんの出張報告書の提出締め切りを延期してあげていることが分かる。よって、男性が申し出ている内容は、(B)「締め切りの延長」である。(B) の extension は「延長」という意味だけでなく、「内線」という意味でも TOEIC によく登場する。

Part 3
① 意図問題

 **11** Woman AU Man UK

Questions 31 through 33 refer to the following conversation.
W: Hi. It's Marg Downey calling. ①I'd like to update my company's catering request for tomorrow.
M: I see ... You must be from Clover Manufacturing. Is that right?
W: Yes, it is. Now, ②the original order was for 60 people ③having a four-course banquet including dessert. ④But, because we'll be supplying our own cake, 18 people say that they no longer want dessert.
M: Let me get this straight. ⑤You want 42 dinners with dessert and 18 without dessert, right?
W: That's right.
M: OK. ⑥We'll be delivering that to the Hepburn Event Hall at 6 P.M.
W: Right, can you send me an updated invoice?
M: ⑦Oh, I'm sorry, but we can't change the price for changes within two days of the event.

問題31-33は次の会話に関するものです。
女性：こんにちは。Marg Downeyといいます。明日の当社の仕出しの依頼内容を更新したいのですが。
男性：なるほど… Clover Manufacturing の方ですよね。違いますか？
女性：ええ、そうです。それで、もともとの注文は、60人分の、デザートを含む4品の食事でした。でも自分たちで用意したケーキも提供するので、18人がデザートはもういらないと言っているんです。
男性：整理させてください。デザート付きのディナーを42人分とデザート無しを18人分ご希望されているということですね？
女性：その通りです。
男性：分かりました。それをHepburn Event Hall へ、午後6時にお届けします。
女性：そう、最新の請求書を送っていただけますか？
男性：ああ、申し訳ございませんが、私どもではイベントから2日以内の変更には料金の変更をいたしかねます。

□update：〜を更新する　□banquet：豪華な食事、宴会　□-course：〜品の

31.
Where most likely is the woman calling?（女性はどこに電話をかけていると考えられますか？）
(A) A hotel（ホテル）
(B) A restaurant（レストラン）
(C) A catering company（仕出し会社）
(D) A cake shop（ケーキ店）

正解：(C)　女性が電話をかけている相手を問う問題。女性は①で「仕出しの依頼内容を更新したい」と電話の目的を伝えている。相手の男性は、③「4品の食事」や⑥「Hepburn Event Hall へ、午後6時にお届けします」と述べている。これら発言から、女性は (C)「仕出し会社」に電話したと判断できる。会話の中に④「ケーキ」は登場するが、女性が「自分たちで用意する」と述べているので、(D) は不適切。

32. **NEW**
What does the man mean when he says, "Let me get this straight"?（男性は "Let me get this straight" と言う際、何を意図していますか？）
(A) He has to put some items in a line.（商品を1列に並べなくてはならない）
(B) He will adjust the cable of his telephone.（電話のケーブルを調節する）
(C) He will offer some advice.（助言を与える）
(D) He wants to clarify an order.（注文内容をはっきりさせたい）

正解：(D)　会話冒頭で女性は「仕出しの依頼内容を更新したい」と述べている。その後、②④で具体的な変更内容を伝えている。その発言を聞き、男性は Let me get this straight と述べ、⑤「デザート付きのディナーを42人分とデザート無しを18人分というご希望でいいか」と女性が伝えた変更内容を確認する発言をしている。よって、男性は、注文内容を正確に把握するためにこの発言をしていると判断できるので、(D) が正解。

33.
Why does the man say he cannot change the price?（男性はなぜ料金を変更できないと言っていますか？）
(A) Package prices are not flexible.（パック料金は融通がきかないから）
(B) The request is too late.（依頼が遅過ぎるから）
(C) There will be additional costs.（追加料金が掛かるから）
(D) The client is not a special member.（その顧客は特別会員ではないから）

正解：(B)　設問 the man say から、男性が料金を変更できない理由を述べることが分かる。「最終の請求書を送ってください」と述べる女性に対し、男性は⑦で「イベントから2日以内は料金の変更ができない」と返答している。つまり、変更を申し出るのが遅過ぎたということになる。よって、正解は (B)「依頼が遅過ぎるから」である。

12 Man US Woman AU

Questions 34 through 36 refer to the following conversation.
M: So, ①Mary, you've been really busy interviewing all those candidates this week — ②how was it?
W: It went well. ③I was pleased with the results. ④I met about five people that we're seriously considering for the position. They all fit the requirements. I don't think we'll rely on experience so much this time.
M: In the end, how will you choose the best one?
W: Actually, I need two, but ⑤I'm going to give them a test to see how well suited they are.

問題34-36は次の会話に関するものです。
男性：それで、Mary、君は候補者全員の面接をするのに今週は大忙しだったね――どうだった？
女性：うまくいったわよ。結果には満足したわ。私たちがその職にどうかと真剣に検討している5人ぐらいの人と面談をしたの。全員条件にぴったりよ。今回、経験はそれほど重視しないと思う。
男性：最終的にはどうやって最高の1人に絞るの？
女性：実際には2人必要なんだけど、試験を実施してどれぐらい適任かを見極めるつもりよ。

□**in the end**：結局、最終的に

34.
What is the conversation mainly about?（会話は主に何に関するものですか？）
(A) Hiring new staff members（新しいスタッフの採用）
(B) Writing an article（記事の執筆）
(C) Reviewing a performance（仕事ぶりの評価）
(D) Choosing a leader（リーダーの選出）

正解：**(A)**　会話のトピックを問う問題。①で男性が「候補者全員の面接」についての話を切り出している。その後、女性は④で「何人と面接したか」など面接の様子を具体的に説明している。よって、2人が話している内容は、(A)「新しいスタッフの採用」についてだと判断できる。本文のcandidate（候補者）の同義語である applicant（応募者、候補者）も TOEIC によく登場する。

35. NEW
What does the woman mean when she says, "It went well"?（女性が "It went well" と言う際、何を意図していますか？）

(A) Her work was successful.（彼女の仕事はうまくいった）
(B) A vehicle ran smoothly.（車がスムーズに走った）
(C) She greeted a visitor.（彼女は来客にあいさつをした）
(D) A device is functioning.（装置が機能している）

正解：**(A)**　男性が②で「どうだった？」と面接の感触を尋ね、女性は It went well と言い、③「結果には満足している」と述べている。つまり、面接はうまくいったと彼女が考えていることが分かる。よって、It went well という発言の意図としてふさわしいのは、(A)である。

36.
How does the woman say she will make a decision?（女性はどのように決定を下すと言っていますか？）
(A) By calling references（照会先に電話をする）
(B) By administering a test（試験を実施する）
(C) By checking qualifications（資格を確かめる）
(D) By holding more interviews（さらに面接を行う）
□**reference**：推薦者、照会先　□**administer**：～を実施する、～を与える

正解：**(B)**　設問の the woman say から女性が決断を下す方法を述べると判断できる。女性は2回目の発言⑤で、「候補者に試験を実施して適性を見極めるつもり」と述べている。よって、正解は (B)「テストを実施する」である。(A) にある reference（照会先）は求人関連の文書や会話によく登場する。

 ヒント⑤にも elision（gonna）あり！**(R)**

「3人の会話」はこんな形式!

1回のテストで1、2セット出る
- Part 3の全13セットの内、1セットか2セットが3人の会話

話し手は3人
- 3人の組み合わせは「男性2人＋女性」か「女性2人＋男性」

設問からはほとんど分からない
- 設問の形にほとんど特徴はないので、先読みでも気づきにくい。主語が the men、または the women と複数になっている設問では、「3人の会話」だと特定できる
- Questions xx through xx refer to the following conversation with three speakers.（問題 ｘｘ－ｘｘは次の3人の話し手による会話に関するものです）という指示文が聞こえて気づくという場合が多い

解説　形式に慣れさえすれば恐れるに足らず

「3人の会話」は新形式の中でも比較的目立つ変更ではありますが、恐れることはありません。「3人」という形式に動揺さえしなければ、2人の会話と同じ取り組み方で対応できる設問ばかりです。本書には3人の会話が8セットあります。本番のテストで指示文の最後、"... with three speakers." を聞いても平常心を保てるよう、十分に練習しましょう。

本書では3人の会話にも意図問題の設問を付けていますが、公開テストで出題される可能性は今のところ低いと見られます。意図問題強化のために、また「この先出題されない」とは断言できないので、これも力を抜かずに取り組んでください。

解説　声の聞き分けはネックにならない

この3人の会話について、受験者がよく口にするのは、同性2人（男性1と男性2、または女性1と女性2）の声を聞き分けられるだろうか、という不安です。でも、心配はいりません。どうやら、声の聞き分けが問題の難易度を上げる要因にならないように、いろいろと「気遣い」がされているらしいのです。

例えば…

【声質・アクセントが違う】
　同性2人は、低めの声の人と高めの声の人を合わせるなど、声質がかなり違うはずです。また、カナダ人男性とオーストラリア人男性のように、アクセントも違います。

【名前を呼ぶ】
　男女2人で会話している場に、別の男性が登場するときには、「トムが来たわ」とその人物の登場を告げたり、「トム！」と名前で呼び止めたりします。受験者はそこで心の準備ができます。また、同性の発言が続くときに名前が呼ばれることもあります。まるで話し手が交代したことをアピールするかのように。

【途中までは「2人？」】
　会話の前半には男女2人しか登場しない（または、発言しない）ケースが結構あります。実際のテストで2人目の同性の話し手が初めて発言したとき、「この人ずっとそこにいたの？」と驚いたりとか、「そうだ、これ、3人の会話だった！」と思い出したなんて話も聞きます。これには、まず1人目の男性（または女性）の声に受験者の耳を慣れさせて、それから2人目の男性（または女性）を登場させる、という意図があるものと思われます。

「3人の会話」攻略の基本

3人の会話に特別な攻略ストラテジーは必要ありません。
P.13「Part 3　攻略の基本」にある、
- 「先読み」を実行しよう
- 誰がヒントを言うのか確認
- 概要を問う設問は後回し

が、そのまま通用するので、ぜひ実行してください。

Part 3 ② 3人の会話 | ドリル

会話を聞き、各設問の解答として最も適切なものを選ぼう。問題の先読み（→P.15）を実践しよう。

37. What does the man mean when he says, "You don't say"?
    (A) He expects a written report.
    (B) He would like to make an announcement himself.
    (C) He has just received some bad news.
    (D) He is pleasantly surprised.

38. What will happen in December?
    (A) A restaurant will be opened.
    (B) A magazine will be published.
    (C) An inspection will be carried out.
    (D) A new menu will be released.

39. What do the women suggest?
    (A) Hiring a new chef
    (B) Renovating a kitchen
    (C) Offering a discount
    (D) Taking out an advertisement

40. What are the speakers mainly discussing?
    (A) Promoting an event
    (B) Attending an exhibition
    (C) Inviting a guest
    (D) Producing a program

41. What does the woman say about the event?
    (A) It was rescheduled.
    (B) Tickets are expensive.
    (C) It is over.
    (D) Many people will attend.

42. What does the woman imply when she says, "she's getting a lot of attention from the media"?
    (A) The artist's work is selling well.
    (B) The artist has been involved in high-profile projects.
    (C) The artist is gaining recognition.
    (D) The artist's works are likely to increase in price.

43. What is the main topic of the conversation?
    (A) A software update
    (B) A new store
    (C) A sales report
    (D) A client appointment

44. What does Bob mean when he says, "We'll be in a meeting until 12 o'clock"?
    (A) He has already completed a job.
    (B) He cannot assist with a problem.
    (C) A conference room will be unavailable.
    (D) He does not need an update urgently.

45. What do the men decide to do?
    (A) Have lunch together
    (B) Demonstrate a device
    (C) Attend a workshop
    (D) Reschedule a meeting

46. Where does the conversation take place?
    (A) At a real estate agency
    (B) In a bank
    (C) In a restaurant
    (D) At a market

47. What does the man imply when he says, "we don't have anything particular in mind"?
    (A) He is in charge of making a decision.
    (B) He has not considered a proposal.
    (C) He has not started planning for an event.
    (D) He is willing to listen to suggestions.

48. What does the man ask?
    (A) The price of an item
    (B) The location of a train station
    (C) The duration of a show
    (D) The name of a business

49. What is the conversation mainly about?
    (A) Reducing the size of an office
    (B) Hiring a new receptionist
    (C) Relocating to a new town
    (D) Renting business equipment

50. What do the men imply about the company?
    (A) It will spend a lot on renovations.
    (B) It will have a shortage of meeting space.
    (C) It has been growing rapidly.
    (D) It needs to offer more employee benefits.

51. Why does the woman say, "You're not wrong"?
    (A) She is a little doubtful.
    (B) She is sorry.
    (C) She feels the same.
    (D) She wonders who made a mistake.

52. Why does the man say, "There's nothing important on the schedule"?
    (A) To set up an appointment
    (B) To point out a problem
    (C) To criticize a staff member
    (D) To explain a decision

53. What do the women imply about Woody's Shopping Center?
    (A) Its stores are offering discounts.
    (B) It is very nearby.
    (C) It was recently renovated.
    (D) Its parking lot is usually full.

54. What will happen on Monday?
    (A) A discount sale
    (B) A retirement party
    (C) A factory inspection
    (D) An opening ceremony

55. What does the man imply when he says, "I heard the tenant next door is moving soon"?
    (A) It will open an overseas branch.
    (B) His company should consider finding a new address.
    (C) His coworkers should organize a party.
    (D) His company should rent neighboring office space.

56. Who most likely is Mr. De Keizer?
    (A) A real estate agent
    (B) A company president
    (C) A landlord
    (D) A client

57. What will the man most likely do next?
    (A) Update a price list
    (B) Leave on a trip
    (C) Make a phone call
    (D) Look for a new job

58. When does the man say the photocopier was purchased?
    (A) Three years ago
    (B) Four years ago
    (C) Five years ago
    (D) Six years ago

59. What does the man mean when he says "I'll give you that"?
    (A) He will provide some equipment.
    (B) He agrees with a point.
    (C) He disagrees with an opinion.
    (D) He does not need a device.

60. What do the women suggest about the tablet computers?
    (A) They are not used enough.
    (B) They have made work much easier.
    (C) They are in need of an upgrade.
    (D) They cannot connect to the network.

Part 3 ②3人の会話　ドリルの解答・解説

 13 | Woman 1 AU | Man UK | Woman 2 CA

Questions 37 through 39 refer to the following conversation with three speakers.

W 1: Hi. I'm glad I found you both together here. ①I just heard that we've won *Dining Out* magazine's Restaurant of the Year award!
M: You don't say! ②I didn't expect such great news after only being in business for 18 months.
W 2: When will it be announced to the public?
W 1: ③In the next issue of *Dining Out*. It's a quarterly—
M: ④So not until December? I want to use this for publicity. It'll really help our reputation and bring in more customers.
W 1: ⑤How about taking out a big advertisement in *Dining Out*?
W 2: ⑥Good idea. We should make sure people notice the award.
M: I'll give them a call and check their advertising rates.

問題37-39は次の3人の話し手による会話に関するものです。
女性1: ねえ。2人一緒にいてくれてよかった。今聞いたんだけど、私たち、*Dining Out* 誌の年間最優秀レストラン賞に選ばれたんですって！
男性: まさか！ 開業からたった18カ月で、そんなすごいニュースは予想していなかったよ。
女性2: それはいつ一般に発表されるの？
女性1: 次号の *Dining Out* よ。季刊誌だから——
男性: じゃあ12月までは出ないってこと？ このことを宣伝に使いたいな。うちの評判を高めてくれて、お客さんも呼び込んでくれるだろうから。
女性1: *Dining Out* に大きな広告を出すのはどうかしら？
女性2: いい考えね。人々に賞のことを知らせるべきだわ。
男性: 僕が電話をして広告料を確認するよ。

□**You don't say！**：まさか！、本当？　□**quarterly**：季刊誌　□**take out an advertisement**：広告を出す

 男性が女性の話を遮って発言する箇所があります。**(R)**

37. NEW
What does the man mean when he says, "You don't say"?（男性は "You don't say" と言う際、何を意図していますか？）
(A) He expects a written report.（書面での報告を期待している）

(B) He would like to make an announcement himself.（自分で発表をしたい）
(C) He has just received some bad news.（悪いニュースを聞いたばかりである）
(D) He is pleasantly surprised.（うれしい驚きを感じている）

正解：(D) 男性のYou don't sayという発言の意図が問われている。①で「私たちが *Dining Out* 誌の年間最優秀レストラン賞に選ばれた」と述べた女性1に、男性は You don't say と述べ、さらに②「開業からたった18カ月で、そんなすごいニュースは予想してなかった」と返答している。つまり、受賞のニュースに驚き、喜んで You don't say! と発言していることが判断できる。よって、(D) が正解。

38.
What will happen in December?（12月には何がありますか？）
(A) A restaurant will be opened.（レストランが開店する）
(B) A magazine will be published.（雑誌が出版される）
(C) An inspection will be carried out.（検査が実施される）
(D) A new menu will be released.（新しいメニューが発表される）
□**inspection**：検査、調査

正解：(B) 12月に起きることが問われている。③で女性1が、「受賞のニュースは、次号の季刊誌 *Dining Out* に掲載される」と述べている。それを受け、男性は④「12月まで出ないということか」と質問している。つまり、12月に *Dining Out* という雑誌が出版されるということが分かるので、正解は (B)。 magazine は quarterly の言い換え。

39.
What do the women suggest?（女性たちは何を提案していますか？）
(A) Hiring a new chef（新しいシェフを雇うこと）
(B) Renovating a kitchen（キッチンをリフォームすること）
(C) Offering a discount（割引をすること）
(D) Taking out an advertisement（広告を出すこと）
□**renovate**：～を改装する、～をリフォームする

正解：(D) 設問文に複数形の women や men が含まれていれば、3人の会話であることの目印。音声が流れる前に心構えをして、「それぞれがどのような役割なのか」ということを考えながら聞こう。女性1は⑤「*Dining Out* に大きな広告を出すのはどうか」と提案している。女性2は⑥「いい考えだ」とそれに同意し、「多くの人に知らせるべきだ」と述べている。よって、2人が提案している内容は (D) である。

036

14 | Man 1 US | Woman AU | Man 2 UK

Questions 40 through 42 refer to the following conversation with three speakers.

M 1: How about going into the city this evening ①to see the art exhibition by Brian Walsh? It was on the news last week, and I thought it looked really interesting.
W: ②That ended on Tuesday.
M 2: ③Yeah, I saw that on their Web site earlier. I'd wanted to see it, too.
W: The gallery is featuring another ④artist now. She's visiting from France.
M 1: That's disappointing. I was looking forward to viewing Brian Walsh's ⑤paintings. ⑥Do you think this French artist is worth checking out, then?
W: Well, she's getting a lot of attention from the media.
M 2: ⑦That's good enough for me.

問題40-42は次の3人の話し手による会話に関するものです。
男性1: 今晩 Brian Walsh の作品展を見に街へ出掛けない？ 先週、ニュースでやっていたんだけど、すごく面白そうだと思ったんだ。
女性: それなら火曜日に終了したわよ。
男性2: うん、この前ウェブサイトで見た。僕も見たかったんだよな。
女性: その画廊は今、別のアーティストを取り上げているわ。フランスから来ている人よ。
男性1: がっかりだな。Brian Walsh の絵を見るのを楽しみにしていたのに。このフランス人アーティストは見る価値あると思う？
女性: そうねえ、彼女はメディアで大きな注目を集めているわ。
男性2: 僕にはそれで十分だ。

□**art exhibition**：美術展、展覧会　□**view**：〜を見る
□**get attention from 〜**：〜の注目を集める

40.
What are the speakers mainly discussing?（話し手たちは主に何について話しているのですか？）
(A) Promoting an event（イベントのプロモーションをすること）
(B) Attending an exhibition（作品展に行くこと）
(C) Inviting a guest（客を招待すること）
(D) Producing a program（番組を制作すること）

正解：(B)　会話の話題を問う問題。男性1は①で「作品展に見に行こう」と提案している。さらに、女性は④「アーティスト」、男性1は⑤「絵」と述べている。その後も、別のアーティストの絵を見に行く話をしていることから、会話のトピックは「作品展を見に行くこと」だと判断できる。よって、(B) が正解。作品展のことを event と言い換えることはできるが、それを promote（宣伝する）ことについて話しているわけではないので、(A) は不適切。

41.
What does the woman say about the event?（女性はイベントについて何と言っていますか？）
(A) It was rescheduled.（予定変更された）
(B) Tickets are expensive.（チケットが高い）
(C) It is over.（終わっている）
(D) Many people will attend.（大勢の人々が行く）

正解：(C)　女性がイベントについて述べている内容が問われている。女性は②で「作品展は火曜日に終わった」と述べている。よって、正解は (C)「終わっている」である。また、②の後に、男性2が③「僕もそれを見たかった」と返答している。この返答からも、女性がイベントは終わったという発言をしたと判断できる。

42. NEW
What does the woman imply when she says, "she's getting a lot of attention from the media"?（女性は "she's getting a lot of attention from the media" と言う際、何を示唆していますか？）
(A) The artist's work is selling well.（そのアーティストの作品はよく売れている）
(B) The artist has been involved in high-profile projects.（そのアーティストは注目を浴びるプロジェクトに関わってきた）
(C) The artist is gaining recognition.（そのアーティストは認められつつある）
(D) The artist's works are likely to increase in price.（そのアーティストの作品は値上がりするだろう）

□**high-profile**：注目を浴びる、知名度の高い　□**gain recognition**：認められる

正解：(C)　⑥で「フランス人画家の作品を見る価値があるか」と尋ねる男性1に対し、女性が she's getting a lot of attention from the media と述べ、男性2は⑦「それで十分だ」と返答している。つまり、男性2に「その画家の作品を見に行こう」と思わせるような発言を女性がしたと考えられる。よって、(C) が正解。会話の中で作品の売れ行きの話はしていないので、(A) も (D) も不適切。プロジェクトに関する話もしていないので、(B) も不可。

Part 3　②3人の会話

037

15　Man 1 US　Woman CA　Man 2 UK

Questions 43 through 45 refer to the following conversation with three speakers.

M 1: ①We need to submit the software updates as soon as possible. A lot of customers are complaining that they can't access important information on their phones.
W: I'm on top of it. ②I've been working on it since I got in this morning. I'm almost finished. Bob, I'll send it to your team for testing as soon as it's ready.
M 2: Thanks, Clair. ③Take your time, though. We'll be in a meeting until 12 o'clock. ④So we won't be able to look at it until after lunch.
M 1: I was hoping we'd be ready before that.
W: I can probably get it done by 11 o'clock.
M 1: ⑤Bob, do you think you could have the meeting in the afternoon instead?
M 2: ⑥Sure. I'll contact everyone now.
M 1: ⑦That'd be best.

問題43-45は次の3人による会話に関するものです。
男性1：ソフトウエアの更新版を至急出す必要がある。たくさんのお客さんが電話の重要な情報にアクセスできないって苦情を言ってきてるよ。
女性：私がちゃんとやってるわ。今朝出社してからずっと掛かりきりよ。もう少しで終わるから。Bob、準備ができ次第、テスト用にあなたのチームへ送るわね。
男性2：ありがとう、Clair。でも急ぐことないよ。僕たち12時まで会議なんだ。だから昼食後までは見られないんだ。
男性1：僕はその前に準備できればと思っていたんだけど。
女性：たぶん11時までにはできるわ。
男性1：Bob、会議を午後にすることはできないかな？
男性2：いいよ。早速みんなに連絡するよ。
男性1：それがいい。

□**be on top of it**：うまくコントロールしている

女性の発言 I'm on top of it. は、状況をコントロールできているという意味。事態は収束に向かっているということです。**(R)**

43.
What is the main topic of the conversation?（会話の主な話題は何ですか？）
(A) A software update（ソフトウエアの更新）
(B) A new store（新店舗）
(C) A sales report（売上報告書）
(D) A client appointment（顧客との約束）

正解：(A)　冒頭①で男性1が「ソフトウエアの更新版が至急必要だ」と述べ、女性が②「朝からそれに掛かりっきりだ」と言っている。その後も、更新の準備に関する話をしていることから、会話の話題は、(A)「ソフトウエアの更新」だと分かる。会話後半には、会議の話が登場する。会議や面会などの「予定」や「約束」を、appointment という単語で言い表すことは可能だが、「顧客との会議」の話をしているわけではないので、(D)は不適切。

44. NEW
What does Bob mean when he says, "We'll be in a meeting until 12 o'clock"?（Bob が "We'll be in a meeting until 12 o'clock" と言う際、何を意図していますか？）
(A) He has already completed a job.（彼はすでに仕事を終えている）
(B) He cannot assist with a problem.（彼は問題に手を貸すことができない）
(C) A conference room will be unavailable.（会議室が使用できなくなる）
(D) He does not need an update urgently.（彼は更新を緊急に必要としているわけではない）

正解：(D)　テスト用ソフトウエアの準備を急いでいる女性に対し、男性2は③「急がなくていい」と述べ、We'll be in a meeting until 12 o'clock と言い、④「だから昼食後まで見ることができない」と述べている。つまり、男性の状況を説明することにより、「急がなくていい」と述べた理由を説明していると判断できる。よって、(D) が正解。前後の内容から、会議室の使用状況を伝えようとしているわけではないことが分かるので、(C)は不適切。

45.
What do the men decide to do?（男性たちは何をすることに決めますか？）
(A) Have lunch together（一緒に昼食を取る）
(B) Demonstrate a device（機器を実際に使ってみせる）
(C) Attend a workshop（研修に出席する）
(D) Reschedule a meeting（会議の予定を変更する）

□**device**：機器、装置

正解：(D)　設問に the men decide to do とあるので、この会話は3人による会話で、男性2人が同じ結論に達することが分かる。男性1は⑤「会議を午後に変更できないか」と男性2に尋ね、男性2は、⑥でみんなに連絡することを申し出ている。それに対し、男性1は⑦「それがいい」と返答している。これらの発言内容から、2人は「会議の時間を変更することにした」と判断できるので、(D)が正解。

16 | Woman 1 CA | Woman 2 AU | Man UK

Questions 46 through 48 refer to the following conversation with three speakers.

W 1: ①Welcome to McGillicutty's Restaurant. My name is Brenda and I'll be serving you this evening. Would you like some more time to look at the menu?
W 2: Thanks, Brenda, but ②I think we'd like to hear your opinion about what's good here.
M: Yeah, we don't have anything particular in mind.
W 1: OK, well, let me see. ③The avocado chicken spaghetti is always very popular. Do you like avocado?
M: I love it.
W 2: Me, too. That's settled. ④We'll take two of them for now, and we'll order drinks when you come back.
W 1: Very well.
M: Oh! Before you go, ⑤could you tell me where the nearest train station is?
W 1: ⑥There's one just across the street.

問題46-48は次の3人による会話に関するものです。
女性1：McGillicutty's Restaurantへようこそ。私はBrendaと申しまして、今晩お二人の担当をさせていただきます。もう少しメニューをご覧になりますか？
女性2：ありがとう、Brenda、でも私たち、この店で何がおいしいのかあなたの意見を聞きたいわ。
男性：そうだね、特にこれというものが思い浮かばないんだ。
女性1：分かりました、ええと、そうですねえ。アボカド・チキン・スパゲティは常に人気があります。アボカドはお好きですか？
男性：大好きだ。
女性2：私も。それに決まりね。取りあえず、それを2人分お願いします、それで、あなたが戻ってきたら飲み物を注文します。
女性1：承知いたしました。
男性：そうだ！ 最寄りの電車の駅を教えてもらえませんか？
女性1：通りの真向かいにありますよ。

□ **That's settled.**:「それは決着した」「それは決まった」

46.

Where does the conversation take place?（この会話はどこで行われていますか？）
(A) At a real estate agency（不動産屋で）
(B) In a bank（銀行で）
(C) In a restaurant（レストランで）
(D) At a market（市場で）

正解:(C) 会話が行われている場所を問う問題。女性1が①で「レストラン」と「メニュー」と言っている。その後も「何を注文するか」という話を中心に会話が行われているので、ウエーターと食事客が「レストランで」会話をしていると判断できる。よって、(C)が正解。serveの名詞 server（給仕係、接客係）と diner（食事客）もTOEICによく登場する。

47. NEW

What does the man imply when he says, "we don't have anything particular in mind"?（男性は "we don't have anything particular in mind" と言う際、何を示唆していますか？）
(A) He is in charge of making a decision.（彼が決断を握っている）
(B) He has not considered a proposal.（彼は提案を検討していない）
(C) He has not started planning for an event.（彼はイベントの計画を始めていない）
(D) He is willing to listen to suggestions.（彼は提案を聞く気がある）

正解:(D) 女性2が②で、レストランのお薦めを尋ね、男性は we don't have anything particular in mind と述べている。2人の発言を聞き、女性1は、③でメニューを提案している。その後、2人は提案されたメニューを注文している（④）。つまり、男性はウエーターの提案を聞いた後に、注文する料理を決めようとしていたことが分かる。よって、(D)が正解。be willing to do は「〜する気がある」という意味のフレーズ。

48.

What does the man ask?（男性は何を尋ねていますか？）
(A) The price of an item（ものの値段）
(B) The location of a train station（駅の場所）
(C) The duration of a show（作品の長さ）
(D) The name of a business（店名）

正解:(B) 設問から、男性が何か質問をすることが分かる。⑤に「〜を教えてくれますか」という表現、could you tell me 〜? がある。男性が尋ねている内容は、「最寄りの駅がどこにあるか」である。よって、正解は(B)「駅の場所」である。男性の発言⑤を聞いて、女性1が⑥で「通りの真向かい」と道順を説明していることからも(B)を選べる。(C)の duration（期間）は重要語。for the duration of 〜（〜の期間中）というフレーズも覚えておこう。

17　Man 1 UK　Woman CA　Man 2 US

Questions 49 through 51 refer to the following conversation with three speakers.

M 1: ①Did you hear that the company will be reducing our office space?
W: Yeah, I heard that they'll stop renting the conference room.
M 1: ②We need that room for meetings.
M 2: ③I know. Where will we meet from now on?
W: Well, the reception area is very large. I suppose they'll divide that.
M 2: Who's going to rent the space we used as a conference room? ④It would only suit a very small company.
W: You're not wrong. ⑤Perhaps a lawyer or someone who works alone will move in.

問題49-51の問題は次の3人による会話に関するものです。
男性1：会社が僕らのオフィスのスペースを減らそうとしているって聞いた？
女性：ええ、会議室を借りるのをやめるって聞いたわ。
男性1：あの部屋は会議に必要だよ。
男性2：そうだよね。これからどこで打ち合わせをすればいいんだろう？
女性：そうねえ、受付のエリアはすごく広いわ。あそこを分割するんじゃないかしら。
男性2：われわれが会議室に使っていたスペースは誰が借りるの？　よほど小さな会社じゃないと合わないよ。
女性：その通りね。たぶん弁護士とか1人で働く人が入るんじゃないかしら。

☐ **from now on**：これから、今後　☐ **divide**：〜を分割する　☐ **suit**：〜に適合する、〜に合う　☐ **You're not wrong.**：「その通り」

> この会話でも going to を gonna と発音する elision が聞こえます。(R)

49.
What is the conversation mainly about?（会話は主に何に関するものですか？）
(A) Reducing the size of an office（オフィスのサイズの削減）
(B) Hiring a new receptionist（新しい受付係の採用）
(C) Relocating to a new town（新しい街への移転）
(D) Renting business equipment（事務機器のレンタル）

☐ **relocate**：移転する

正解：(A)　会話の話題を問う問題。冒頭①で男性1は、「会社がオフィススペースを減らそうとしていることを知っているか」と2人に尋ねている。その後、オフィススペースがなくなった後に会議を行う場所（③）や使用してきたスペースの使い道（④、⑤）などについて話している。よって、この会話の話題は、(A)「オフィスのサイズの削減」だと分かる。「移転」については述べられていないので、(C)は不適切。

50.
What do the men imply about the company?（男性たちは会社について何を示唆していますか？）
(A) It will spend a lot on renovations.（リフォームにたくさんのお金を使う）
(B) It will have a shortage of meeting space.（会議スペースが足りなくなる）
(C) It has been growing rapidly.（急成長している）
(D) It needs to offer more employee benefits.（もっと福利厚生を提供すべきである）

正解：(B)　男性たちの発言に関する「暗示問題」。話者の発言から、示唆されている内容を推測する必要がある。冒頭で「会社が会議室を借りるのをやめる可能性がある」と述べられた。それを聞き、男性1は②「あの部屋は会議に必要だ」と述べ、男性2はそれに同意し、③「今後の会議をどこで行うのか」と尋ねている。これらの発言から、男性たちは会社について「会議用の場所が不足する」ということをほのめかしていると分かるので、(B)が正解。

51. NEW
Why does the woman say, "You're not wrong"?（女性はなぜ "You're not wrong" と言っていますか？）
(A) She is a little doubtful.（少し疑わしいから）
(B) She is sorry.（気の毒に感じるから）
(C) She feels the same.（同じ気持ちだから）
(D) She wonders who made a mistake.（誰が間違いを犯したのか知りたいと思うから）

正解：(C)　女性の You're not wrong という発言の意図を問う問題。④「（そのスペースは）よほど小さな会社でなければ合わない」と述べる男性2に対し、女性は You're not wrong. と言い、その後に⑤「1人で働く人が使うのではないか」と男性2と同じような意見を述べている。よって、男性Bに賛同する意味でこの発言をしたことが分かるので、(C)が正解。

18 | Woman 1 CA | Man UK | Woman 2 AU

Questions 52 through 54 refer to the following conversation with three speakers.

W 1: Peter, ①would you mind if Zoe and I took some time off this afternoon?
M: ②Fine by me. There's nothing important on the schedule. Where are you off to?
W 2: ③We'd just like to go to Woody's Shopping Center before it closes — this is the last day of the spring sales.
W 1: ④We want to take advantage of the bargains.
M: I see. Well, have fun!
W 2: We will.
M: ⑤Oh, and don't forget, we'll all be meeting at the Greenvale Convention Center on Monday rather than in the office.
W 1: ⑥That's right! We have to prepare for Mr. Kruger's retirement party.

問題52-54は次の3人による会話に関するものです。
女性1：Peter、今日の午後、Zoeと私、休みをもらってもいいかしら？
男性：僕は構わないよ。予定には重要なことは何もないし。君たちどこへ行くの？
女性2：Woody's Shopping Centerが閉まる前に行きたいのよ——今日が春のセールの最終日なの。
女性1：バーゲンを利用したいというわけ。
男性：なるほど。まあ、楽しんでおいでよ！
女性2：そうさせてもらうわ。
男性：あっ、忘れないで、月曜はオフィスじゃなくて、僕ら全員Greenvale Convention Centerで会うんだからね。
女性1：そうだわ！ Krugerさんの退職パーティーの準備をしなくちゃいけないのよね。

□ **take advantage of 〜**：〜を利用する、〜に乗じる

> この会話には want to の elision（省略）、wanna が女性1の発言に登場します。**(R)**

52. NEW

Why does the man say, "There's nothing important on the schedule"?（男性はなぜ "There's nothing important on the schedule" と言っていますか？）
(A) To set up an appointment（アポイントを取るため）
(B) To point out a problem（問題を指摘するため）
(C) To criticize a staff member（職員を批判するため）
(D) To explain a decision（決断を説明するため）

正解：(D) 新形式の「意図問題」。女性1は①で、男性から休みの許可を得ようとしている。それを受け、男性は②「構わない」と述べているので、女性1たちに休みを与えたことが分かる。その発言の後に、There's nothing important on the schedule. と述べている。つまり「重要な予定はない」と言うことで、休みを与えた理由を説明するしようとしていることが分かる。よって、その言い換えとしてふさわしい(D)「決断を説明するため」が正解。

53.

What do the women imply about Woody's Shopping Center?（女性たちはWoody's Shopping Centerについて何を示唆していますか？）
(A) Its stores are offering discounts.（店が割引を提供している）
(B) It is very nearby.（非常に近くにある）
(C) It was recently renovated.（最近改装された）
(D) Its parking lot is usually full.（そこの駐車場は大抵満車である）

正解：(A) 設問に the women imply とあるので、女性たちがWoody's Shopping Centerに関する発言をすることが分かる。女性2の③「今日がWoody's Shopping Center春のセール最終日」、女性1の④「バーゲンを利用したい」という発言から、このショッピングセンターではセールが行われていると判断することができる。よって、それを「店が割引を提供している」と言い換えた(A)が正解。

54.

What will happen on Monday?（月曜に何が起きますか？）
(A) A discount sale（割引セール）
(B) A retirement party（退職パーティー）
(C) A factory inspection（工場の視察）
(D) An opening ceremony（開場式典）

正解：(B) 設問と選択肢から、月曜日に何かの行事があることが分かる。男性が⑤で「月曜はオフィスではなくGreenvale Convention Centerで会う」と女性たちに念を押している。それを受け、女性1が⑥「Krugerさんの退職パーティーの準備をしなくては」と述べている。よって、正解は(B)。定年退職など理由に「退職する」場合は、(B) retirementの動詞、retireが使われ、自らの意思で仕事を「辞める」場合は、quitやleaveが使われる。

19 Woman 1 AU Man UK Woman 2 CA

Questions 55 through 57 refer to the following conversation with three speakers.

W 1: ①I feel like it's time to get some new offices. We're running out of space.
M: I heard the tenant next door is moving soon.
W 1: Me, too. ②We could really use that room.
W 2: Yeah. ③Well, let's talk to the company president about it. He might already be considering it.
W 1: ④That's right. Mr. De Keizer mentioned that he wanted to expand the company over the next few years.
W 2: ⑤Tim, you should give him a call.
M: ⑥I'll do that.

問題55-57は次の3人による会話に関するものです。
女性1：私、新しいオフィスを持つべき時期じゃないかと感じてるの。スペースが足りていないもの。
男性：隣のテナントが近々移転するって聞いたよ。
女性1：私も聞いた。あの部屋があったら本当にいいわよね。
女性2：そうよね。じゃあ、社長にこのことを話してみましょうよ。彼もすでに検討しているかもしれないわ。
女性1：その通りだわ。De Keizer さんは今後3年で会社を拡大したいって言ってたもの。
女性2：Tim、あなたが彼に電話をすべきだわ。
男性：そうするよ。

55. NEW
What does the man imply when he says, "I heard the tenant next door is moving soon"?（男性は "I heard the tenant next door is moving soon" と言う際、何を示唆していますか？）
(A) It will open an overseas branch.（そのテナントは海外支社を開く）
(B) His company should consider finding a new address.（彼の会社は新しい住所を探すことを検討すべきだ）
(C) His coworkers should organize a party.（彼の同僚たちはパーティーを開くべきだ）
(D) His company should rent neighboring office space.（彼の会社は隣接するオフィス・スペースを借りるべきだ）
☐**neighboring**：隣接する、近隣の

正解：(D) この会話における、I heard the tenant next door is moving soon という男性の発言の意図が問われている。男性は、女性1の①「スペースが足りないので、新しいオフィスを持つべき」という提案を受けて、I heard the tenant next door is moving soon と述べている。女性1はそれに対し、②「あの部屋があったらいい」と返答している。この流れから、男性の発言は「近々空くと聞いた隣のスペースを借りるのはどうか」ということだと解釈できるので、(D)が正解。

56.
Who most likely is Mr. De Keizer?（De Keizer さんとは誰であると考えられますか？）
(A) A real estate agent（不動産業者）
(B) A company president（会社社長）
(C) A landlord（家主）
(D) A client（顧客）
☐**real estate agent**：不動産業者

正解：(B) 女性2は③「（隣を借りることを）社長も検討しているかもしれない」と述べ、女性1は④で、その発言に同意し、「De Keizer 氏が会社を拡大したいと言っていた」と述べている。これらの発言内容から、De Keizer 氏は「会社の社長」と考えられるので、正解は(B)。彼は部屋を借りる立場なので、(A) や (C) は不適切。(A) の real estate agent は TOEIC に頻出するが、他にも、travel agent（旅行代理店）や advertising agent（広告代理店）などの「代理店」がよく登場する。

57.
What will the man most likely do next?（男性は次に何をすると考えられますか？）
(A) Update a price list（価格表を更新する）
(B) Leave on a trip（旅行に出掛ける）
(C) Make a phone call（電話をかける）
(D) Look for a new job（新しい仕事を探す）

正解：(C) 男性の「次の行動」が問われている。Part 3 の会話は、男性・女性が会話の後に「何をするか」を述べて終わることも多い。この設問があったら、会話の最後の方にある予定や意志を伝える表現に注意しよう。⑤で女性2が「De Keizer 氏に電話すべきだ」と男性に伝えている。それを受け、男性は、⑥I'll 〜（私が〜する）という表現を使って、De Keizer 氏に連絡するということを述べている。よって、(C)が正解。

🔊 20 | Woman 1 AU | Man US | Woman 2 CA

Questions 58 through 60 refer to the following conversation with three speakers.

W 1: We need to get a new photocopier for the general affairs office.
M: But ①that's the newest photocopier in the whole company. We bought it about three years ago.
W 1: Well, they have to print out a lot of memos for the whole company. ②So, their copier gets a lot more use than the machines in other departments.
M: I'll give you that. ③But photocopiers aren't cheap.
W 2: Yeah ... ④Let's talk to them about some alternatives. Every member of the staff has a tablet computer. Can't they make use of them more to send memos? It'd save paper, too.
W 1: ⑤I was thinking that.
M: Let's swap their copier with one in another department for now.
W 2: Great. Then, let's talk to them about using the tablet computers more.

問題58-60は次の3人の話し手による会話に関するものです。
女性1：総務部用に新しいコピー機を入れる必要があります。
男性：でも、あれは社内で一番新しいコピー機だよ。3年くらい前に購入したんだから。
女性1：まあ、彼らは全社用の連絡メモをたくさん出力しなくてはなりませんから。彼らのコピー機は、他の部のコピー機よりもたくさん使われるんですよ。
男性：その点は認める。でもコピー機は安くはないからね。
女性2：そうですね…彼らと代替案について話をしてみましょう。スタッフは各自タブレットコンピューターを持っています。メモを送るのにはもっとそれを活用できないでしょうか？紙の節約にもなりますし。
女性1：私もそれを考えていました。
男性：ひとまずは彼らのコピー機を他の部のものと交換しよう。
女性2：それはいいですね。それから、タブレットコンピューターをもっと活用することを彼らと話し合いましょう。

☐ **general affairs office**：総務部　☐ **I'll give you that.**：「その点は認めます」、「その点は確かにその通りです」
☐ **alternative**：選択肢、代替案　☐ **for now**：差し当たり、ひとまず

58.
When does the man say the photocopier was purchased?（男性はコピー機がいつ購入されたと言っていますか？）

(A) Three years ago（3年前）
(B) Four years ago（4年前）
(C) Five years ago（5年前）
(D) Six years ago（6年前）

正解：(A)　設問の the man say から、男性がコピー機を購入した日時を述べることが分かる。①で男性は「あれは社内で一番新しいコピー機で、約3年前に購入した」と述べている。よって、正解は (A)「3年前」。この会話では1回しか登場しなかったが、選択肢に時刻や曜日などが並んでいる場合、会話の中で複数の時刻や曜日が出てくることもあるので、集中して聞き取るようにしよう。

---

59. NEW
What does the man mean when he says "I'll give you that"?（男性は "I'll give you that" と言う際、何を意図していますか？）

(A) He will provide some equipment.（備品を与えるつもりである）
(B) He agrees with a point.（ある点について同意する）
(C) He disagrees with an opinion.（意見に反対である）
(D) He does not need a device.（装置は必要ではない）

正解：(B)　新しいコピー機を買うことに消極的な男性に、女性1は②で使用量の違いを説明している。その後、男性は I'll give you that. と述べ、③「でもコピー機は安くない」と付け加えている。つまり、安くないので、すぐに購入しようとは言っていないが、購入する必要があることには同意をしていると判断できる。よって、正解は (B)。反対意見を述べたのなら、③で But を加えずに「高いから必要ない」という内容が続いていないと不自然なので、(C) は不適切。

60.
What do the women suggest about the tablet computers?（女性たちはタブレットコンピューターについて何を示唆していますか？）

(A) They are not used enough.（十分に活用されていない）
(B) They have made work much easier.（仕事を楽にしてくれた）
(C) They are in need of an upgrade.（アップグレードが必要である）
(D) They cannot connect to the network.（ネット

043

ワークに接続ができない)
□**in need of ～**：～を必要として

正解：(A)　設問 the women suggest から、女性2人がタブレットコンピューターに関する発言をすることが分かる。女性2は④で、「新しいコピー機を買う代わりに、各自が持っているタブレットコンピューターをもっと活用しよう」と提案している。それに対し、女性1も⑤で「同じことを考えていた」と述べている。これらの発言には、「現在はタブレットコンピューターが十分に活用されていない」ということがほのめかされているので、(A) が正解。

Part 3

② 3人の会話

グラフィック問題はこんな問題！

1回のテストで2、3問出題される
- 意図問題と合わせて5問
- グラフィック付きのセットが登場するのは、Part 3 の最後

フォーマットも設問も独特
- 表や図が1問目の設問よりも前に置かれているので嫌でも目に入る
- グラフィックと関係する設問は3問中の1問だけ。必ず Look at the graphic.(図を見てください) で始まる

解答時間が長い
- 通常、Part 3 の問題の解答には1問当たり8秒が与えられるが、グラフィック問題は12秒に設定されている

解説　音だけでは解けない！

　グラフィック問題の graphic とはグラフのことではありません。何らかのビジュアル・イメージのことです。視覚的なインパクトはありますが、決して難問というわけではありません。今のところ、「商品名と値段」「電車と発車時刻」のような、シンプルな表形式のものが圧倒的（約8割）です。その他、数は少ないですが、何かのクーポン券や地図、見取り図のようなものが出ることもあります。グラフィック問題は、音だけ聞いても解けません。音とグラフィック、両方の情報を統合して初めて解ける作りになっています。
　次のような表と設問があったとします。

「シンポジウム：講演予定」

月曜	タカシ・トヤマ
火曜	スーザン・カーター
水曜	ジョディ・ウォン
木曜	マイケル・ロペス

設問：水曜日に講演するのは誰ですか？

　さらに、「水曜日に講演するウォンさんに、そろそろハンドアウトを送ってもらわなくちゃ」という情報が聞こえたとしたらどうでしょう。音だけでもグラフィックだけでも設問に答えることができますね。このような、音だけ、またはグラフィック中の情報だけで解けてしまう問題がグラフィック問題として出題されることはありません。

「グラフィック問題」攻略の基本

● グラフィック問題の先読み

グラフィック問題でも先読みは必須ですが、最も重要なのは、「パートナー情報」に目を向けることです。
[パートナー情報の例]

| 選択肢 | 「シンポジウム：講演予定」 |

選択肢
(A) 月曜
(B) 火曜
(C) 水曜
(D) 木曜

月曜	タカシ・トヤマ
火曜	スーザン・カーター
水曜	ジョディ・ウォン
木曜	マイケル・ロペス

← パートナー情報

上のように、選択肢には曜日が並んでいて、リストにも同じ月～木の曜日が存在するとします。グラフィックには、多くの場合このように、選択肢と一致する情報があります。このときの、選択肢と共通していない方の情報が「パートナー情報」（ここでは人名）です。会話を聞くときには、このパートナー情報を見ながら聞くことをお勧めします。パートナー情報は会話に音として登場する可能性が高く、問題が解きやすくなるからです（ただし、グラフィックに関係しない2問を解くには、それらの選択肢を見てください）。グラフィック問題以外では、（違う形に言い換えられているとしても）正解の選択肢が音として会話に登場しますが、グラフィック問題においては、そのような現象はめったに起きません。

地図のようなグラフィックでも、先読みのやり方は基本的に同じです。リストのように情報が整然と配置されていない分、多少の読みにくさはありますが、この場合も、選択肢とグラフィックの共通項ではない方の情報に注意を向けましょう。

★グラフィック問題については、P.74～75でも説明されています

Part 3　③グラフィック問題　ドリル

会話を聞き、各設問の解答として最も適切なものを選ぼう。問題の先読み（→P.15）を実践しよう。

Stinson Concert Hall — Schedule	
June 2 ~ June 7	Stark Brothers Band
June 8 ~ June 12	Mombasa Beat
June 13 ~ June 17	New York Blues
June 19 ~ June 25	Grunge Revival

Grade	Price
Set 1 (blue)	$320
Set 2 (red)	$270
Set 3 (blue)	$160
Set 4 (red)	$110

61. Why is Mr. Fields calling?
    (A) To order additional tickets
    (B) To request a refund
    (C) To cancel a reservation
    (D) To discuss a mistake

62. Look at the graphic. What show does Mr. Fields want to attend?
    (A) Stark Brothers Band
    (B) Mombasa Beat
    (C) New York Blues
    (D) Grunge Revival

63. What does the woman ask Mr. Fields to do?
    (A) Make a new reservation
    (B) Complete a form
    (C) Dispose of some tickets
    (D) Contact a concert venue

64. What does the man say he will buy?
    (A) Trophies
    (B) Sporting equipment
    (C) Event tickets
    (D) Furniture

65. Look at the graphic. Which set will the man most likely purchase?
    (A) Set 1
    (B) Set 2
    (C) Set 3
    (D) Set 4

66. What does the woman ask the man to do?
    (A) Describe a product
    (B) Conduct a survey
    (C) Fill out a request
    (D) Send a report

Membership	Provides access to:
Grey	Treadmills and Bikes
Blue	Grey level plus Pool
Red	Grey Level plus Aerobics
Green	Grey Level plus Weights

Average Precipitation for Barnaby City

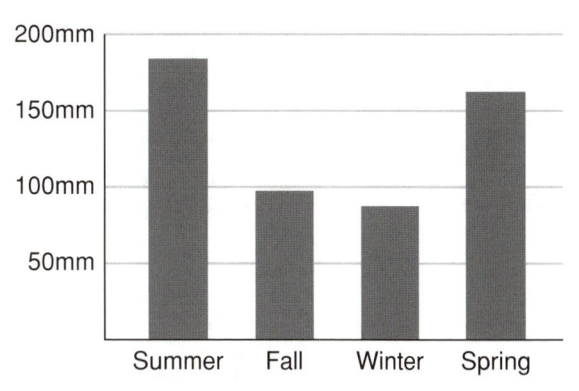

(Bar chart showing: Summer ~185mm, Fall ~95mm, Winter ~85mm, Spring ~160mm)

67. Why does the woman thank the man?
    (A) For bringing her to the gym
    (B) For finding her member card
    (C) For lending her a book
    (D) For showing her around a facility

68. Look at the graphic. What level of membership will the woman most likely purchase?
    (A) Grey
    (B) Blue
    (C) Red
    (D) Green

69. How can people get a discount on membership?
    (A) By introducing another customer
    (B) By signing up for six months
    (C) By completing a survey
    (D) By winning a competition

70. Where most likely does the conversation take place?
    (A) At a production company
    (B) At a tourist resort
    (C) At a manufacturing plant
    (D) At a convention center

71. Look at the graphic. According to the woman, when should the man start work?
    (A) In summer
    (B) In fall
    (C) In winter
    (D) In spring

72. What will the man most likely do next?
    (A) Respond to an e-mail
    (B) Meet with an accountant
    (C) Check a weather forecast
    (D) Make a presentation

GO ON TO THE NEXT PAGE

Timpson National Park

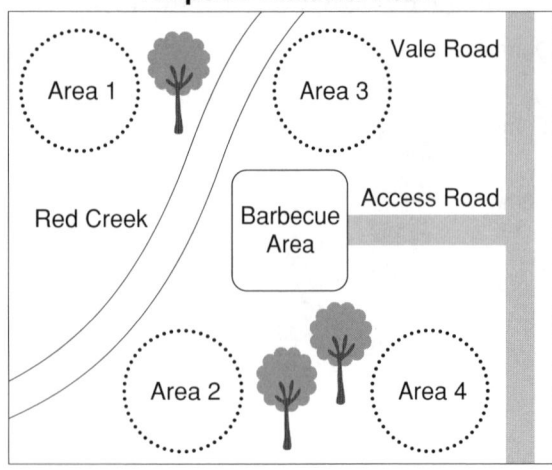

(Map showing Area 1, Area 3, Vale Road, Red Creek, Barbecue Area, Access Road, Area 2, Area 4)

Survey Results

(Bar chart: Prices ~2.2, Service ~4.0, Cleanliness ~3.3, Location ~2.7)

Note: High scores show greater satisfaction

73. Who most likely are the speakers?
    (A) Campers
    (B) Council members
    (C) Tour guides
    (D) Park managers

74. What does the man say about the woman's suggestion?
    (A) It will take too long to finish.
    (B) It has already been tried.
    (C) It will save money.
    (D) It is popular with survey respondents.

75. Look at the graphic. Where most likely will the campground be built?
    (A) In Area 1
    (B) In Area 2
    (C) In Area 3
    (D) In Area 4

76. Where most likely does the conversation take place?
    (A) In a concert hall
    (B) In a college
    (C) In a restaurant
    (D) In a factory

77. What does the woman agree to do?
    (A) Pay for a meal
    (B) Conduct another survey
    (C) Schedule a meeting
    (D) Make a presentation

78. Look at the graphic. What does the man propose improving first?
    (A) Prices
    (B) Service
    (C) Cleanliness
    (D) Location

Single Bedroom Accommodation	
Hotel	Cost per night
Green Garden Hotel (Standard)	$127
Buffay Towers (Standard)	$132
Tribbiani's (Executive)	$145
Hotel Geller (Luxury)	$260

Candidate — Shortlist	
Morgan Webb	3 years
Taylor Moody	5 years
Cleo Spiros	7 years
Alex Chang	12 years

79. Who most likely is Mr. Anthony?
    (A) An author
    (B) An actor
    (C) A director
    (D) A producer

80. Look at the graphic. Which hotel will the woman most likely choose?
    (A) Green Garden Hotel
    (B) Buffay Towers
    (C) Tribbiani's
    (D) Hotel Geller

81. How does the man say he will contact Mr. Anthony?
    (A) By e-mail
    (B) By telephone
    (C) By text message
    (D) By letter

82. What did the woman ask for?
    (A) Some reports
    (B) Repair work
    (C) Some equipment
    (D) A holiday

83. Look at the graphic. Which applicant does the man choose?
    (A) Morgan Webb
    (B) Taylor Moody
    (C) Cleo Spiros
    (D) Alex Chang

84. What does the man suggest about the successful applicant?
    (A) She is friendly.
    (B) She has many qualifications.
    (C) She has lived abroad.
    (D) She has never worked in advertising.

GO ON TO THE NEXT PAGE

PIZZA KING

Free Garlic Bread and Chili Sauce
(Only with orders over $22)

Expires: October 5
Mermaid Waters store only
Not valid for take-out orders

Floor Guide

1. Lobby
2. Conference Rooms
3. ~ 14. Guest Rooms
15. Restaurants

No access to the 15th floor after 11 P.M.
Maximum Capacity: 7 People
(600 kilograms)

---

85. What does the woman ask the man about?
    (A) Membership details
    (B) Topping preferences
    (C) Payment method
    (D) Coupon type

86. Look at the graphic. Why is the voucher rejected?
    (A) The expiry date has passed.
    (B) It is for a different store.
    (C) The order is too small.
    (D) The man requested a take-out meal.

87. What does the man say he will do?
    (A) Read a magazine
    (B) Buy some groceries
    (C) Check a Web site
    (D) Use a different coupon

88. What does the woman say about the hotel lobby?
    (A) There are not enough elevators.
    (B) It is very luxurious.
    (C) There are few people there.
    (D) It has a lot of information for tourists.

89. What does the man say he wanted to do?
    (A) Make a reservation
    (B) Revise a menu
    (C) View a presentation
    (D) Discuss a plan

90. Look at the graphic. Why is the woman unable to use the button?
    (A) There are too many people in the elevator.
    (B) It is too late in the evening.
    (C) There is a malfunction.
    (D) She has inserted the wrong key.

Part 3 ③グラフィック問題 | ドリルの解答・解説

◎ 21 Woman AU Man US

Questions 61 through 63 refer to the following conversation and schedule.

W: Hello, Stinson Concert Hall. My name is Kate. What can I do for you?
M: Hello, ①I think you've sent me the wrong tickets. ②I ordered tickets for June twelfth, ③but these are for the thirteenth.
W: ④I'm sorry about that. Can you give me your name and registration number so that I can check our records?
M: Sure. It's Randy Fields, and the number is 762309.
W: Let me see. Yes, it ⑤seems that the error is on our end. ⑥Please throw those tickets away. I'll send the replacements to your home address. They should arrive tomorrow.
M: That'll be fine.

問題61-63の問題は次の会話と予定表に関するものです。
女性：もしもし、Stinson Concert Hall です。私は Kate です。ご用件を承ります。
男性：どうも、間違ったチケットが送られてきたようです。6月12日のチケットを注文したのに、届いたのは13日のものです。
女性：申し訳ございません。記録を確認いたしますので、お名前と登録番号をいただけますか？
男性：はい。Randy Fields です。番号は762309です。
女性：そうですねえ。はい、こちらの間違いのようです。そのチケットは破棄してください。交換のチケットをご自宅の住所にお送りします。明日には届くと思います。
男性：それで結構です。

Stinson Concert Hall — Schedule	
June 2 ~ June 7	Stark Brothers Band
⑦June 8 ~ June 12	Mombasa Beat
June 13 ~ June 17	New York Blues
June 19 ~ June 25	Grunge Revival

Stinson Concert Hall　予定表	
6月2日～6月7日	Stark Brothers Band
6月8日～6月12日	Mombasa Beat
6月13日～6月17日	New York Blues
6月19日～6月25日	Grunge Revival

61.
Why is Mr. Fields calling?（Fields さんはなぜ電話をしているのですか？）
(A) To order additional tickets（追加のチケットを注文するため）
(B) To request a refund（返金を求めるため）
(C) To cancel a reservation（予約を取り消すため）
(D) To discuss a mistake（間違いについて話をするため）

正解：(D)　電話の目的を問う問題。男性は①②③で「注文した日付とは異なる日付のチケットが届いた」と説明している。それを受け、女性は④で男性に謝罪し、彼には非がないことを伝えている（⑤）。つまり、Fields さんは、間違いについて話をするために電話をかけている、と言い表すことができる。よって、(D) が正解。⑤on our end は「こちら側、当方、当社」という表現。

62. NEW
Look at the graphic. What show does Mr. Fields want to attend?（図を見てください。Fields さんが行きたいのはどのコンサートですか？）
(A) Stark Brothers Band
(B) Mombasa Beat
(C) New York Blues
(D) Grunge Revival

正解：(B)　グラフィック問題は、会話の内容と図にある情報を組み合わせて解答する必要があるため、選択肢の内容が会話の中で直接言及される可能性は低い。よって、図の中の、選択肢と共通する情報以外の箇所（ここでは左側の日付）を見ながら音声を聞くことが攻略の近道である。男性は②「6月12日のチケットを注文した」と伝えている。表の⑦から、6月12日にあるコンサートは Mombasa Beat だと分かるので、(B)が正解。

63.
What does the woman ask Mr. Fields to do?（女性は Fields さんに何をするよう求めていますか？）
(A) Make a new reservation（新規の予約をする）
(B) Complete a form（用紙に記入する）
(C) Dispose of some tickets（チケットを捨てる）
(D) Contact a concert venue（コンサート会場に連絡をする）

☐**dispose of ~**：〜を捨てる、〜を処分する
☐**venue**：開催地、会場

正解：(C)　設問から、女性が男性に何らかの依頼をすることが分かる。女性は⑥で Please（〜してください）と述べ、続けてチケットを破棄するように言っている。よって、依頼内容は(C)「チケットを捨てる」である。(C) dispose of が本文 throw away（捨てる）の言い換えになっている。

053

🔊 22　Man US　Woman CA

Questions 64 through 66 refer to the following conversation and list.

M: ①I'm about to order a set of trophies for the company bowling competition. I've found a Web site that specializes in them. They come in sets. What do you think?

W: Well, our logo is blue, so if they have something in blue, that would be best. In the end, this is just a fun occasion, so try not to spend too much money.

M: Sure. ②I'll get the cheapest blue ones they have, then.

W: ③Send me a purchase report when you're done, though.

問題64-66は次の会話とリストに関するものです。
男性：そろそろ社内ボウリング大会用にトロフィーのセットを注文しようと思います。専門に扱うウェブサイトを見つけました。セットで売られています。どう思いますか？
女性：そうねえ、うちのロゴは青だから、もし何か青いのがあれば、それが一番いいと思うわ。結局のところ、これは遊びの行事だから、あまりお金を使わないようにしましょう。
男性：分かりました。それなら、彼らの売っている物で一番安くて青いものにします。
女性：注文が済んだら購入報告書を私に送ってね。

Grade	Price
Set 1 (blue)	$320
Set 2 (red)	$270
④Set 3 (blue)	$160
Set 4 (red)	$110

等級	価格
セット1（青）	320ドル
セット2（赤）	270ドル
セット3（青）	160ドル
セット4（赤）	110ドル

□**trophy**：トロフィー　□**specialize in ~**：~を専門に扱う　□**come in ~**：~の形で提供される　□**occasion**：行事、機会

64.
What does the man say he will buy?（男性は何を買うと言っていますか？）
(A) Trophies（トロフィー）
(B) Sporting equipment（スポーツ用品）
(C) Event tickets（イベントのチケット）
(D) Furniture（家具）

正解：(A)　設問に the man say とあるので、男性がヒントを言うことが分かる。冒頭①で男性は「トロフィーのセットを注文しようと思う」と述べている。よって、正解は (A)「トロフィー」。①にある be about to ~ は「まさに~しようとしている」という意味のフレーズ。①で「ボウリング」と述べているが、ボウリングで使用するものを購入すると言っているわけではないので、(B)「スポーツ用品」は不適切。

65. NEW
Look at the graphic. Which set will the man most likely purchase?（図を見てください。男性はどのセットを買うと考えられますか？）
(A) Set 1（セット1）
(B) Set 2（セット2）
(C) Set 3（セット3）
(D) Set 4（セット4）

正解：(C)　新形式の「グラフィック問題」。選択肢とリストの共通情報は、セット番号である。よって、それ以外の情報、すなわち色と価格に関する情報が流れるのでは、と予測する。会話前半で、「会社のロゴが青なので、青いトロフィーがベストだが、お金はかけられない」と女性が述べている。それを受け、男性は②で「一番安く、青いものにする」と述べている。図によると、青いものは Set 1 と Set 3 で、より安いのは160ドルの後者なので、正解は (C)「セット3」である。

66.
What does the woman ask the man to do?（女性は男性に何をするよう依頼していますか？）
(A) Describe a product（商品を描写する）
(B) Conduct a survey（調査を実施する）
(C) Fill out a request（依頼書に記入する）
(D) Send a report（報告書を送る）
□**request**：依頼書、要求書

正解：(D)　女性が男性に依頼している内容を問う問題。女性は③で「購入報告書を送って」と述べている。よって、正解は (D)「報告書を送る」である。本文の purchase（購入）は make a purchase で「購入する」というフレーズでも登場する。また、purchase には「~を購入する」という動詞の用法もあるので覚えておこう。

23 Woman CA Man US

Questions 67 through 69 refer to the following conversation and brochure.

W: ①Thanks for showing me around the gym. I can see that you have a lot of great programs.
M: We certainly do. Would you like to sign up for membership so that you can get started training?
W: Can you tell me a little about your membership levels?
M: Well, they're all explained in this brochure. Why don't you take a look for a moment to make up your mind?
W: ②Thanks. Um, well, I like to swim so I guess I'll take this one. How much is it?
M: ③It's $70 a month, but we're running a campaign this week. You can get 20% off if you sign up for six months of membership.

問題67-69は次の会話とパンフレットに関するものです。
女性：ジムを案内してくれてありがとう。素晴らしいプログラムがたくさんありますね。
男性：そうなんですよ。トレーニングを始められるように、会員に申し込まれますか？
女性：会員のレベルについて少し教えてもらえますか？
男性：ええと、このパンフレットの中で説明されています。少しの間ご覧になってお決めになってはいかがですか？
女性：ありがとう。うーん、そうねえ、私は泳ぐのが好きだから、これにしようかしら。これはいくらですか？
男性：月70ドルですが、今週はキャンペーン中です。6カ月会員にお申し込みいただければ、20パーセントの割引になりますよ。

Membership	Provides access to:
Grey	Treadmills and Bikes
④Blue	Grey level plus Pool
Red	Grey Level plus Aerobics
Green	Grey Level plus Weights

会員	利用できるもの：
グレー	ランニングマシンとバイク
ブルー	グレー・レベルにプール
レッド	グレー・レベルにエアロビクス
グリーン	グレー・レベルに ウエート

67.
Why does the woman thank the man?（女性はなぜ男性に感謝していますか？）
(A) For bringing her to the gym（ジムに連れてきてくれたから）
(B) For finding her member card（彼女の会員証を見つけてくれたから）
(C) For lending her a book（本を貸してくれたから）
(D) For showing her around a facility（施設を案内してくれたから）

正解：(D)　女性が男性に感謝している理由が問われている。女性の発言①では Thank you for ～（～をありがとう）と始まり、「ジムを案内してくれて」と続いているので、正解は (D)「施設を案内してくれたから」。(D) facility（施設）が会話中の gym（ジム）の言い換えになっている。show around は「見せて回る、案内する」という表現。男性が女性をジムに連れてきたとは述べられていないので、(A) は不適切。

68. NEW
Look at the graphic. What level of membership will the woman most likely purchase?（図を見てください。女性はどのレベルの会員を選ぶと考えられますか？）
(A) Grey（グレー）　　(C) Red（レッド）
(B) Blue（ブルー）　　(D) Green（グリーン）

正解：(B)　表と選択肢の共通情報は、会員のレベルである。よって、右側の「利用できるもの」に関する情報が、会話の中に登場する。女性は②で「泳ぐことが好きなので、これにする」と述べている。この発言から、彼女はプールが使えるプログラムに申し込もうとしていることが分かる。「利用できるもの」の中で、プールがあるのは④「ブルー」だけなので、女性が申し込もうとしているのは(B)だと判断できる。

69.
How can people get a discount on membership?（どうすれば会員費の割引を受けられますか？）
(A) By introducing another customer（別の客の紹介する）
(B) By signing up for six months（6カ月に申し込む）
(C) By completing a survey（アンケートに答える）
(D) By winning a competition（コンテストで優勝する）

正解：(B)　割引を得られる手段を問う問題。③で男性は、キャンペーンを行っていると述べ、その内容を「6カ月会員に申し込めば、20パーセント割引」と説明している。よって、正解は (B)「6カ月に申し込む」。

24 Woman AU Man UK

Questions 70 through 72 refer to the following conversation and chart.

W: ①I'm pleased to inform you that Field's Television Productions has approved your script and we would like to fund the production of your children's movie.
M: That's great news. I hope we can get started as soon as possible.
W: That might be a little difficult. Many of the scenes are set outside, and ②rainfall is just too high at this time of year. Look at this data. ③In a few weeks, rainfall will be much lower and that would be the safest time to begin filming.
M: Good idea. We'll save money if the production goes smoothly.
W: Great. ④Well, I'd like you to meet Mr. Ling in the accounting department now. He'll explain the budget.
M: ⑤Thanks.

問題70-72は次の会話と図表に関するものです。
女性：Field's Television Productions があなたの脚本を承認したことをお伝えします。そして、私たちはあなたの児童向け映画の制作に資金提供をしたいと思います。
男性：それは素晴らしい知らせです。一刻も早く始められるといいのですが。
女性：それは少し難しいかもしれません。シーンの多くが屋外の設定ですし、1年の中でもこの時期は、降雨量がとにかく多過ぎます。このデータをみてください。数週間後には降雨量も減って、撮影を開始するのに最も安全な時期になるでしょう。
男性：良い考えです。制作が順調にいけば、お金の節約になりますね。
女性：良かったわ。では、経理部の Ling さんに会ってください。彼が予算を説明しますから。
男性：ありがとうございます。

Average Precipitation for Barnaby City
Barnaby City の平均降水量

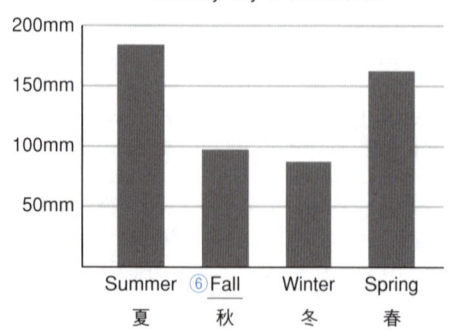

	Summer	⑥Fall	Winter	Spring
	夏	秋	冬	春

□**rainfall**：降水（量）、降雨（量）
【図表】□**precipitation**：降水（量）、降雨（量）

70.
Where most likely does the conversation take place?（会話はどこで行われていると考えられますか？）
(A) At a production company（制作会社で）
(B) At a tourist resort（観光リゾートで）
(C) At a manufacturing plant（製造工場で）
(D) At a convention center（会議場で）

正解：(A)　会話が行われている場所を問う問題。女性が①で「Field's Television Productions はあなたの脚本を承認したことをお伝えします」と具体的なプロダクション会社の名前を述べ、その後も「映画の制作」に関する話をしていることから、この会話は (A)「制作会社で」行われているものだと判断できる。

71. NEW
Look at the graphic. According to the woman, when should the man start work?（図を見てください。女性によれば、男性はいつ仕事に取り掛かるべきですか？）

(A) In summer（夏に）　　(C) In winter（冬に）
(B) In fall（秋に）　　(D) In spring（春に）

正解：(B)　選択肢とグラフの共通情報は、季節なので、降水量に関する情報が会話の中に登場すると予測する。②で女性が「今の時期は降雨量が多い」と述べているので、会話が行われているのは、春か夏だと判断できる。その後、女性が③「数週間たてば、雨の量が減り、撮影を開始できる」と述べている。よって今は夏だ。今後は降雨量が減り、その時期に仕事に取り掛かるべきと述べていることになる。これらの条件に合うのは⑥「秋」なので、(B) が正解。

72.
What will the man most likely do next?（男性は次に何をすると考えられますか？）
(A) Respond to an e-mail（E メールに返信する）
(B) Meet with an accountant（経理担当者に会う）
(C) Check a weather forecast（天気予報を確認する）
(D) Make a presentation（プレゼンテーションをする）

正解：(B)　男性の「次の行動」を問う問題。女性が男性に、④「経理部の Ling さんが予算を説明するので彼と会ってください」と伝えている。男性はお礼を述べることによって（⑤）、それを了承している。よって、男性はこれから (B)「経理担当者に会う」と判断できる。(B) accountant は「経理担当者」以外にも「会計士」という意味でも重要。

25 Woman CA Man US

Questions 73 through 75 refer to the following conversation and map.

W: ①The council has given us some money to create a campground at Timpson National Park. ②I think we should use the same access road as the barbecue area.
M: ③Yeah, we'll save a lot of money that way. I took a look at the map of proposed sites you e-mailed me earlier. ④I think Area 3 is too close to the barbecue site and Area 4 is too close to Vale Road.
W: Yeah, people will want to experience nature without hearing other people or traffic.
M: ⑤How about using the area on the other side of the creek?
W: ⑥Fine, but do we have funds to build a bridge?
M: ⑦No problem.

問題73-75は次の会話と地図に関するものです。
女性：評議会が Timpson National Park にキャンプ場を造る資金をくれたの。私はバーベキュー場と同じ連絡道路を使うべきだと思うわ。
男性：うん、それならお金をたくさん節約できるね。君が前にメールで送ってくれた候補地の地図を見てみたよ。第3エリアはバーベキュー場に近過ぎるし、第4エリアは Vale Road に近過ぎるね。
女性：ええ、人々は他人の声や車の音を聞かずに自然を体験したいと思うでしょうしね。
男性：小川の反対側のエリアを使うのはどう？
女性：いいわね、でも橋を造る資金はあるかしら？
男性：問題ないよ。

Timpson National Park

（地図：Area 1, Area 3, Vale Road, Red Creek, Barbecue Area バーベキュー場, Access Road 連絡道路, Area 2, Area 4）

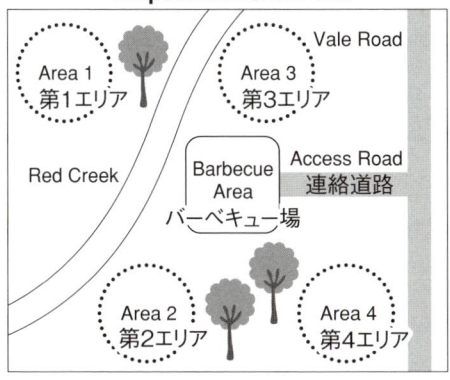

□council：評議会 □campground：キャンプ場
□access road：連絡道路 □creek：小川

73.
Who most likely are the speakers?（話し手たちは誰であると考えられますか？）
(A) Campers（キャンプをする人）
(B) Council members（評議会のメンバー）
(C) Tour guides（ツアーガイド）
(D) Park managers（公園管理者）

正解：(D)　女性が冒頭①で「評議会が Timpson National Park にキャンプ場を造る資金をくれた」と述べている。その後も、④と⑤で公園内のキャンプ場の候補地、⑥で橋を造ることについて話している。よって、話し手たちは公園内の設備や管理に携わる仕事をしていると判断できるので、正解は (D)。キャンプをする側ではないので、(A) は不適切。また、(B) の「評議会のメンバー」は話し手たちに資金を渡す方なので、これも不可。

74.
What does the man say about the woman's suggestion?（男性は女性の提案について何と言っていますか？）
(A) It will take too long to finish.（完成するのに時間がかかり過ぎるだろう）
(B) It has already been tried.（すでに試した）
(C) It will save money.（金の節約になるだろう）
(D) It is popular with survey respondents.（調査の回答者たちの人気が高い）

正解：(C)　設問に the man say とあるので、男性が女性の提案に対し、何か言及することが分かる。まず女性が②で「バーベキュー場と同じ連絡道路を使うべきだ」と述べている。それに対し、男性は③で彼女の意見に同意し、「その方法ならお金を節約できる」と返答している。この内容を「金の節約になるだろう」と言い換えた (C) が正解。

75. NEW
Look at the graphic. Where most likely will the campground be built?（図を見てください。キャンプ場が作られるのはどこだと考えられますか？）
(A) In Area 1（第1エリア）
(B) In Area 2（第2エリア）
(C) In Area 3（第3エリア）
(D) In Area 4（第4エリア）
□campsite：キャンプ場

正解：(A)　地図などのレイアウトを表すグラフィックが出てきた場合は、設問が流れる前に「どこに何があるか」を大まかに把握しておこう。④で「第3と第4エリアはキャンプ場

に向いていない」と述べられたので、それぞれ不適切。男性は⑤で「小川の反対側のエリア」を提案し、女性もその案に同意している（⑥）。そして、そのエリアに行くためには橋を使わないといけないことが⑥と⑦から分かる。よって、この条件に合う⑧の(A)「第1エリア」が正解。

🔘 **26** Woman AU　Man UK

Questions 76 through 78 refer to the following conversation and chart.

W: Hi Joe. Look, I've graphed the results of ① the diner satisfaction survey we conducted last week. ②This is only from dinner patrons but I'm sure lunch would be similar.
M: I see. ③Perhaps we should conduct one at ④lunch time just to be sure, though. ⑤Maybe next week.
W: ⑥Fine. I'll get on it. Anyway, look at this. Higher scores show greater satisfaction. It's pretty clear what we need to work on, isn't it?
M: Well, not really. I knew our prices were comparatively high. I don't plan to do anything about that because most of our customers can afford them.
W: So, ⑦what do you think we should improve first?
M: ⑧This one. It has our second highest rating, but it should be higher and it's something we can easily fix.

問題76-78は次の会話と図に関するものです。
女性：ねえ、Joe。見て、先週実施した食事客満足度調査の結果をグラフにしたの。これはディナーの常連客のみだけど、ランチについてもきっと似たものになると思うわ。
男性：なるほど。でも念のため、ランチタイムにも実施した方がいいんじゃないかな。来週にでも。
女性：分かった。すぐに取り掛かるわ。ともかく、これを見て。点数が高いほど満足度が高いことを表しているの。われわれが何に取り組まなくてはならないか一目瞭然よね？
男性：うーん、そうでもないな。うちの値段が比較的高いというのは知ってたよ。それについて何かするつもりはないんだ。だって大抵のうちのお客さまはそれを払えるんだから。
女性：じゃあ、まず何を改善すべきだと思う？
男性：これだよ。2番目に高い評価を受けているけど、もっと高くあるべきだし、簡単に解決できることだからね。

Survey Results 調査結果

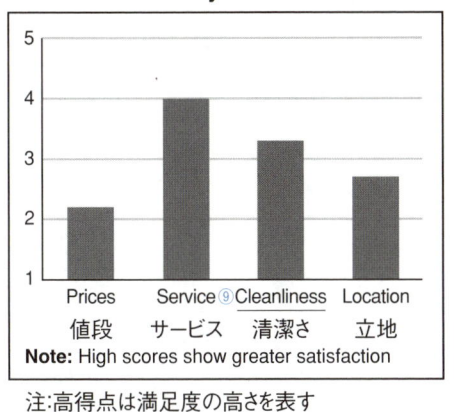

```
5 |
4 |      ■
3 |      ■    ■
2 |  ■   ■    ■    ■
1 |  ■   ■    ■    ■
   Prices Service ⑨Cleanliness Location
    値段  サービス   清潔さ    立地
Note: High scores show greater satisfaction
```
注:高得点は満足度の高さを表す

□**diner**:食事客　□**graph**:〜をグラフに描く、〜のグラフを作成する　□**patron**:常連客、得意客　□**just to be sure**:念のため　□**get on 〜**:〜にすぐ取り掛かる、〜をどんどん進める

76. Where most likely does the conversation take place?（この会話はどこで行われていると考えられますか？）
(A) In a concert hall（コンサートホールで）
(B) In a college（大学で）
(C) In a restaurant（レストランで）
(D) In a factory（工場で）

正解：(C)　会話が行われている場所を問う問題。女性が①で「食事客満足度調査」、②で「その調査はディナーの常連客に行った」と述べている。さらに、④で男性は「ランチタイム」と言っている。その後も、この調査結果に基づいた会話をしていることから、2人はレストランの関係者で、レストラン内でこの会話は行われていると判断できる。よって、(C)が正解。

77.
What does the woman agree to do?（女性は何をすることに同意していますか？）
(A) Pay for a meal（食事代を払う）
(B) Conduct another survey（調査を実施する）
(C) Schedule a meeting（会議を計画する）
(D) Make a presentation（プレゼンテーションを行う）

正解：(B)　設問の the woman agree から、男性が述べた内容を聞き、女性がそれに合意することが分かる。よって、男性の発言にも解答のヒントがある。男性は⑤「来週のランチタイムにも調査ができたらいい」と述べている。それを受け、女性は⑥「すぐに取り掛かる」と返答している。つまり、「調査を行った方がいい」という男性の発言に同意していることが分かるので、女性が同意したことは (B)「調査を実施する」である。

78. NEW
Look at the graphic. What does the man propose improving first?（図を見てください。男性は最初に何を改善すべきだと提案していますか？）
(A) Prices（値段）
(B) Service（サービス）
(C) Cleanliness（清潔さ）
(D) Location（立地）
□**cleanliness**:清潔さ、清潔にしておくこと

正解：(C)　選択肢は「調査項目」で、グラフの横軸に並んでいる。よって、音声として聞こえる情報は、縦軸に関連するものだと予測する。⑦で「どの項目を最初に改善すべきか」と尋ねる女性に対し、男性は⑧「これだ。この項目が2番目に高い」と述べている。表によると、2番目に高い項目は⑨「清潔さ」だと分かる。よって、(C) が正解。「価格」の満足度が1番低いが、それに対して男性は「何もしない」と述べているので、(A) は不適切。

27 Man UK Woman CA

Questions 79 through 81 refer to the following conversation and list.

M: Hi, Rebecca. We need to start talking about preparations for Jim Anthony's visit. He's agreed to promote the new television show by doing some press interviews.

W: Oh, that's right. ①He wrote the novel that our new television drama is based on.

M: Yeah. Anyway, I'd like to put you in charge of looking after him. First, you should arrange some accommodation. We'll be paying the bill, so don't choose anything too expensive.

W: What's the maximum we can afford per night?

M: ②Let me see, um, well, $150, I suppose. Use the usual Web site and ③get the best room you can for that price.

W: Should I e-mail Mr. Anthony with the details directly, or send them to you first?

M: ④Send them to me. I'll speak with him on the phone this evening and I'll mention it then.

W: No problem.

問題79-81は次の会話とリストに関するものです。
男性：やあ、Rebecca。Jim Anthony の来訪の準備について相談を始めなくてはいけないね。彼は何回か記者会見をして、新しいテレビ番組の宣伝をすることに同意してくれているんだ。
女性：ああ、そうでしたね。彼はうちの局のドラマの基になっている小説を書いたんですよね。
男性：そうなんだ。ともかく、君に彼の世話を任せたいんだよ。まず、宿泊施設の手配からしてもらおうか。勘定はうちが負担することになるから、高過ぎるところは選ばないでくれよ。
女性：われわれが出せる上限は1泊当たりいくらですか？
男性：そうだなぁ、うーん、まあ、150ドルかな。いつものウェブサイトを使って、その料金で一番いい部屋を取ってくれ。
女性：詳細は私から Anthony さんに直接メールを送りますか、それともまずあなたに送りますか？
男性：私に送ってくれ。今夜彼と電話で話をするから、そのときにそのことについて話すよ。
女性：分かりました。

Single Bedroom Accommodation	
Hotel	Cost per night
Green Garden Hotel (Standard)	$127
Buffay Towers (Standard)	$132
⑤Tribbiani's (Executive)	$145
Hotel Geller (Luxury)	$260

シングルルームの宿泊	
ホテル	1泊当たりの料金
Green Garden Hotel（標準）	127ドル
Buffay Towers（標準）	132ドル
Tribbiani's（エグゼクティブ）	145ドル
Hotel Geller（高級）	260ドル

□**press interview**：記者会見　□**be based on ～**：～に基づいている　□**put ～ in charge of ...**：～に…を任せる、～に…を担当させる　□**look after ～**：～の世話をする、～の面倒を見る　□**accommodation**：宿泊、宿泊施設　□**pay the bill**：勘定を支払う　□**maximum**：最高限度、最大限

79.
Who most likely is Mr. Anthony?（Anthony さんとは誰だと考えられますか？）
(A) An author（作家）
(B) An actor（俳優）
(C) A director（監督）
(D) A producer（プロデューサー）

正解：(A)　Anthony さんの職業を問う問題。Anthony という名前は、男性の最初の発言に登場する。その後、女性が①で「彼はドラマの基になった小説を書いた」と述べている。つまり、Anthonyさんは小説を書く人間、すなわち作家だと考えることができるので、(A)「作家」が正解。

80. NEW
Look at the graphic. Which hotel will the woman most likely choose?（図を見てください。女性はどのホテルを選ぶと考えられますか？）
(A) Green Garden Hotel
(B) Buffay Towers
(C) Tribbiani's
(D) Hotel Geller

正解：(C)　選択肢とリストの共通情報はホテル名なので、ホテル名以外の情報が会話に登場すると考えられる。女性が1泊当たりの予算を尋ね、それに対し、男性は②「150ドル」と返答している。さらに、③でその料金内で最もいい部屋を選ぶよう、女性に指示している。表の右側を見ると、3行目の145ドルの部屋が、男性が提示した条件に合う。⑤からそのホテル名は「Tribbiani's」だと分かるので、正解は (C)。

81.
How does the man say he will contact
Mr. Anthony?（男性は Anthony さんにどうやって連絡を取ると言っていますか？）
(A) By e-mail（E メールで）
(B) By telephone（電話で）
(C) By text message（携帯メールで）
(D) By letter（手紙で）

正解：(B)　設問から、男性が Anthony さんに連絡を取ることが分かる。男性は④で「今夜、彼と電話で話をする」と述べている。よって、正解は (B)「電話で」。(A)「E メールで」は宿泊の詳細を送る手段として会話の中に登場するが、「女性」が言及した連絡手段なので、不適切。

🔵 **28**　Woman AU　Man UK

Questions 82 through 84 refer to the following conversation and list.

W: ①Have you completed those customer satisfaction reports I asked for yet?
M: Ms. West, I just haven't had time. I've been looking for a replacement for Joe Thorne and we're all doing extra work until a new employee starts.
W: Oh. That explains it. Sorry to put so much pressure on you. How have the interviews been going?
M: ②All done. Here's the shortlist of candidates. I don't remember her name, but I chose the one with five years' experience.
W: Why? There are others with more experience in advertising.
M: ③She seems really knowledgeable and easy to communicate with. I'm sure she'll get along well with the rest of the team.

問題82-84は次の会話とリストに関するものです。
女性：私がお願いした顧客満足度の報告書はもう完成してるかしら？
男性：West さん、本当に時間がなくって。Joe Thorne の後任を探しているんですが、新しい社員が働き始めるまで、われわれみんな余分に仕事をしているんです。
女性：まあ。そういうことだったのね。あなたに大変な負担をかけてごめんなさい。面接はどんな感じですか？
男性：全て終わりました。これが最終候補者のリストです。彼女の名前は覚えていませんが、5年の経験を持つ人物を選びました。
女性：どうして？　広告業界でもっと経験のある人たちが他にいるじゃない。
男性：彼女は非常に知識豊富でコミュニケーションが取りやすいようです。チームの他の人たちともきっとうまくやるだろうと思います。

Candidate — Shortlist	
Morgan Webb	3 years
④Taylor Moody	5 years
Cleo Spiros	7 years
Alex Chang	12 years

候補者 — 最終リスト	
Morgan Webb	3年
Taylor Moody	5年
Cleo Spiros	7年
Alex Chang	12年

□**replacement**：後任、交代要員　　□**put pressure on ~**：~に負担をかける　　□**shortlist**：最終候補リスト　　□**knowledgeable**：博識な、知識豊富な　　□**get along with ~**：~とうまく付き合う、~と仲良くやる

82.
What did the woman ask for?（女性は何を求めましたか？）
(A) Some reports（報告書）
(B) Repair work（修理作業）
(C) Some equipment（備品）
(D) A holiday（休暇）

正解：**(A)**　女性が必要としているものを問う問題。冒頭で女性は、①「頼んだ顧客満足度調査の報告書は完成しているか」と男性に尋ねている。よって、正解は (A)「報告書」。report には「報告書」以外に、動詞の用法もある。report to work で「職場に出勤する」と report to＋人で「（~の）直属の部下になる」はフレーズとして覚えておこう。

83. NEW
Look at the graphic. Which applicant does the man choose?（図を見てください。男性はどの応募者を選んでいますか？）
(A) Morgan Webb
(B) Taylor Moody
(C) Cleo Spiros
(D) Alex Chang

正解：**(B)**　選択肢とリストの共通情報は、候補者の氏名である。よって、リストの候補者の氏名以外、つまり、年数に関する情報が会話の中で登場すると考えられる。男性は②で「5年の経験を持つ人物を選んだ」と述べている。表④から、5年の経験があるのは「Taylor Moody」だと分かるので、(B) が正解。

84.
What does the man suggest about the successful applicant?（男性は合格者について何を示唆していますか？）
(A) She is friendly.（彼女は感じがいい）
(B) She has many qualifications.（彼女は多くの資格を持っている）

(C) She has lived abroad.（彼女は海外に住んだことがある）
(D) She has never worked in advertising.（彼女は広告業界で働いたことは一度もない）
□**successful applicant**：合格者

正解：**(A)**　男性の発言に関する「暗示問題」。合格者のことを男性は③で「彼女はコミュニケーションが取りやすそうで、チームの他の人たちともきっとうまくやるだろう」と述べている。この発言から、彼女は「感じのいい人」であると考えることができる。よって、正解は (A)。②で「5年の経験がある」と述べられているので、(D) は不適切。その他の選択肢にある内容は述べられていないので、(B) も (C) も不適切。

29 Woman UK　Man US

Questions 85 through 87 refer to the following conversation and voucher.

W: OK, ①two medium pizzas and a bottle of soda to go ... that comes to a total of $36. ②How will you be paying for that? We accept credit card or cash.
M: I'll pay cash, thanks. Can I use this voucher I found in the newspaper?
W: Let me see. ③Oh, sorry, you can't. See here?
M: I see. ④I want to take it home, so I'll go without the garlic bread. How long will it take to prepare?
W: Oh, about five to ten minutes, I guess.
M: OK. I'll come back then. ⑤I need to buy some groceries next door.

問題85-87は次の会話と割引券に関するものです。
女性：それでは、ピザの中が2枚と炭酸水1本をお持ち帰りですので…合計36ドルです。お支払いはどのようにされますか？　当店はクレジットカードか現金をお取り扱いしています。
男性：現金で払います。新聞で見つけたこの割引券は使えますか？
女性：拝見します。ああ、申し訳ありませんが、お使いいただけません。ここをご覧ください。
男性：なるほど。持ち帰りたいので、ガーリックブレッドはいいです。用意にどれくらいかかりますか？
女性：ああ、5分から10分程度でしょう。
男性：分かりました。ではそのころ戻ってきます。お隣で食料品を買うので。

PIZZA KING

**Free Garlic Bread and Chili Sauce
(Only with orders over $22)**

⑥ Expires: October 5
　Mermaid Waters store only
⑦ Not valid for take-out orders

有効期限：10月5日
Mermaid Waters 店のみ
持ち帰りのご注文には無効

☐**voucher**：割引券　　☐**pay cash**：現金で支払う
【図表】☐**valid**：有効な

85.
What does the woman ask the man about?（女性は男性に何について尋ねていますか？）
(A) Membership details（会員資格の詳細）
(B) Topping preferences（トッピングの好み）
(C) Payment method（支払い方法）
(D) Coupon type（クーポンの種類）
☐**topping**：トッピング、上に乗せるもの
☐**preference**：好み　　☐**coupon**：クーポン、割引券

正解：(C)　設問から、女性が男性に質問をすることが分かる。女性は最初の発言で、注文内容を男性に伝えている。その後、②「お支払いはどのようにされますか」と尋ね、選択できる支払い方法を述べている。よって、彼女が尋ねている内容としてふさわしいのは、(C)「支払い方法」である。

86. NEW
Look at the graphic. Why is the voucher rejected?（図を見てください。割引券はなぜ受け取ってもらえないのですか？）
(A) The expiry date has passed.（終了日を過ぎているから）
(B) It is for a different store.（違う店のものだから）
(C) The order is too small.（注文が少な過ぎるから）
(D) The man requested a take-out meal.（男性は持ち帰りの食事を頼んだから）
☐**expiry**：満期、終了

正解：(D)　割引券が使えるかと尋ねる男性に、女性は③「使えない」と返答し、See here? と券を見るよう促している。割引券の使用に関する条件は⑥「有効期限」と⑦「持ち帰り注文無効」の2つがある。注文内容を確認する女性の発言①の to go、男性の④「持ち帰りたい」という発言から、男性がテークアウトを頼んだことが分かる。男性の注文は⑦に該当するので、(D) が正解。

87.
What does the man say he will do?（男性は何をすると言っていますか？）
(A) Read a magazine（雑誌を読む）
(B) Buy some groceries（食料品を買う）
(C) Check a Web site（ウェブサイトを確認する）
(D) Use a different coupon（違う割引券を使う）

正解：(B)　男性は最後の発言⑤で「隣で食料品を買う必要がある」と述べている。よって、(B)「食料品を買う」が正解。男性は③で「割引券は使えない」と言われたが、別のものを使うということは言っていないので、(D) は不適切。

③グラフィック問題

30 Man US Woman CA

Questions 88 through 90 refer to the following conversation and floor guide.
M: I'd never have guessed that ①we'd arrive around midnight.
W: Right. That flight delay has really ruined our evening. We should have gotten to the hotel hours ago. ②We're the only two people in the lobby.
M: Yeah, ③I was hoping to spend some time discussing our plans for tomorrow's presentation over dinner.
W: Let's have something to eat before we go to our rooms, or would you like to ...
M: ... Look at this sign. ④There are restaurants. Could you push the button for that floor?
W: ⑤It doesn't work.
M: ⑥Oh, yeah. Look what it says here.

問題88-90は次の会話とフロア案内に関するものです。
男性：真夜中近くに到着するなんて思いもしなかったよ。
女性：本当よね。あの飛行機の遅れで夜が台無しになったわ。数時間前にはホテルに着いているはずだったのに。ロビーにいるのは私たち2人だけよ。
男性：うん、夕食を取りながら、明日のプレゼンのプランについて話す時間をつくりたいと思ってたんだけどな。
女性：部屋へ行く前に何か食べましょうよ、それとも…
男性：…この表示を見て。レストランがある。15階のボタンを押してくれる？
女性：押せないわよ。
男性：ああ、そういうことか。ここに書いてあることを見て。

Floor Guide フロア案内

1.	Lobby	1階	ロビー
2.	Conference Rooms	2階	会議室
3.~14.	Guest Rooms	3～14階	客室
⑦15.	Restaurants	15階	レストラン

⑧No access to the 15th floor after 11 P.M.
Maximum Capacity: 7 People
(600 kilograms)

午後11時以降、15階には行けません。
最大定員：7人
（600キログラム）

男性が女性の話を遮って発言する箇所があります。現実のコミュニケーションでもよくあることです。**(R)**

88.
What does the woman say about the hotel lobby?（女性はホテルのロビーについて何と言っていますか？）
(A) There are not enough elevators.（エレベーターの数が十分ではない）
(B) It is very luxurious.（非常に高級感がある）
(C) There are few people there.（人がほとんどいない）
(D) It has a lot of information for tourists.（旅行客のための情報がたくさんある）

正解：(C) 女性がロビーについて言及した内容を問う問題。女性は②で「ロビーにいるのは私たち2人だけ」と述べているので、それを「人がほとんどいない」と言い表した (C) が正解。その他の選択肢の内容は述べられていないので、どれも不適切。

89.
What does the man say he wanted to do?（男性は何がしたかったと言っていますか？）
(A) Make a reservation（予約をする）
(B) Revise a menu（メニューを見直す）
(C) View a presentation（プレゼンテーションを見る）
(D) Discuss a plan（プランについて話し合う）

正解：(D) 冒頭の内容から、2人は予定よりも遅くホテルに到着したことが分かる。男性は③I was hoping to ~（~がしたかった）と述べ、「明日のプレゼンテーションの話し合い」と続いている。よって、その言い換えとしてふさわしい (D) が正解。③「プレゼンテーション」という単語は会話に出てくるが、2人がそれを見るということは述べられていないので、(C)は不適切。

90. NEW
Look at the graphic. Why is the woman unable to use the button?（図を見てください。なぜ女性はボタンを使えないのですか？）
(A) There are too many people in the elevator.（エレベーターに人が乗り過ぎているから）
(B) It is too late in the evening.（夜遅過ぎるから）
(C) There is a malfunction.（故障だから）
(D) She has inserted the wrong key.（違う鍵を差し込んだから）

正解：(B) 男性は④で「レストランに行こう」と言い、ボタンを押すよう女性に頼む。⑦から、女性が押そうとしたのはレストランがある15階のボタンだと分かる。⑤「押せない」と言う女性に男性は女性に案内を見るよう促す（⑥）。案内の⑧に「11時以降は15階に行けない」とある。①から今は真夜中に近い時間だと分かるので、ボタンが押せない理由は、(B)「夜遅過ぎるから」である。

意図問題に強くなる
特製プログラム！
「3文トレーニング」のススメ
ヒロ前田

　P. 13でボクは、今回の形式変更について「受験者本人の英語力に変動がなければ、アップデート前と同様のスコアを取ることができるはずだ」と書きました。そうは言っても、形式に慣れていないせいでスコアを落とす人はいるはずですし、これまでの英語学習の取り組み方によって、変更の影響の大きさには個人差があると思っています。

　その差が最も出るのがこの意図問題です。意図問題は英語体験が豊富な人ほど有利です。普段からテレビや映画、洋書などで生きた英語のコミュニケーションに触れている人なら、特別な対策をとる必要はなく、むしろ「意図問題は楽勝」と感じるはずです。一方で、これまで「英語力」よりも「受験力」の強化に重点を置いた学習をしてきた人や、TOEICに特化した学習しかしてこなかった人にとっては、ハードルの高い問題です。しかも意図問題は、Part 3、4、7の3パートで約7問も出題されます。

　発言者の意図や気持ちをくみ取る力というのは短期間で身につくものではありませんが、意図問題に不安を感じている人がいるなら、少しでも力になりたいと思い、ボクとロスとでこの**「3文トレーニング」**を考案しました。意図問題のエッセンスをギュっと凝縮させた、気軽に取り組むことができるトレーニングです。

　Part 3のトレーニングは次頁から始まりますが、Part 4(P. 92～)、Part 7(P. 180～)のトレーニングにもぜひ挑戦してください。合計36のターゲット文から、72通りもの「意図や気持ち」を学べます。

「3文トレーニング」のやり方

このトレーニングは基本的に**文字だけで行います**。

- あるターゲット文について、3文から成る2つの会話（またはトーク、チャット）が用意されています。それぞれの会話において、話し手はどのような意図や気持ちでターゲット文を発言しているのか考えます。

- 直下にある3つの選択肢から、それぞれの文脈に合うものを1つ選んでください。

- 「解答・解説」ページで答え合わせと復習をしましょう。

※会話（トーク、チャット）部分の音声を聞くことも可能です。「3文トレーニング」の音声はCDには収録されていません。P. 10の案内に従って音声ファイルをダウンロードしてください

ひたすら意図問題！
3文トレーニング [Part 3編]

各セット内の下線部①②について最も適切なものを (A) ～ (C) から選ぼう。
音声を聞く場合はダウンロード・コンテンツの該当するファイル番号を再生してください。
例) 🔊 01　ダウンロード・コンテンツのファイル「01」

▶▶▶ SET 1　🔊 01

会話1

Man: Do you think the merger with JGF Industries will go ahead?
Woman: ①It's simply a matter of time. Everyone has agreed to the terms and both firms have a lot to gain.

会話2

Man: Can you tell me why the reports from your department are always late?
Woman: ②It's simply a matter of time. There's too much information to analyze by Friday each week.

What does the woman mean when she says, "It's simply a matter of time"?
(A) She does not have long enough to complete a project.
(B) The deadline for a manuscript is approaching.
(C) A result will be achieved eventually.

①_____ ②_____

▶▶▶ SET 2　🔊 02

会話1

Woman: There's a shipping firm in Illinois that has some trucks heading back there empty after making a delivery to New York. They'll give us a huge discount because they're making the trip anyway.
Man: ①I wish I'd thought of that.

会話2

Woman: Customers preferred the old packaging. If you'd conducted a survey before changing the design, you could have saved a lot of money.
Man: ②I wish I'd thought of that.

Why does the man say, "I wish I'd thought of that"?
(A) He has found a problem.
(B) He is surprised by a good idea.
(C) He is sorry for making a mistake.

①_____ ②_____

▶▶▶ SET 3　🔊 03

会話1

Man: I'm worried about whether or not there's enough money left in the budget to buy a new printing machine.
Woman: ①There's no getting around it. The current machine is not repairable.

会話2

Man: There's not enough money left in the budget for a new printing machine.
Woman: ②There's no getting around it. We'll just have to wait until next year.

What does the woman mean when she says, "There's no getting around it"?
(A) Some equipment cannot be replaced.
(B) An expense cannot be avoided.
(C) She has to pass through a busy area.

①_____ ②_____

※解答・解説は P. 70 ～ 73 にあります

▶▶▶ SET 4   🔊 04

会話 1

Man: Will the factory be ready in time to start production in May?
Woman: ①Thanks for asking. Well, of course, but I wanted to mention that we're considering a backup plan in case there are any setbacks.

会話 2

Man: Do you think you could join us on a trip to inspect the factory in May?
Woman: ②Thanks for asking. I'd love to go along with you.

Why does the woman say, "Thanks for asking"?
(A) She is happy to be invited.
(B) She will examine some suggestions.
(C) She wanted to talk about a topic.

①_____ ②_____

▶▶▶ SET 5   🔊 05

会話 1

Woman: We should attend that industry conference in Colorado this year. ①A lot of potential clients will be there.
Man: I know, but I'll be too busy on those dates.

会話 2

Woman: I know you were thinking of taking a vacation, but I really need you to attend the product launch on Friday. ②A lot of potential clients will be there.
Man: I guess I'll take my holidays a few days later.

Why does the woman say, "A lot of potential clients will be there"?
(A) To sell tickets to an event
(B) To stress the importance of a trip
(C) To explain a work assignment

①_____ ②_____

▶▶▶ SET 6   🔊 06

会話 1

Woman: About your idea, I don't think we'll be able to offer customers free Internet access.
Man: ①Why can't we? Is it too expensive or something?

会話 2

Woman: Look, the café across the street has started providing free Internet access.
Man: ②Why can't we? It might help keep our regular customers.

Why does the man say, "Why can't we"?
(A) He wants to follow an example.
(B) A strategy seems unrealistic.
(C) His suggestion has been rejected.

①_____ ②_____

▶▶▶ SET 7 🔊 07

会話1

Woman: ①I've been meaning to call you all week. I've reviewed your application to hire a new salesperson, and given it my approval.
Man: Thanks, Kelly. When can I hire the new employee?

会話2

Man: I'm waiting on the data from the factory inspection but no one's been in touch.
Woman: ②I've been meaning to call you all week. It's just not ready yet, I'm afraid.

Why does the woman say, "I've been meaning to call you all week"?
(A) She has made a decision.
(B) She regrets not contacting the man earlier.
(C) She has not met the man for a long time.

①_____ ②_____

▶▶▶ SET 8 🔊 08

会話1

Woman: We should call an interior decorator and have the office refurbished, don't you think?
Man: ①It's not as easy as that. We need to get permission from head office and they'll insist that all the branch offices look similar.

会話2

Woman: This new software looks just like Financia Plus.
Man: ②It's not as easy as that. There are a lot of complicated settings that you have to learn before you can use it well.

What does the man imply when he says, "It's not as easy as that"?
(A) A new product is harder to use.
(B) A plan is too costly to put into practice.
(C) A task is more difficult than it seems.

①_____ ②_____

▶▶▶ SET 9 🔊 09

会話1

Man: I'm thinking 9 A.M. might be the best time to leave tomorrow morning.
Woman: ①Do you know how long it takes to get to New York? We wouldn't get there until 11 A.M.

会話2

Man: The train looks a lot cheaper than taking a flight, but you shouldn't waste too much time getting there.
Woman: ②Do you know how long it takes to get to New York? I'll only spend the extra money if the time difference is significant.

What does the woman imply when she says, "Do you know how long it takes to get to New York"?
(A) She thinks a schedule is unrealistic.
(B) She is trying to choose a mode of transportation.
(C) There has been a change to a schedule.

①_____ ②_____

▶▶▶ SET 10 🔊 10

会話1

Man: Why are we using Linden Corporation's paper in the copiers instead of Kingsway Supplies?
Woman: ①Oh, I had nothing to do with it. I guess management was looking for a way to save money.

会話2

Man: Sales in the gardening equipment section have risen sharply this year so I guess you're doing something different.
Woman: ②Oh, I had nothing to do with it. There have been a lot of gardening shows on television and sales have improved everywhere.

What does the woman imply when she says, "Oh, I had nothing to do with it"?
(A) She was not busy at the time.
(B) She did not take part in a decision.
(C) She should not receive any praise.

①_____ ②_____

▶▶▶ SET 11 🔊 11

会話1

Woman: The cost of fuel has gone up; so why don't we adjust our prices to stay profitable?
Man: Actually, we should probably lower them. ①There are a lot of other bus companies in the area.

会話2

Woman: A friend of mine is looking for a job starting this May.
Man: I'm sorry we're not hiring at the moment. ②There are a lot of other bus companies in the area.

What does the man imply when he says, "There are a lot of other bus companies in the area"?
(A) Bus companies are in heavy competition.
(B) There may be some employment opportunities.
(C) Prices for transportation are too low.

①_____ ②_____

▶▶▶ SET 12 🔊 12

会話1

Man: Can you come with me to the hardware store this afternoon and help me choose a few things?
Woman: ①I need to get this job done by Friday. I'm sure Claire has some time now that her project is finished.

会話2

Man: We still don't know how many pages will be included in the brochure.
Woman: ②I need to get this job done by Friday. Can you ask Claire to tell me how many pages I can use?

What does the woman imply when she says, "I need to get this job done by Friday"?
(A) She has received a promotion.
(B) She is too busy to help a colleague.
(C) She needs some information urgently.

①_____ ②_____

3文トレーニングの解答・解説

▶▶▶ SET 1

会話1
男性：JGFとの合併は進展すると思う？
女性：①単に時間の問題よ。誰もが条件に同意しているし、両社にとって得るものは大きいわ。

会話2
男性：あなたの部署の報告書はどうしていつも遅れるのか教えてくれませんか？
女性：②単に時間の問題です。毎週金曜日までに分析するには情報が多過ぎます。

女性は"It's simply a matter of time"と言う際、何を意図していますか？
(A) 業務を完了させるのに十分な時間がない。
(B) 原稿の締め切りが近づいている。
(C) 成果はそのうち得られるだろう。

【解説】会話1で女性は、①の直後に「誰もが条件に同意している」「両社が得るものは大きい」と述べているので、合併が実現すると思っている。よって、(C) が正解。この文脈における It's simply a matter of time. は、文字通り「時間の問題」という意味。会話2では、情報が多過ぎて処理が間に合わない状況、つまり、時間が足りないことを問題視した発言なので、正解は (A) だ。(B) の deadline も「時間」に関連するが、「原稿」はどちらの会話にも関係がない。
正解：①(C) ②(A)

▶▶▶ SET 2

会話1
女性：New Yorkへの配達の後、空っぽのトラックが何台か戻ってくる運送会社が Illinois にあるの。どっちにしろ移動はするのだからというわけで、彼らがうちに大幅な割引をしてくれるって。
男性：①その手があったか。

会話2
女性：消費者は昔のパッケージの方が好きだったのよ。デザインを変える前に調査をしていたら、すごくお金を節約できたのに。
男性：②それを思い付いていれば良かったです。

男性はなぜ"I wish I'd thought of that"と言っていますか。
(A) 問題を発見したから。
(B) 良い考えに驚いたから。
(C) 失敗したことを申し訳ないと思っているから。

【解説】I wish I'd ~ は、現実には起きなかったことに対して「~だったら良かったのに」と願う表現。会話1で、女性の話を聞いた男性は、予想外の案に驚き、「(それを) 自分が思い付いていれば良かった」という気持ちを込めて①を発言している。よって、(B) が適切。一方、②では経費を節減する方法があったのに、自分が思い付かなかったことを嘆いているため、(C) が正解。
正解：①(B) ②(C)

▶▶▶ SET 3

会話1
男性：新しいコピー機を購入するのに十分な予算が残っているのかどうか心配なんだけど。
女性：①買うしかないじゃない。今のコピー機は修理のしようがないんだから。

会話2
男性：新しいコピー機に十分なお金なんて予算には残ってないよ。
女性：②ないものは仕方ないわ。来年まで待つしかないわね。

女性は"There's no getting around it"と言う際、何を意味していますか？
(A) 機材を交換することはできない。
(B) 出費は避けられない。
(C) 混雑した地区を通らなければならない。

【解説】ターゲット文の意味は、「それを避けることはできない」だ。日本語の「仕方がない」に近い。女性は①の後で、コピー機が修理できる状態ではないと述べている。つまり、「買うしかない」という意味で①の発言をしているので、(B) が適切。一方の会話2では、「来年まで待つしかない」と補足している。これは「(今は) 買えない」ことを意味しているので (A) が正解。(C) は、「迂回路がない」という文脈では正解になり得る。
正解：①(B) ②(A)

▶▶▶ **SET 4**

会話1

男性：工場は5月の生産開始に間に合うよう準備できそうですか？
女性：①よくぞ聞いてくださいました。そうですね、準備はもちろんですが、何か妨げがあった場合に備えて、予備案も検討中だということを申し上げたかったんです。

会話2

男性：5月の工場視察の出張にあなたも同行していただくことはできますか？
女性：②お誘いありがとうございます。ぜひご一緒させていただきたいです。

女性はなぜ"Thanks for asking"と言っていますか？
(A) 誘われてうれしいから。
(B) いくつかの提案を検討するつもりだから。
(C) ある話題について話したいと思っていたから。

【解説】動詞の ask をどう解釈するかがポイント。会話1では、男性の質問が、予備案を検討していたことを伝えるきっかけになったことを喜んで①を言っている。よって、(C) が正解だ。会話2での男性の質問は提案に近い。女性は、出張への同行を誘う (ask) 男性に感謝しているので、(A) が正解。女性は「(複数の) 提案を検討する」ためにターゲット文を言っているわけではないので、(B) は不適切。
正解：①(C)　②(A)

▶▶▶ **SET 5**

会話1

女性：私たち、今年は Colorado で開かれるあの産業会議へ行くべきだわ。①たくさんの見込み客がいるわよ。
男性：分かってる、でもその期間、僕はすごく忙しいんだ。

会話2

女性：休暇を取ろうとしていたのは分かっているんだけど、金曜の製品発表会にはあなたにどうしても出席してほしいのよ。②たくさんの見込み客が来るだろうから。
男性：休暇は数日後に取ることにしましょう。

女性はなぜ、"A lot of potential clients will be there"と言っていますか？
(A) イベントのチケットを売るため
(B) 出張の目的を強調するため
(C) 業務の割り当てを説明するため

【解説】ターゲット文の意味は「たくさんの見込み客がそこにいる」だ。会話1では、「そこ」は Colorado で開かれる産業会議であり、多くの見込み客が来るから出張するべきだと女性は述べている。よって、①の発言の理由は (B) だ。会話2では、女性は男性に金曜日に休暇を取ってほしくない理由を説明しているため、(C) が正解。(A) は、彼らがイベントのチケットを売る立場であれば成立する。
正解：①(B)　②(C)

▶▶▶ **SET 6**

会話1

女性：あなたの案についてだけど、お客さまに無料のインターネット接続を提供できるようになるとは思わないわ。
男性：①どうしてできないんですか？　高過ぎるとかそういうことでしょうか？

会話2

女性：ねえ、通りの向かい側にあるカフェが無料のインターネット接続を始めたわよ。
男性：②僕らもやらない？　常連客を維持する助けになるかもしれない。

男性はなぜ"Why can't we"と言っていますか？
(A) 例にならいたいから。
(B) 戦略が非現実的に見えるから。
(C) 提案が却下されたから。

【解説】①と②では意味が大きく違う。男性は、インターネット接続を無料で提供するという自分の案が無理である理由を知りたくて①を発言している。会話2では、他店のサービスを取り入れることを提案しているので、「自分たちはできない」という意味ではない。なお、①と②を発音する場合は語尾 (we?) のイントネーションが違う。①は下がり調子、②は上がり調子にするのが適切。(※音声を聞いてみてください)
正解：①(C)　②(A)

▶▶▶ SET 7

会話1

女性：①今週ずっとあなたに電話するつもりだったのよ。新しい販売部員を採用するというあなたの申請書に目を通して、承認をしました。
男性：ありがとう、Kelly。新しい従業員はいつから採用できますか？

会話2

男性：工場検査のデータを待っているのですが、誰からも連絡がありません。
女性：②今週ずっとお電話するつもりだったんです。申し訳ありませんが、まだ準備できていないんです。

女性はなぜ "I've been meaning to call you all week" と言っていますか？
(A) ある決定をした。
(B) 男性にもっと早く連絡しなかったことを反省している。
(C) 男性には長い間会っていない。

【解説】mean to ~ は「~するつもりだ」という意味。会話1では、女性の①直後の発言から、男性の申請を承認したことを伝えようとしていたと分かる。よって、正解は (A) だ。会話2では、「連絡を待っている」と言う男性の発言に対して女性はターゲット文を述べている。相手を待たせたことを悪いと思っているので、②の発言意図は (B) だ。(C)は、どちらの文脈にも合わない。
正解：①(A)　②(B)

▶▶▶ SET 8

会話1

女性：インテリアデザイナーを呼んで、オフィスを改装してしてもらうべきだと思わない？
男性：①それってそんなに簡単じゃないよ。本社の許可を得る必要があるけど、彼らは全ての支社のオフィスは同じように見えるべきだと主張するだろうからね。

会話2

女性：この新しいソフトウエアって Financia Plus にそっくりね。
男性：②あれほど単純じゃないよ。ちゃんと使えるようになる前に、学ばないといけない複雑な設定がたくさんあるんだ。

男性は "It's not as easy as that" と言う際、何を示唆していますか？
(A) 新製品は使うのが難しい。
(B) 計画は実行に移すのに経費が掛かり過ぎる。
(C) 課題は見掛けよりも困難である。

【解説】会話1で、男性は①に続いて We need to get permission ... と述べている。オフィスの改装には本社の許可が必要なので、「(言うのは簡単だが) 実行するのは簡単ではない」ということだ。よって、(C) が正解。会話2では、新しいソフトウエアが Financia Plus ほどには「簡単に使えない」という意味で②を発言している。よって、(A)が正解。(B)は、costly の部分がどちらの会話にも関係ない。
正解：①(C)　②(A)

▶▶▶ SET 9

会話1

男性：明日の朝は9時に出発するのが一番いいんじゃないかな。
女性：①New York まで行くのにどれくらいかかるか分かってるの？　午前11時まで着かないわ。

会話2

男性：鉄道は飛行機で行くより安そうだけど、あちらへ行く時間を無駄にすべきじゃないよ。
女性：②New York まではどのくらいかかるか知ってる？　時間の差が大きいなら、その分のお金を出すつもりなんだけど。

女性が "Do you know how long it takes to get to New York" と言う際、何を示唆していますか？
(A) 計画は非現実的だと思う。
(B) 交通手段を選ぼうとしている。
(C) 予定に変更があった。

【解説】Do you know how long ... ? という質問には2つの意味がある。1つは所要時間を尋ねる純粋な「質問」だ。男性に New York までの時間を尋ねている②がこれに該当する。女性は男性の答えを聞いてから移動手段を決めるつもりなので、(B) が正解。もう1つは的外れだったり浅はかな発言に対する「批判」だ。これには①が該当する。①の直後の発言から、女性は New York まで長時間かかることを知っており、(A) が適切。(C)は、どちらの文脈にも合わない。
正解：①(A)　②(B)

▶▶▶ SET 10

会話1
男性：どうしてうちは Kingsway Supplies じゃなくて、コピーに Linden Corporation の用紙を使っているの？
女性：①あら、私は関係ないわ。経営陣が経費を削減する方法を探していたんじゃないかしら。

会話2
男性：今年は園芸用具コーナーの売り上げが急増してるね。君が何か違うことをしたに違いないね。
女性：②あら、私は関係ないわ。テレビでガーデニング番組がたくさんやっているから、どこでも売り上げは伸びているのよ。

女性は"Oh, I had nothing to do with it"と言う際、何を意図していますか？
(A) 当時は忙しくなかった。
(B) 決定に加わらなかった。
(C) 何の称賛も受けるべきではない。

【解説】会話1で、女性はターゲット文の後、経営陣が経費削減策を探していたのだろうと述べることで、自分は無関係だったことを示唆している。よって、(B) が正解。会話2でもターゲット文の意味は同じだが、意図は男性の推測を否定することだ。売り上げ増は自分の功績ではなく、市場環境の影響だと言っている。よって、(C) が適切。(A) は、ターゲット文を「やることがなく暇だった」と解釈してしまった人には魅力的な誤答だ。
正解：①(B) ②(C)

▶▶▶ SET 11

会話1
女性：燃料費が値上がりしているので、利益性を維持するために料金を調整してはどうでしょう？
男性：むしろ、われわれは下げるべきなんだ。①この辺りにはバス会社がたくさんあるからね。

会話2
女性：友人が5月から始まる仕事を探しているんです。
男性：残念だけど、うちでは今のところ採用はないな。②この辺りには他にもバス会社はたくさんあるよ。

男性は"There are a lot of other bus companies in the area"と言う際、何を示唆していますか？
(A) バス会社は激しく競い合っている。
(B) 雇用の機会があるかもしれない。
(C) 運賃は安過ぎる。

【解説】会話1で値上げを提案する女性に、男性は値下げするべきだと述べている。ターゲット文はその主張の根拠だ。競合他社が多く存在するから値下げを提案するということは、競争が厳しいということだ。よって、(A) が正解。(C) は「値下げするべき」という発言とかみ合わない。会話2の②は、友人のための職を探している女性に対する発言なので、正解は (B)。
正解：①(A) ②(B)

▶▶▶ SET 12

会話1
男性：今日の午後、ホームセンターに一緒に来て、いつくか物を選ぶのを手伝ってくれない？
女性：①この仕事を金曜日までに終わらせなくちゃいけないの。Clair はプロジェクトが終わっているから、今ならきっと時間があると思うわ。

会話2
男性：このパンフレットは何ページあるのか、われわれはまだ知らないよね。
女性：②この仕事は金曜日までに終わらせなくちゃいけないのよ。私は何ページ使えるのか教えてくれるよう Clair に頼んでもらえる？

女性は"I need to get this job done by Friday"と言う際、何を示唆していますか？
(A) 昇進した。
(B) 忙しくて同僚を助けることができない。
(C) 至急情報を必要としている。

【解説】会話1では、手伝いを要請してきた男性に対してターゲット文を述べ、他のスタッフに依頼するよう促している。つまり「自分は手伝えない」ことを示唆しており、(B) が正解。会話2では、パンフレットのページ数に言及した男性に対して、ターゲット文を述べ、さらに、ページ数を調べるよう依頼しているため、(C) が適切だ。この2人は同じ仕事に取り組んでいる。
正解：①(B) ②(C)

Part 4 のまとめ
ヒロ前田

Part 4 はココが変わった！

新しい問題形式が登場
- 問題数は30問（3問×10セット）と変更ないが、新たに意図問題とグラフィック問題が導入された。計5問出題される計算。どちらも Part 3 のものと同じアプローチでOK
- グラフィック問題が出るのは最後

より自然な英語が話される
- Part 3 と比べるとカジュアルさは低いが、以前の Part 4 よりも自然な英語を含む
- 言いよどみや言い直しは Part 3 よりも起きがち。これらの現象ではわずかな空白が生まれるため、むしろ「リスニングが楽になった」と感じる受験者も少なくない

解説　グラフィック問題の「トラップ」にご用心！

　Part 3 にも共通することですが、グラフィック問題には実に巧妙なトラップが仕組まれています。本番でつまずくことのないよう、その代表的なパターンを紹介しておきます。次のようなグラフィックと選択肢の付いた問題があるとしましょう。まずは、トラップのないノーマルなパターンです。

3:00 P.M.	社長のスピーチ
4:00 P.M.	清掃
5:00 P.M.	営業会議
6:00 P.M.	パーティー

(A) 3:00 P.M.
(B) 4:00 P.M.
(C) 5:00 P.M.
(D) 6:00 P.M.

　ジョンがメアリーの留守番電話にメッセージを残しています。
　ジョン：メアリー、今度のプレゼンに間に合うように、会社のロゴマークについて打ち合わせをしようよ。夕方に営業会議の予定があったけど、キャンセルになって1時間空いたんだ。その時間にしよう。
　「打ち合わせは何時からですか？」という問いの正解は、(C) の「5時」です。

①「ずらし」のトラップ

ジョン：メアリー、今日、ロゴマークの打ち合わせをしようよ。時間はある？ オフィスの清掃に立ち会わなくてはいけないけど、その後なら時間をとれるよ。

「打ち合わせは何時からですか？」という問いに対して、「清掃」という単語を聞き取っただけで、ストーリーを理解していない人は、グラフィックを見て「4時」を選んでしまいます。ジョンは「清掃の後なら」と言っているので、正解は「5時」にずれます。

②「ぼかし」のトラップ

会話やトーク中の情報（＝音声）と選択肢との間で、言い換えや抽象化はこれまでも頻繁に起きていました。グラフィック問題では、このような情報のぼかしが音声とグラフィックとの間で起きるのです。左頁の例なら、グラフィックにある「社長のスピーチ（President's address）」が、音声では speech や presentation といった言葉で言い換えられている可能性があります。

③「だまし」のトラップ

ジョン：メアリー、ロゴマークの打ち合わせをしようよ。来週にはプレゼンもしなくちゃいけないし。6時にパーティーがあるね。その前に予定されていた営業会議がキャンセルになったから、その時間にしよう。

ジョンは、重要度の極めて低い「6時」という情報をわざわざ口に出しています。「6時」は音として聞き取りやすい上、選択肢にも存在しているので、コレだ！、と飛びついてしまう人がかなりいるはずです。まさに「だまし」ですね。「聞こえたから6時」で正解になるような問題はグラフィック問題ではありません。グラフィック問題の正解は、音とグラフィックの情報を統合して初めて導かれるものなのです。裏を返せば、「聞こえた単語をそのまま選んだら不正解になる」（だから選んじゃダメ！）という、Part 3・4共通の攻略法でもあります。

Part4 攻略の基本

実際の試験では、Part 3の終了後にPart 4のDirections（指示）の音声が流れます。この間の30秒という時間を活用して、直後に解くことになる数セット分の設問（余裕があれば選択肢も）に目を通します。これは、従来形式のころから、多くの受験者が実行していることです。でも、これだけではありません。Part 3の最後の設問をマークし終わった直後から始めれば、30秒どころか40秒近い時間を確保することができます。最初の1セットの先読みは、このうちの最後の10〜15秒を充てれば十分です。

● Directions の間に意図問題・グラフィック問題の先読み

そこで推奨するのが、意図問題・グラフィック問題を狙い撃ちした先読みです。優先順位は、意図問題が上です。意図問題はPart 4 に2、3問出題されますが、フルセンテンスの長い選択肢が多いのです。その場合は、設問だけでなく、選択肢も先読みする価値があります。

グラフィック問題の先読みでは、選択肢と共通していないグラフィック中の情報（＝「パートナー情報」→ P. 47）に目を向けましょう。

Part 4 | ドリル

トークを聞き、各設問の解答として最も適切なものを選ぼう。問題の先読み（→P.15）を実践しよう。

1. What is the purpose of the message?
   (A) To arrange a rental car
   (B) To report a problem
   (C) To change a meal order
   (D) To cancel an appointment

2. What does the speaker mean when he says, "I've had it"?
   (A) He has forgotten where he left something.
   (B) He already owns a piece of equipment.
   (C) He has tried the meal himself.
   (D) He is very dissatisfied with a situation.

3. What is the listener asked to do?
   (A) Check a map
   (B) Organize a meeting
   (C) Send a staff member
   (D) Provide directions

4. Where do the listeners most likely work?
   (A) At a hotel
   (B) At a restaurant
   (C) At a plumbing company
   (D) At a government office

5. What does the speaker imply when he says, "I wonder if anyone here can reach him"?
   (A) He needs someone to pick up an employee.
   (B) He supposes a worker will volunteer to take part.
   (C) He is encouraging employees to compete for an award.
   (D) He hopes someone will be able to contact a coworker.

6. According to the speaker, what can affected staff do?
   (A) Charge a meal to the company
   (B) Receive free tickets for a show
   (C) Leave work early
   (D) Attend a promotional event

7. What is the purpose of the broadcast?
   (A) To seek performers for an event
   (B) To publicize a music concert
   (C) To warn of traffic congestion
   (D) To notify members of an update to a Web site

8. What does the woman imply when she says, "But this year's list of performers will be hard to beat"?
   (A) Future events are unlikely to have such well-known entertainers.
   (B) The musicians participating are expected to win a prize.
   (C) There are more performers than there have been in the past.
   (D) It is still unclear how many people will be performing at the event.

9. What does the woman say about tickets?
   (A) They are likely to sell out quickly.
   (B) They are cheaper than they were last year.
   (C) They are available for purchase at the venue.
   (D) They can be returned until the day of the event.

10. What is the message mainly about?
    (A) A presentation
    (B) A workshop
    (C) A report
    (D) A sale

11. What does the speaker mean when she says, "I missed the point"?
    (A) She arrived too late.
    (B) She felt sad about leaving somewhere.
    (C) She did not understand a purpose.
    (D) She forgot to mention one topic.

12. What is the listener encouraged to do tonight?
    (A) Compare prices online
    (B) Review sales figures
    (C) Make amendments to some slides
    (D) Buy some competitors' products

13. Who are Protel Mobile's main clients?
    (A) Educational institutions
    (B) Students
    (C) Government departments
    (D) Businesses

14. Why does the speaker say, "come to Protel Mobile"?
    (A) To offer listeners a factory tour
    (B) To give a free consultation to customers
    (C) To propose an alternative provider
    (D) To promote a special class on technology

15. What can customers receive at no extra cost this week?
    (A) Insurance coverage
    (B) A protective case
    (C) A software application
    (D) Instruction on usage

Flight#	Destination	Departing
DA382	Denver	7:15 P.M.
GT991	Boise	7:22 P.M.
YU932	Seattle	7:30 P.M.
OI249	Toledo	7:38 P.M.

16. Look at the graphic. Which flight will likely leave next?
    (A) DA382
    (B) GT991
    (C) YU932
    (D) OI249

17. What should customers with connecting flights do?
    (A) Hurry to their boarding gate
    (B) Wait for more information
    (C) Check their ticket details
    (D) Contact airline representatives

18. Why should Mr. Cox go to the third floor?
    (A) To meet an airline official
    (B) To deliver some baggage
    (C) To get a replacement ticket
    (D) To pick up an item

GO ON TO THE NEXT PAGE

Agenda	Speaker
Sales campaign	Greg Dalton
Company logo	Linda Park
Recruiting project	Janice Suzuki
Office renovation	Anton Gupta

Purchasing Request		
Quotation from supplier — Carpet World		
Pure Wool Business Grade Carpet (Blue)	25 meters	$2,100
Delivery and installation		$200
	TOTAL	$2,300
Estimated completion date: May 17		

19. Look at the graphic. What will be discussed next week?
    (A) Sales campaign
    (B) Company logo
    (C) Recruiting project
    (D) Office renovation

20. What kind of products does the company produce?
    (A) Baggage
    (B) Pharmaceuticals
    (C) Vehicles
    (D) Appliances

21. According to the speaker, what will the company do next week?
    (A) Provide a discount
    (B) Welcome a guest
    (C) Hire some new staff members
    (D) Launch a new product line

22. What does the speaker say about the company's offices?
    (A) They have been occupied for a long time.
    (B) They are going to be rebuilt.
    (C) The rent is too expensive.
    (D) The location is inconvenient.

23. Look at the graphic. Why might the request be rejected?
    (A) It is not necessary.
    (B) It is over budget.
    (C) It cannot be completed in time.
    (D) It is not for an approved supplier.

24. Who should employees contact before making a purchase?
    (A) An interior decorator
    (B) An online discount store
    (C) The general affairs department
    (D) Their department supervisor

Tullox BFM25X

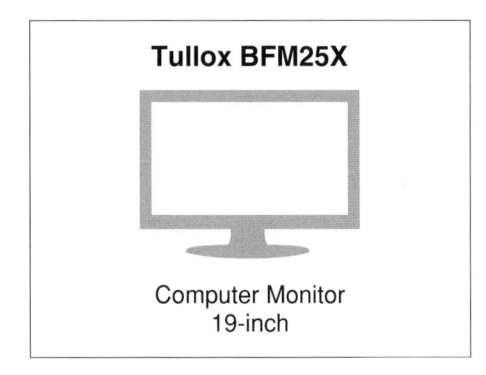

Computer Monitor
19-inch

Schedule	
Friday	Winter Sale Day 1
Saturday	Winter Sale Day 2
Sunday	Restocking
Monday	Spring Fair

25. What is the purpose of the message?
    (A) To update an order
    (B) To reply to a request
    (C) To explain a procedure
    (D) To offer a suggestion

26. Look at the graphic. To which department will the device be delivered?
    (A) Administration
    (B) Reception
    (C) Cafeteria
    (D) Nursing

27. What is the listener asked to do?
    (A) Install a device
    (B) Return a call
    (C) Send a catalog
    (D) Carry out repairs

28. What kind of items does the store sell?
    (A) Food
    (B) Cookware
    (C) Electronics
    (D) Clothing

29. What is available free of charge?
    (A) Home delivery
    (B) Gift-wrapping
    (C) Professional installation
    (D) International shipping

30. Look at the graphic. What time will the store close on Saturday?
    (A) At 4:00 P.M.
    (B) At 5:00 P.M.
    (C) At 6:00 P.M.
    (D) At 9:00 P.M.

Part 4 | ドリルの解答・解説

🔊 31 Man UK

Questions 1 through 3 refer to the following telephone message.
M: Hi, Kate. It's Fred calling. I'm on my way out to deliver a meal to a customer in Springwood. ①Well, um, the delivery van has broken down again. I'm about a kilometer from the customer's address, so I'm going to walk the rest of the way. And, of course, because of our policy, if I don't get there in a few minutes, the food is free. ②Anyway — I've had it. ③This is the second time the van has broken down this week. We have to buy a new one. I'll be at the corner of Ford Street and Holden Street in about 10 minutes. ④Can you ask one of the other staff to come and get me?

問題1-3は次の電話メッセージに関するものです。
男性：どうも、Kate。Fred です。Springwood のお客さまのところへ料理を届けに行く途中です。ええと、あの、配達用のバンがまた故障してしまいました。お客さまの住所から1キロほどのところにいるので、あとは歩きます。そうなるともちろん、うちのポリシーがありますから、あと2、3分で着かないと、料理はただです。とにかく、うんざりです。バンが故障したのは、今週これで2度目です。われわれは新しい車を買う必要があります。取りあえず、10分後ぐらいには、Ford Street と Holden Street の角にいますから。迎えに来てくれるよう、スタッフの誰かに頼んでもらえますか？

☐ **on one's way out to ~**：〜へ行く途中で　☐ **van**：(ライト) バン、ワゴン車　☐ **I've had it.**：「うんざりだ」、「もうたくさんだ」

1.
What is the purpose of the message?（このメッセージの目的は何ですか？）
(A) To arrange a rental car（レンタカーを手配すること）
(B) To report a problem（問題を報告すること）
(C) To change a meal order（食事の注文を変更すること）
(D) To cancel an appointment（約束を取りやめること）

正解：(B)　電話メッセージの目的を問う問題。話者は①で「配達用のバンがまた故障した」とトラブルがあったことを述べている。その後も、バンが故障したせいで徒歩で配達先に向かうことや、配達時間に間に合わない可能性があることなどを述べている。よって、話者は「問題を報告する」ために電話をかけたと判断できるので、(B) が正解。迎えの手配は頼んではいるが、レンタカーの手配ではないので、(A) は不適切。

2. NEW
What does the speaker mean when he says, "I've had it"?（話し手は "I've had it" と言う際、何を意図していますか？）
(A) He has forgotten where he left something.（何かを置いた場所を忘れてしまった）
(B) He already owns a piece of equipment.（すでに道具を1つ持っている）
(C) He has tried the meal himself.（その料理を自分でも食べてみたことがある）
(D) He is very dissatisfied with a situation.（状況に強い不満を抱いている）

正解：(D)　このメッセージにおける、I've had it という発言の意図を問う問題。前半で話し手は、「バンが再び故障したせいで、配達先まで歩いて行く」と述べている。その後、②「とにかく」と切り出し、I've had it と言い、③「これで2度目なので、新しい車を買う必要がある」と述べている。つまり、この発言は「バンが再び壊れた状況にうんざりしている」ということを意図していると判断できるので、(D) が正解。

3.
What is the listener asked to do?（聞き手は何をするよう依頼されていますか？）
(A) Check a map（地図を確認する）
(B) Organize a meeting（会議を計画する）
(C) Send a staff member（スタッフを行かせる）
(D) Provide directions（道を教える）

正解：(C)　聞き手が依頼されている内容を問う問題。④に Can you ~?（〜してくれませんか）という依頼表現があり、「スタッフの誰かに迎えに来てもらうよう頼む」と続いている。よって、その言い換えとしてふさわしい (C)「スタッフを行かせる」が正解である。迎えに来る場所を指定しているが、地図を見ることは頼んでいないので、(A) は不適切。

080

32 Man US

Questions 4 through 6 refer to the following talk.

M: Could I just have everyone's attention for a moment? ①We've been asked to help repair some pipes at the Oxenford Hotel. It's a big job and we'll need two or three people to go up there and find out what the problem is and ②get their water supply working again. ③Philip Smith is doing a job in the area right now, but he doesn't have his work phone switched on. I wonder if anyone here can reach him. ④Perhaps you know his private number or something. Anyway, there's a good chance that'll require us to work until late, ⑤so anyone involved can charge their dinner expenses to the company.

問題4-6は次のトークに関するものです。
男性: ちょっと皆さん聞いてもらえますか？ Oxenford Hotel の配管の修理を支援するよう依頼がありました。大掛かりな作業なので、2、3人に現地へ出向いて、何が問題なのかを突き止め、給水設備を再稼働させてもらう必要があります。Philip Smith が現在その地区で作業中なのですが、彼は業務用電話の電源を入れていません。ここにいるどなたか、彼に連絡がつかないでしょうか。もしかすると彼の私用電話番号か何かご存じかもしれませんね。とにかく、遅くまで作業しなくてはいけなくなる可能性が高いので、関係する方は、夕食の経費を会社に請求していただいて構いません。

□**water supply**：給水（設備）、飲料水の供給　□**have ~ switched on**：~の電源を入れている　□**there's a good chance ~**：~という可能性が高い　□**charge ~ to ...**：~を…の負担にする、~を…の勘定として請求する　□**expense**：費用、出費

4.
Where do the listeners most likely work?（聞き手はどこで働いていると考えられますか？）
(A) At a hotel（ホテルで）
(B) At a restaurant（レストランで）
(C) At a plumbing company（配管工事会社で）
(D) At a government office（官庁で）
□**plumbing**：配管工事

正解：(C)　聞き手の職業を問う問題。①から話し手と聞き手は、ホテルに配管の修理を頼まれたことが分かる。②で聞き手は、「給水設備を再稼働させる」と修理の詳細を伝えられている。よって、このトークの聞き手は (C)「配管工事会社で」働いていると判断できる。「ホテル」は聞き手がこれから作業を行う場所なので、(A) は不適切。

5. NEW
What does the speaker imply when he says, "I wonder if anyone here can reach him"?（話し手は "I wonder if anyone here can reach him" と言う際、何を示唆していますか？）
(A) He needs someone to pick up an employee.（誰かにある従業員を迎えに行ってほしい）
(B) He supposes a worker will volunteer to take part.（従業員が進んで参加することを想定している）
(C) He is encouraging employees to compete for an award.（従業員たちが賞を競うことを奨励している）
(D) He hopes someone will be able to contact a coworker.（誰かがある同僚に連絡を取れることを願っている）

正解：(D)　話し手は③「Philip Smithの仕事用の電話に連絡がつかない」と述べた後、I wonder if anyone here can reach him. と言い、④「彼の私用の番号を知っているなら、そちらでもいい」と述べている。つまり、話し手は「誰かが Philip Smith と連絡が取れたらいい」と思っていることが分かる。よって、(D) が正解。reach には「連絡を取る」以外にも、「手を伸ばす」や「（目的地に）到着する」などの意味がある。

6.
According to the speaker, what can affected staff do?（話し手によると、影響を受ける社員は何をすることができますか？）
(A) Charge a meal to the company（食事を会社の負担にする）
(B) Receive free tickets for a show（公演の無料チケットを受け取る）
(C) Leave work early（仕事を早退する）
(D) Attend a promotional event（販促イベントに出席する）
□**affected**：影響を受ける　□**promotional**：販売促進の、販促用の

正解：(A)　トークの最後で、話し手は「遅くまで作業をする可能性がある」と述べている。そして、⑤で「遅くまで働くことになった人は、夕食代を会社に請求していい」と聞き手に伝えている。よって、それを「食事を会社の負担にする」と表した (A) が正解。本文 a good chance の good は、ここでは「十分な」という意味で使われている。

33 Woman UK

Questions 7 through 9 refer to the following excerpt from a broadcast.

W: You're listening to Triple Z Radio, Normandy's most popular radio station. ①Every summer for the last three years, we've invited five bands to perform at a rock and roll concert at Sunbury Park. Every year, more and more of the performers are major international bands. But this year's list of performers will be hard to beat. ②The headline act is none other than world-famous rock musician, Rod Moon. Tickets are already on sale online ③but get in quick because they're expected to sell out in hours.

問題7-9は次の放送の一部に関するものです。
女性：お聞きの放送は Triple Z Radio、Normandy で最も人気があるラジオ局です。過去3年、夏になると、われわれは5組のバンドに Sunbury Park でのロックロール・コンサートへの出演を依頼してきました。年々、メジャーな国際的バンドが出演者に増えています。でも今年の出演者のリストは、この上なく素晴らしいものになるでしょう。メーン・アクトは、世界的に有名なロック・ミュージシャン、Rod Moon にほかなりません。チケットはすでに発売中ですが、お急ぎください。数時間後には売り切れることが予想されます。

□**hard to beat**：この上なく素晴らしい、強敵である
□**headline act**：メーン・アクト　□**none other than ~**：~にほかならない　□**world-famous**：世界的に有名な

7.
What is the purpose of the broadcast?（このお知らせの目的は何ですか？）
(A) To seek performers for an event（イベントの出演者を探すこと）
(B) To publicize a music concert（コンサートを宣伝すること）
(C) To warn of traffic congestion（交通渋滞に注意を呼び掛ける）
(D) To notify members of an update to a Web site（ウェブサイトの更新を会員に知らせる）
□**publicize**：~を宣伝する、~を公表する　□**warn of ~**：~を警告する、~に注意を呼び掛ける　□**traffic congestion**：交通渋滞

正解：(B)　話し手は①で、今までに開催されてきたコンサートについて話している。その後、今年のコンサートの出演者のことや、チケットが発売中であることを述べている。よって、これを「コンサートを宣伝すること」と表した (B) が正解。今年の出演者はすでに決まっているので、(A) は不適切。

8. NEW
What does the woman imply when she says, "But this year's list of performers will be hard to beat"?（女性は "But this year's list of performers will be hard to beat" と言う際、何を示唆していますか？）
(A) Future events are unlikely to have such well-known entertainers.（今後のイベントにこれほど有名な出演者がそろうことはないだろう）
(B) The musicians participating are expected to win a prize.（参加ミュージシャンは賞を取ることが予想される）
(C) There are more performers than there have been in the past.（かつてよりも多くの出演者がいる）
(D) It is still unclear how many people will be performing at the event.（イベントに何人出演するのかはまだ不明である）

正解：(A)　話し手はトーク前半で「年々、メジャーなバンドの出演者が増えている」と述べている。その後、But this year's list of performers will be hard to beat と述べ、②で世界的に有名なミュージシャンの出演を発表している。つまり、この発言は「今年の出演者以上に豪華な人はいない」という意図で述べられたと判断できる。よって、(A) が正解。出演者数に関することは述べていないので、(C) は不適切。

9.
What does the woman say about tickets?（話し手はチケットについて何と言っていますか？）
(A) They are likely to sell out quickly.（すぐに売り切れる可能性がある）
(B) They are cheaper than they were last year.（昨年よりも安い）
(C) They are available for purchase at the venue.（会場で購入することが可能である）
(D) They can be returned until the day of the event.（イベントの当日まで返品できる）
□**venue**：会場、開催地

正解：(A)　チケットに関する情報を問う問題。話し手は最後に、③「チケットは数時間後には売り切れることが予想される」と述べている。よって、その言い換えとしてふさわしい (A)「すぐに売り切れる可能性がある」が正解。その他の選択肢の内容について話者は触れていないので、それぞれ不適切。

34 Woman AU

Questions 10 through 12 refer to the following telephone message.

W: ①Hi, Joe. It's Ming Lee. I'm calling to leave you some feedback on your rehearsal for the presentation today. All in all, I was quite impressed. Your use of images and graphs made the data very easy to understand. ②As for the brief introduction featuring our corporate history. Well ... I missed the point. To be honest, ③there's no reason to talk about it and the clients won't be interested. I think it's more important to stress the strength of our products because they'll compare us with rival companies. ④I recommend you make revisions to the slides tonight. I'll check them in the morning.

問題10-12は次の電話メッセージに関するものです。
女性：どうも、Joe。Ming Lee です。今日のあなたのプレゼンの練習について感想を伝えるために電話しました。全体としてはとても感心しました。画像やグラフを使うことで、データが非常に理解しやすかったです。わが社の歴史を紹介する簡潔な導入部についてなんですが。その…要点がつかめませんでした。率直に言って、それについて話す理由がないし、クライアントは関心を持たないでしょう。わが社の製品の強みを強調することの方が重要だと思います。彼らはわが社を競合企業と比較するでしょうから。今夜のうちにスライドに変更を加えることをお勧めします。私が午前中に確認します。

□**feedback**：意見、感想　□**rehearsal**：練習、リハーサル　□**all in all**：全体として、大体において　□**be impressed**：感心する　□**as for ~**：~に関して　□**corporate history**：社史、会社の歴史　□**miss the point**：要点がつかめない　□**to be honest**：率直に言って　□**make a revision to ~**：~に変更を加える

10.
What is the message mainly about?（このメッセージは主に何に関するものですか？）
(A) A presentation（プレゼンテーション）
(B) A workshop（研修）
(C) A report（報告書）
(D) A sale（特売）

正解：**(A)**　会話の概要を問う問題。冒頭①で、話し手は「あなたのプレゼンテーションのリハーサルの感想を伝えるために電話した」と述べている。その後、プレゼンテーションの内容やそれを見た感想などを伝えていることから、この会話の主な内容は (A)「プレゼンテーション」についてだと判断できる。

11. NEW
What does the speaker mean when she says, "I missed the point"?（話し手が "I missed the point" と言う際、何を意図していますか？）
(A) She arrived too late.（到着したのが遅過ぎた）
(B) She felt sad about leaving somewhere.（どこかから去ることが悲しかった）
(C) She did not understand a purpose.（目的が理解できなかった）
(D) She forgot to mention one topic.（ある話題に触れるのを忘れた）

正解：**(C)**　話し手は②で「プレゼンテーションのわが社の歴史を紹介する部分」の話を切り出し、I missed the point と言い、③「クライアントが興味を持たないと思うから、それを話す必要がない」と言っている。つまり、話し手は「自社の歴史について話す必要がない」と思っているので、聞き手がなぜそれについて話したのか、その狙いを理解できなかったことが分かる。よって、(C) が正解。

12.
What is the listener encouraged to do tonight?（聞き手は今夜何をすることを勧められていますか？）
(A) Compare prices online（インターネットで価格を比較する）
(B) Review sales figures（売上高を見直す）
(C) Make amendments to some slides（スライドに変更を加える）
(D) Buy some competitors' products（競合企業の製品を購入する）
□**make an amendment to ~**：~に変更を加える

正解：**(C)**　話し手は④で I recommend you ~（あなたに~することを勧める）という表現を使い、聞き手に「スライドに変更を加えること」を促している。よって、正解は (C) である。(C) amendment が本文 revision の言い換えである。その他にも、adjustment（調整）、change（変更）、modification（修正）も同義語として覚えておこう。

083

35 Man UK

Questions 13 through 15 refer to the following advertisement.

M: Protel Mobile is a mobile telephone network with a difference. ①Our discount connection plans are specially designed for companies who equip large numbers of their employees with mobile phones. ②If you're unhappy with the service from ③your business's current mobile phone service, come to Protel Mobile. You name it, we can do it. ④We stock a wide variety of makes and models and have a plan ⑤to suit any size firm at the lowest prices. ⑥Clients who sign up with Protel Mobile this week will receive free plastic covers to keep their new phones safe and clean. We have excellent insurance plans and expert staff, so we'll ⑦make sure your company gets the best deal possible.

問題13-15は次の宣伝に関するものです。
男性：Protel Mobile は一味違う携帯電話ネットワークです。当社の割引接続プランは、多くの社員に携帯電話を持たせている企業向けに特別に考案されています。もしあなたが、御社の現在使用されている携帯電話サービスに満足していないなら、Protel Mobile にお越しください。おっしゃっていただければ、何でも対応します。当社では、幅広いメーカーとモデルの在庫を置いており、どんな規模の企業にも合うプランを最安値で用意しています。今週 Protel Mobile と契約されるお客さまには、新しい電話を安全で清潔に保つことのできる無料のプラスチックカバーを差し上げます。当社では優れた保険プランと専門スタッフをそろえておりますので、御社に可能な限り最良の契約を結んでいただけます。

□**equip ~ with ...**：～に…を身に付けさせる　□**you name it**：何でも、どんなものでも　□**make**：製造者、メーカー　□**plastic**：ビニール、プラスチック

13.
Who are Protel Mobile's main clients?（Protel Mobile の主な顧客は誰ですか？）
(A) Educational institutions（教育機関）
(B) Students（学生）
(C) Government departments（政府機関）
(D) Businesses（企業）
□**institution**：機関、施設

正解：(D)　話し手は①で「当社の割引接続プランは社員に携帯電話を持たせている企業向け」と述べている。さらに③「あなたのビジネス」、⑤「どんな規模の企業にも合う」、⑦「あなたの会社」という発言から、この宣伝は「企業」に向けてのものだと判断できる。よって、Protel Mobile の主な顧客は (D)「企業」である。

14. NEW
Why does the speaker say, "come to Protel Mobile"?（話し手はなぜ "come to Protel Mobile" と言っていますか？）
(A) To offer listeners a factory tour（聞き手に工場見学を提案するため）
(B) To give a free consultation to customers（顧客への無料相談を行うため）
(C) To propose an alternative provider（別のプロバイダーを提案するため）
(D) To promote a special class on technology（技術に関する特別講座を宣伝するため）
□**consultation**：相談

正解：(C)　この会話における come to Protel Mobile という発言の意図が問われている。話し手は②の文で「現在の携帯電話サービスに満足していないなら」と言い、come to Protel Mobile と付け加えている。その後、提供しているサービスや特典の内容を説明している（④）。つまり、「Protel Mobile に来たら、他の会社とは異なる携帯電話サービスを提供できる」という意図でこの発言をしたと考えられる。よって、(C) が正解。

15.
What can customers receive at no extra cost this week?（顧客は今週、追加費用無しで何を受け取ることができますか？）
(A) Insurance coverage（保険の補償）
(B) A protective case（保護ケース）
(C) A software application（アプリケーション・ソフト）
(D) Instruction on usage（使い方の説明書）
□**insurance coverage**：保険の補償、保険金
□**protective**：保護の、保護用の　□**usage**：使用法、使用

正解：(B)　話し手は⑥で「今週 Protel Mobile と契約したお客さまには、新しい電話を安全で清潔に保てる無料のプラスチックカバーを差し上げる」と言っているので、「プラスチックカバー」を「保護ケース」と表した (B) が正解。トーク中の free を設問では no extra cost と言い換えている。complimentary（無料の）という単語も言い換え表現として覚えておこう。その他の選択肢に関する内容は述べられていないので、不適切。

36 Woman AU

Questions 16 through 18 refer to the following announcement and timetable.

W: Good evening, travelers. ①The current time in Dallas is 7:05 P.M. ②The Devine Air flight for Denver that was scheduled for departure at 7:15 is going to be delayed for over an hour — There were some maintenance issues. The staff of Devine Air would like to offer passengers their sincere apologies. ③If you have connecting flights in Denver that may be affected, please contact the staff at our service counter. ④If passenger Mr. Jason Cox is in the airport terminal, he should make his way to the lost and found department on the third floor. ⑤One of his possessions has been delivered there.

問題13-15は次のお知らせと予定表に関するものです。
女性：ご旅行中の皆さま、今晩は。Dallas の現在の時刻は午後7時5分です。7時15分に出発が予定されていた Devine 航空 Denver 行きは、1時間以上遅れる予定です。メンテナンスの問題が発生したためです。Devine 航空の従業員一同、お客さまには心よりおわび申し上げます。Denver での乗り継ぎに影響を受ける可能性のあるお客さまは、当社サービスカウンターのスタッフにご連絡ください。お客さまの Jason Cox 様、空港ターミナル内にいらっしゃいましたら、3階の遺失物係までお越しください。落とし物がそちらに届いております。

便名	行き先	出発
Flight#	Destination	Departing
⑥DA382	Denver	7:15 P.M.
⑦GT991	Boise	7:22 P.M.
YU932	Seattle	7:30 P.M.
OI249	Toledo	7:38 P.M.

□**sincere**：誠実な、心からの　□**apology**：謝罪
□**connecting flight**：接続便、乗り継ぎ便　□**make one's way to ~**：~へ向かう　□**lost and found department**：遺失物係　□**possession**：所有物

16. NEW
Look at the graphic. Which flight will likely leave next?（図を見てください。次に出発すると考えられるのはどの便ですか？）
(A) DA382

(B) GT991
(C) YU932
(D) OI249

正解：(B)　グラフィック問題は音声と図表内の情報を組み合わせて解答するので、選択肢にある情報が、音声の中でそのまま正解として登場する可能性は低い。選択肢は「便名」なので、表の「行き先」と「出発時刻」に関する情報が聞こえると予測する。②に「7:15発 Denver 行きの出発が1時間遅れる」とあるので、表の⑥から、DA382 の出発時刻が8:15になると分かる。よって、①の現在時刻と表⑦から、次に出発する便は (B) GT991だと分かる。

17.
What should customers with connecting flights do?（乗り継ぎ便のある利用客は何をすべきですか？）
(A) Hurry to their boarding gate（搭乗口へ急ぐ）
(B) Wait for more information（さらに情報を待つ）
(C) Check their ticket details（チケットの詳細を確認する）
(D) Contact airline representatives（航空会社の担当者に連絡する）

□**boarding gate**：搭乗口、搭乗ゲート
□**representative**：係員、担当者

正解：(D)　③で「Denver での乗り継ぎに影響を受ける可能性のあるお客さまは」とある。その後に、please ~（~してください）という依頼表現を使って、「サービススタッフに連絡する」という内容が続いている。よって、(D) が正解。

18.
Why should Mr. Cox go to the third floor?（Cox さんはなぜ3階へ行くべきですか？）
(A) To meet an airline official（航空会社関係者に会うため）
(B) To deliver some baggage（荷物を届けるため）
(C) To get a replacement ticket（代わりのチケットを入手するため）
(D) To pick up an item（物を受け取るため）
□**official**：職員

正解：(D)　Cox という名前は④で登場する。話し手は「Jason Cox 様は3階の遺失物係までお越しください」と述べている。その後、その理由を⑤「落とし物が届いている」と述べている。よって、正解は (D)「物を受け取るため」である。(D) item がトーク中の possession(s) の言い換えである。one of + 複数名詞で「~のうちの1つ」という意味。Cox 氏の荷物は届けられた方なので、(B) は不適切。

37 Man US

Questions 19 through 21 refer to the following excerpt from a meeting and agenda.

M: ①Before starting the weekly meeting, I should tell you ②Linda Park just called to say she wouldn't be able to join us today. It seems that her train's been delayed on account of the snow. So ③we'll hear about the updates from her next time. Now, as you all know, the ongoing Internet marketing strategy has generated a lot of ④interest in our luggage and travel items. Greg, I'd like you to talk about how we'll translate that public interest into sales because ⑤next week we'll be launching a line of exciting ⑥leather suitcases and shoulder bags.

問題19-21は次の会議の一部と議題に関するものです。
男性：週一会議を始める前に、先ほどLinda Parkから今日は出席できないという電話があったのでお知らせしておきます。雪のせいで電車が遅れているようです。そういうわけで、彼女の最新情報の報告は次回聞くことにしましょう。さて、皆さんご存じの通り、進行中のインターネットによるマーケティング戦略が、わが社の旅行かばんや旅行用品に対する大きな関心を生んでいます。Greg、その世間の関心をどうやって売り上げにつなげるのかを話してもらえますか。来週われわれは素晴らしい革製のスーツケースとショルダーバッグのシリーズを発売するわけですから。

議題	発言者
Agenda	**Speaker**
Sales campaign 販売キャンペーン	Greg Dalton
⑦Company logo 会社のロゴ	Linda Park
Recruiting project 求人プロジェクト	Janice Suzuki
Office renovation オフィスの改築	Anton Gupta

□**on account of** 〜：〜の理由で、〜のせいで
□**update**：最新情報　□**ongoing**：進行中の、現在行われている　□**generate** 〜：〜を生む、〜を引き起こす
□**translate** 〜 **into** ...：〜を…につなげる

19. NEW
Look at the graphic. What will be discussed next week?（図を見てください。来週は何について議論さ れますか？）
(A) Sales campaign（販売キャンペーン）
(B) Company logo（会社のロゴ）
(C) Recruiting project（求人プロジェクト）
(D) Office renovation（オフィスの改築）
□**recruiting**：求人活動

正解：(B)　選択肢と表の共通情報は「議題」なので、表右側の「発言者」を見ながら、「来週」に関連する情報を聞き取る。冒頭①から、会議は毎週行われていることが分かる。その後、②で「Linda Parkが今日出席できない」、③で「彼女の最新情報は次回聞こう」と述べられている。これらの発言から、Park氏が話す予定だった⑦「会社のロゴ」が来週、議論されることが分かる。よって、(B)が正解。

20.
What kind of products does the company produce?（この企業はどのような種類の商品を製造していますか？）
(A) Baggage（手荷物入れ）
(B) Pharmaceuticals（薬剤）
(C) Vehicles（車）
(D) Appliances（電化製品）
□**baggage**：(旅行用の)手荷物　□**pharmaceutical**：薬剤　□**appliance**：電化製品、電気器具

正解：(A)　話し手の企業が製造している商品を選ぶ問題。④の「わが社の旅行かばんや旅行用品」と⑥の「革製のスーツケースとショルダーバッグ」という発言から、この企業は(A)「手荷物入れ」を製造していることが分かる。その他の選択肢に関する情報は述べられていないので、それぞれ不適切。

21.
According to the speaker, what will the company do next week?（話し手によれば、この会社は来週何をしますか？）
(A) Provide a discount（割引を行う）
(B) Welcome a guest（来客を迎える）
(C) Hire some new staff members（新しい職員を雇う）
(D) Launch a new product line（新しい製品シリーズを発売する）

正解：(D)　設問にnext weekといった具体的な時期を示す表現がある場合は、その情報に注意して聞こう。⑤で「来週、スーツケースとショルダーバッグのシリーズを発売する」とある。よって、正解は(D)「新しい製品シリーズを発売する」である。launchは動詞で「開始する」という意味で、startの言い換えとしても登場する。また、動詞だけでなく「開始、発売」という意味の名詞としても使われる。

38　Man　UK

Questions 22 through 24 refer to the following excerpt from a meeting and order form.

M: ①It's been ten years since we moved into this building and the age is starting to show. We've decided to renovate the workplace a little this year. ②Each department will be given a two-thousand-dollar allocation to use for that purpose. You're expected to spend the money on replacing any worn-out pieces of furniture or anything else that'll improve the offices' appearance. The general affairs department gets a lot more visitors than other departments so it's been agreed that they will spend their allocation on a new carpet. Marketing, product development, and manufacturing can spend the money as they like. However, ③employees are asked not to make any purchases without permission from their department supervisor.

問題22-24は次の会議の抜粋と注文フォームに関するものです。
男性：私たちがこのビルに移ってきてから10年たちますが、その年月が表れ始めています。私たちは今年、仕事場を少しリフォームすることを決めました。各部署にはその目的に使う2000ドルの割り当てがあります。そのお金は、古くなった家具の買い替えやオフィスの景観を改善するものに使うことになるでしょう。総務部には他の部署よりもずっと多くの来客があるので、割当金を新しいカーペットに使うことになっています。営業部、商品開発部、製造部は自由にそのお金を使うことができます。ただし、社員の方々は、ご自分の部の管理者の許可を得ずに購入をしないようお願いします。

Purchasing Request		
Quotation from supplier — Carpet World		
Pure Wool Business Grade Carpet (Blue)	25 meters	$2,100
Delivery and installation		$200
	④TOTAL	$2,300
Estimated completion date: May 17		

購入申請書		
納入業者からの見積書 — Carpet World		
純毛事業所用カーペット（青）	25メートル	2100ドル
配達と設置		200ドル
	合計	2300ドル
作業完了予定日：5月17日		

☐**renovate**：〜を修理する、〜をリフォームする
☐**allocation**：割り当て、配分　☐**worn-out**：使い古された、擦り切れた　☐**supervisor**：管理者、責任者

22.

What does the speaker say about the company's offices?（話し手はその会社のオフィスについて何と言っていますか？）

(A) They have been occupied for a long time.（長い間使っている）
(B) They are going to be rebuilt.（建て直される予定である）
(C) The rent is too expensive.（賃貸料が高過ぎる）
(D) The location is inconvenient.（立地が不便である）

正解：(A)　話し手はビルの様子を冒頭①で、「このビルに移ってきてから10年たち、それが建物に表れて始めている」と述べている。よって、この発言を「長い間使っている」と言い換えた (A) が正解。「職場を改装する」とは言っているが、「建て直す」とは言っていないので、(B) は不適切。renovate の言い換えとして、remodel（〜を改装する）、repair（〜を修理する）、restore（〜を修理する）も覚えておこう。

23. NEW

Look at the graphic. Why might the request be rejected?（図を見てください。この申請はなぜ却下される可能性がありますか？）
(A) It is not necessary.（必要ないから）
(B) It is over budget.（予算を上回っているから）
(C) It cannot be completed in time.（期限内に完了させることができないから）
(D) It is not for an approved supplier.（認められている納入業者ではないから）

正解：(B)　設問から、この申請は何らかの条件を満たしていないことが分かるので、その内容を聞き取る。話し手は②で「各部署には2000ドルが割り当てられる」と述べて

087

いる。表④を見ると、この注文の合計金額は2300ドルなので、予算を上回っていることが分かる。よって、正解は (B) である。カーペットが必要な理由は述べられているので、(A) は不適切。(C) と (D) に関することも述べられていないので、それぞれ不適切。

24.
Who should employees contact before making a purchase?（社員は購入する前に誰に連絡を取るべきですか？）
(A) An interior decorator（インテリアデザイナー）
(B) An online discount store（インターネットのディスカウントストア）
(C) The general affairs department（総務部）
(D) Their department supervisor（部の管理者）
□**interior decorator**：インテリアデザイナー、インテリアコーディネーター

正解：(D)　話し手は③「部の管理者の許可を得てから購入するように」と述べている。よって、社員は商品を購入する前に「部の管理者」に連絡しないといけないことが分かるので、(D) が正解。(C)「総務部」は、「すでにカーペットを購入することが決まっている」と述べられているだけなので、不適切。その他の選択肢の内容も言及されていないので、それぞれ不適切。

🔊 39　Woman AU

Questions 25 through 27 refer to the following telephone message and label.

W: Hi, it's Gina Prinz from Hadfield Hospital. ①I called earlier to order some monitors for some of our departments. I'm sorry, but I need to change the order a little. Administration and reception will keep their orders as they are, ②but the cafeteria staff have informed me that they would prefer a 19-inch model because they don't have much space. And finally, nursing wants 24-inch screens. Our maintenance staff will deliver the monitors to each department, so please mark them clearly. ③Can you give me a call back to let me know you've heard this? Thanks, bye.

問題25-27は次の電話メッセージとラベルに関するものです。
女性：もしもし、Hadfield Hospital の Gina Prinz です。先ほど、当院の複数の部門用にモニターを注文するお電話をした者です。申し訳ありませんが、注文を少し変更しなくてはなりません。事務局と受付の注文はそのままですが、食堂の職員から、スペースがあまりないので、19インチ型の方が良いとの連絡がありました。そして最後になりますが、看護部門は24インチ画面を希望しています。当院の保守担当者がモニターを各部門に届けることになるので、分かりやすく表示してください。これをお聞きになったらお電話でお知らせいただけますか？ お願いします、それでは。

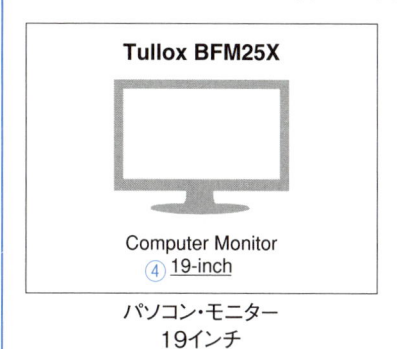

```
           Tullox BFM25X
         ┌─────────────────┐
         │                 │
         │                 │
         │                 │
         └─────────────────┘
            Computer Monitor
              ④ 19-inch
```
パソコン・モニター
19インチ

☐**administration**：管理、運営　　☐**nursing**：看護

25.
What is the purpose of the message?（このメッセージの目的は何ですか？）
(A) To update an order（注文を更新すること）
(B) To reply to a request（依頼に回答すること）
(C) To explain a procedure（手順を説明すること）
(D) To offer a suggestion（提案をすること）
☐**procedure**：手順、手続き

正解：(A)　メッセージの目的を問う問題。話し手は冒頭①で「先ほど、モニターの注文をしたが、注文を少し変更しないといけない」という内容を述べている。その後、具体的な変更内容を説明していることからも、このメッセージの目的は (A)「注文を更新すること」である。

26. NEW
Look at the graphic. To which department will the device be delivered?（図を見てください。この機器はどこの部門へ届けられますか？）
(A) Administration（事務局）
(B) Reception（受付）
(C) Cafeteria（食堂）
(D) Nursing（看護部）
☐**device**：機器、装置

正解：(C)　選択肢とグラフィックに共通する情報がないので、それぞれの内容が直接トークの中で言及されると考えられる。話し手は②で「食堂のスタッフから19インチ型が欲しいと連絡があった」と述べている。ラベル④に「19インチ」とあるので、この機器は「食堂」に届けられることが分かる。よって、(C) が正解。(D)「看護部」に関して話し手は、「24インチ画面を希望している」と言っているので、不適切。

27.
What is the listener asked to do?（聞き手は何をするよう依頼されていますか？）
(A) Install a device（機器を設置する）
(B) Return a call（折り返し電話をする）
(C) Send a catalog（カタログを送る）
(D) Carry out repairs（修理をする）
☐**install**：～を設置する、～を取り付ける　☐**carry out**：～を実行する

正解：(B)　聞き手が依頼されている内容が問われている。依頼内容を問う問題が出たら、依頼表現に注意して聞こう。③に Can you ～?（～してくれませんか）で始まる依頼表現があり、その後、give me a call back（私に電話をかけ直す）と続いている。よって、聞き手が依頼されているのは、(B)「折り返し電話をする」ことである。

40　Woman　CA

Questions 28 through 30 refer to the following announcement and schedule.

W: Good morning shoppers, and welcome to ①Max's Appliance Warehouse. We have a wide range of products at heavily discounted prices. ②Washing machines, dryers, dishwashers, computers, audio equipment — we've got it all, including games, software, and all the latest gadgets. We offer major brands at lower than half-price. ③There's even free gift-wrapping at the service counter. ④Remember, though, the winter sale is today and tomorrow only, so take advantage before it's too late. Today doors close at 9 P.M.
⑤Tomorrow we'll be closing at 4 P.M. to start preparations for our spring fair. Then we'll be back to our regular closing time of 5 P.M.

問題28-30は次のお知らせと予定表に関するものです。
女性： お買い物中の 皆さま、おはようございます、Max's Appliance Warehouseへようこそ。当店ではさまざまな商品を、大幅値引き価格で取りそろえています。洗濯機、乾燥機、食器洗い機、コンピューター、音響機器――ゲーム、ソフトウエアなどの最新機器も全てございます。大手メーカーの商品も半額を下回る価格で提供しています。サービスカウンターでは、無料のギフトラッピングも承っています。ただし、冬のセールは今日と明日限りですので、お早めにご利用ください。本日は午後9時に閉店します。明日は春フェアの準備に取り掛かるため、午後4時に閉店します。それ以降は通常の閉店時間の午後5時に戻ります。

Schedule	
⑥Friday	Winter Sale Day 1
⑦Saturday	Winter Sale Day 2
Sunday	Restocking
Monday	Spring Fair

スケジュール	
金曜日	冬セール1日目
土曜日	冬セール2日目
日曜日	在庫補充
月曜日	春フェア

☐**appliance**：電化製品　☐**washing machine**：洗濯機　☐**dryer**：乾燥機　☐**dishwasher**：食器洗い機　☐**gift-wrapping**：ギフト用の包装
【図表】☐**restocking**：在庫補充

28.
What kind of items does the store sell?（この店はどんな商品を販売していますか？）
(A) Food（食品）
(B) Cookware（調理器具）
(C) Electronics（電化製品）
(D) Clothing（衣料品）

正解：(C)　話し手は、まず①で「Max's Appliance Warehouseへようこそ」と述べているので、applianceが「電化製品」という意味だと知っていれば、(C)「電化製品」を即選ぶことができる。その後も②で、「洗濯機」や「コンピューター」などのさまざまな電化製品の名前が出てくるので、判断は容易なはずだ。warehouseには「倉庫」という意味もあるが、ここでは「大規模な店舗」という意味で使われている。

29.
What is available free of charge?（無料で利用できるのは何ですか？）
(A) Home delivery（宅配）
(B) Gift-wrapping（ギフト包装）
(C) Professional installation（プロによる設置）
(D) International shipping（海外配送）

正解：(B)　③で「無料のギフトラッピングも承っている」とあるので、正解は (B)「ギフト包装」である。その他の選択肢に関する内容は述べられていないので、それぞれ不適切。

30. NEW
Look at the graphic. What time will the store close on Saturday?（図を見てください。この店は土曜日には何時に閉店しますか？）
(A) At 4:00 P.M.（午後4時）
(B) At 5:00 P.M.（午後5時）
(C) At 6:00 P.M.（午後6時）
(D) At 9:00 P.M.（午後9時）

正解：(A)　選択肢とグラフィックに共通する情報がないため、両方に注意を払いながら、しっかりトークを聞くことに集中しよう。④で「冬のセールは今日と明日限り」と述べているので、表の⑥⑦から今日が金曜日だと分かる。その後、⑤で「明日は4時に閉まる」と言っているので、正解は(A)「午後4時」である。

Part 4

ひたすら意図問題！
3文トレーニング [Part 4編]

各セット内の下線部①②について最も適切なものを (A) 〜 (C) から選ぼう。
音声を聞く場合はダウンロード・コンテンツの該当するファイル番号を再生してください。

▶▶▶ **SET 1** 🔊 13

トーク1

Woman: We're in a difficult situation today. We've announced to all the participants that the meeting will be on September 9 from 4 P.M., but that might be difficult. ①The conference room has already been booked.

トーク2

Woman: I'm about to send out the invitations for the meeting of committee members. ②The conference room has already been booked. Is there anything else I need to take care of before the invitation goes out?

What does the speaker mean when she says, "The conference room has already been booked"?
(A) A new facility is proving popular.
(B) A preparation has been made.
(C) A venue is not available.

①_____ ②_____

▶▶▶ **SET 2** 🔊 14

トーク1

Man: I received an e-mail from a client who wanted to know about the details of our warranty. I work in sales and marketing so ... ①I'm not the one to ask. If I forward the e-mail to you, would you mind replying to her?

トーク2

Man: I understand that you want to schedule the campaign launch for Sunday next week, but ... ②I'm not the one to ask. Jake Takeda is in charge of planning. So, I'm not authorized to make a decision of that kind.

What does the speaker mean when he says, "I'm not the one to ask"?
(A) He cannot provide permission for something.
(B) He is not familiar with a topic.
(C) He is not able to access his computer.

①_____ ②_____

▶▶▶ **SET 3** 🔊 15

トーク1

Woman: I know you want to include an ice-breaking session on the first evening of the retreat, but there is already a lot on the agenda. ①Ten o'clock is very late. Is there something we can put off until the following day?

トーク2

Woman: I realize that it was impossible to predict the high demand we're experiencing this month. But I'm finding it hard to get people to work the extra hours to meet the revised target. ②Ten o'clock is very late.

Why does the speaker say, "Ten o'clock is very late"?
(A) To explain a staffing difficulty
(B) To suggest a schedule change
(C) To draw attention to an amendment

①_____ ②_____

※解答・解説は P. 96 〜 99 にあります

▶▶ SET 4 🔊 16

トーク1

Man: Regarding the scheduling of the year-end party, ①I'll leave that with you. Please just keep in mind that many people will be on holidays after December 20. So, sometime before that would be best.

トーク2

Man: I won't be back from my trip to Asia for about four months. My office is going to be relocated while I'm away, so I need somewhere to keep my document cabinet. ②I'll leave that with you if you don't mind.

What does the speaker mean when he says, "I'll leave that with you"?
(A) He would like the listener to store something.
(B) He wants a coworker to pay a bill.
(C) He will let the listener make a decision.

①_____ ②_____

▶▶ SET 5 🔊 17

トーク1

Woman: I know a lot of you are wondering why the company chose to hold the party on June 19 rather than June 25. ①Here's the deal. Some important guests won't be available on the twenty-fifth, so we had to change it.

トーク2

Woman: We're still interested in purchasing the property at 24 Borden Street, but there are a lot of costs involved so we'd like to agree to a price below the amount you're asking. ②Here's the deal. I hope you will consider it seriously.

Why does the speaker say, "Here's the deal"?
(A) To explain a reason
(B) To request assistance
(C) To present an offer

①_____ ②_____

▶▶ SET 6 🔊 18

トーク1

Man: We should definitely take a map when we visit the Bradfield office. I've been there before, but ... ①it's been a while. We'll probably get lost.

トーク2

Man: Ms. Little seems to be very reliable and knows her way around the office. I suppose it is only natural. ②It's been a while ... since she came to us.

What does the speaker imply when he says, "it's been a while"?
(A) He has forgotten how to get to a branch office.
(B) A colleague is accustomed to her new position.
(C) He has been waiting for a long time.

①_____ ②_____

▶▶▶ **SET 7** 🔊 19

トーク1

Woman: Steve, I'm calling about the Houston trip. I know we'd planned to go separately, but my car has broken down, and I need a ride. ①Let me know when you're leaving.

トーク2

Woman: It's Rebecca Smalls from Springfield Mechanics calling. I'll be bringing your car back in time for you to use for your trip to New York. ②Let me know when you're leaving.

What does the woman imply when she says, "Let me know when you're leaving"?
(A) She has to plan a farewell party.
(B) She needs a deadline for returning a vehicle.
(C) She would like to accompany the man.

①_____ ②_____

▶▶▶ **SET 8** 🔊 20

トーク1

Man: My name is Troy Barnes and I'll be leading the orientation workshop. If you have any questions, don't hesitate to ask. ①I've been here for more than 15 years, so I should be able to answer.

トーク2

Man: At my performance review, I'm going to ask for a promotion. ②I've been here more than 15 years. At the moment, I feel as though my career is not developing at all.

What does the speaker mean when he says, "I've been here for more than 15 years"?
(A) He is familiar with the company.
(B) He would like to work in a new location.
(C) He needs more responsibility.

①_____ ②_____

▶▶▶ **SET 9** 🔊 21

トーク1

Woman: Even though the furniture is a little old and much of it was used as a display in the store, they're only offering us 10 percent off. ①This isn't the kind of discount I was hoping for. I suggest we look at some other furniture stores first.

トーク2

Woman: The manager at the furniture store has offered us 75 percent off the total. ②This isn't the kind of discount I was hoping for. I thought the best we could hope for would be a voucher for a future purchase or something.

What does the speaker mean when she says, "This isn't the kind of discount I was hoping for"?
(A) She is surprised at the length of negotiations.
(B) She expected the price to be much higher.
(C) She thought the store would provide a bigger reduction.

①_____ ②_____

▶▶ **SET 10** 🔊 22

トーク1

Woman: I'm still at the airport and Mr. Hammond hasn't appeared. ①It's been an hour now. I'm going to come in to the office because I don't think he's coming.

トーク2

Woman: When I called earlier, I was asked to wait a few minutes for a maintenance worker to come and check the plumbing. ②It's been an hour now, and no one has spoken to me about it. Can you call me back with an update?

What does the speaker imply when she says, "It's been an hour now"?
(A) Service is taking too long.
(B) A visitor is unlikely to show up.
(C) A plan should be avoided.

① _____ ② _____

▶▶ **SET 11** 🔊 23

トーク1

Man: I understand Mr. Singh is running a little late. As soon as he arrives, please lead him upstairs to start the workshop. ①Everyone's gathered in the meeting room.

トーク2

Man: ②Everyone's gathered in the meeting room whenever the CEO pays us a visit. He always addresses all of the staff about his goals for the next few months. Then, he takes a tour of the offices with the local manager.

Why does the speaker say, "Everyone's gathered in the meeting room"?
(A) He is explaining a company policy.
(B) Employees are ready for a visitor.
(C) An announcement will be made.

① _____ ② _____

▶▶ **SET 12** 🔊 24

トーク1

Woman: I know how busy you are and I really understand that this is not the best time of year to ask you to make a trip. ①Who else could we ask? You're the only person in the company with experience in bridge engineering.

トーク2

Woman: I've looked over the people you've suggested to take over when Mr. Simpson leaves, but I really don't think any of them are qualified. ②Who else could we ask? You can look outside the company if you need to.

What does the speaker imply when she says, "Who else could we ask"?
(A) She would like to advertise more.
(B) There is only one qualified person.
(C) She is unhappy with some candidates.

① _____ ② _____

3文トレーニングの解答・解説

▶▶▶ SET 1

トーク1
女性：今日われわれは厄介な状況にあります。会議は9月9日の午後4時からだと出席者全員に知らせてありますが、それは難しいかもしれません。①会議室はすでに予約が入っているんです。

トーク2
女性：そろそろ委員会メンバーの会合の招待状を送ろうと思います。②会議室はもう予約してあります。招待状を発送する前に、すべきことは他にありますか？

話し手は "The conference room has already been booked" と言う際、何を意図していますか？
(A) 新しい施設が人気を博している。
(B) 用意はできている。
(C) 会場が使えない。

【解説】トーク1で話し手は、会議を予定通りの日時に開くことが難しいと述べている。ターゲット文は、その理由だ。つまり、他の人が会議室を予約したので自分たちは使えないということ。よって、(C) が正解。トーク2では、自分たちが使う会議室を確保したことを伝えているので、(B) が正解。(A) は、会議室を貸し出す商売を営む人の発言としてなど、文脈次第では正解となる。
正解：①(C)　②(B)

▶▶▶ SET 2

トーク1
男性：わが社の保証の詳細について知りたいというクライアントからのEメールを受信しました。私は販売宣伝部で働いているので…①質問を受ける立場にありません。メールを転送したら、回答していただけますか？

トーク2
男性：あなたがキャンペーンの開始を来週の日曜にしたがっているのは分かりますが…②私は頼まれる立場にありません。Jake Takeda が企画の責任者です。ですから、私にはそのような決断を下す権限がないんです。

話し手は "I'm not the one to ask" と言う際、何を意図していますか？
(A) 彼は何かのための許可を与えることができない。
(B) 彼は話題になじみがない。
(C) 彼は自分のパソコンにアクセスすることができない。

【解説】トーク1では、warranty（保証）に関する問い合わせを受けた話し手が、販売宣伝部に所属していると述べている。つまり、「保証について自分は詳しくない」と言いたいと判断できる。よって、(B) が正解。トーク2の話し手は、ある案に対する承認を求められていることが分かる。それに対し、「そのような決断を下す権限がない」と言っているので、正解は (A) だ。
正解：①(B)　②(A)

▶▶▶ SET 3

トーク1
女性：あなたが社員旅行の最初の夜に懇親会を盛り込みたがっているのは知っているけど、予定にはすでにいろいろあります。①10時というのは相当遅いわ。何か翌日にずらせるものはある？

トーク2
女性：われわれが今月経験している高い需要を予測することが不可能だったというのは理解しています。でも修正された目標を達成するため、皆に残業してもらうのは大変だと思います。②10時というのはかなり遅いですよ。

話し手はなぜ "Ten o'clock is very late" と言っていますか？
(A) 職員配置の難しさを説明するため
(B) スケジュールの変更を提案するため
(C) 修正に関心を集めるため

【解説】トーク1で話し手は、懇親会を初日に開くことに難色を示しているが、後で、翌日にずらせる案件がないか尋ねている。つまり、予定の一部を変更して懇親会の時間をつくろうとしているので、(B) が正解。トーク2では、従業員に残業させることに否定的な発言をしてからターゲット文を述べている。残業を強要できない理由として「10時は遅い」と述べているため、(A) が正解。
正解：①(B)　②(A)

▶▶▶ SET 4

トーク1

男性：年末パーティーのスケジュールの件ですが、①あなたに任せます。12月20日以降は休暇を取る人が多いということだけ忘れないでください。だから、その前がいいでしょうね。

トーク2

男性：アジアへの出張 からは4カ月ほど戻りません。私のオフィスは留守中に移転するので、私の書類キャビネットをどこかに置いておく必要があります。もしよければ、②あなたのところに置いていきます。

話し手は "I'll leave that with you" と言う際、何を意図していますか？
(A) 聞き手に何かを保管してほしい。
(B) 同僚に勘定を支払ってほしい。
(C) 聞き手に決断をさせる。

【解説】動詞 leave の異なる意味が問われている。目的語の that が何を指すかが解答のポイント。トーク1では、that はターゲット文の前にある schedule を指す。「スケジュールをあなたに任せる」という意味で leave が使われているので、(C) が正解。トーク2では、that は書類キャビネットを指している。聞き手にそれを預けるという意味なので、(A) が正解。that が請求書を指す場合なら、(B) は正解になり得る。
正解：①(C)　②(A)

▶▶▶ SET 5

トーク1

女性：皆さんの多くが、社はなぜ6月25日ではなく6月19日にパーティーを開くことを選んだのだろうかと思っているのは分かっています。①こういうことなんです。重要な来賓が25日は出席できないので、変更しなくてはなりませんでした。

トーク2

女性：われわれは今も 24 Borden Street の不動産の購入に関心があるのですが、多くの費用が掛かるので、そちらが提示している金額よりも安い価格で同意したいと思います。②こちらが条件です。本気で検討していただけることを願っています。

話し手はなぜ "Here's the deal" と言っていますか？
(A) 理由を説明するため
(B) 助けを依頼するため
(C) 値段を示す

【解説】トーク1では、ターゲット文の前後にあるのは「結論」と「理由」なので、(A) が正解。この Here's the deal. は「実はですね」や「こういうことです」のような前置きとして使われる表現だ。トーク2は、話し手が最後に I hope you will consider it seriously. と言っているので、it が指す何かを聞き手に見せている。ここでは文脈から、希望価格を提示していると考えられるため、(C) が正解。
正解：①(A)　②(C)

▶▶▶ SET 6

トーク1

男性：Bradfield 支店を訪問するときには絶対に地図を持っていくべきだ。前に行ったことがあるけど…①ずいぶんたっているからな。おそらく道に迷うだろう。

トーク2

男性：Little さんはとても頼りになるし、オフィスのことをよく分かっている。当然なんだろうな。②だいぶたつからね… 彼女がうちに来てから。

話し手は "it's been a while" と言う際、何を示唆していますか？
(A) 彼は支店への行き方を忘れてしまった。
(B) 同僚は新しい仕事に慣れている。
(C) 彼は長い間待っている。

【解説】トーク1のターゲット文の前後で、話し手は「Bradfield 支店に行ったことがある」と言いつつ、「おそらく道に迷う」とも言っている。よって、「ずいぶんたっている」は「(久しぶりの訪問だから) 道を忘れた」ことをほのめかしており、(A) が正解だ。トーク2での「だいぶたった」は、Littleさんが頼りになるのは当然であるという前半の発言に理由を添える役割を果たしている。よって、(B) が正解。
正解：①(A)　②(B)

▶▶▶ SET 7

トーク1

女性：Steve、Houston の出張のことで電話しています。私たち別々に行くことになっていたけど、私の車が故障してしまって、乗せてもらわなくてはなりません。①いつ出発するのか教えてください。

トーク2

女性：こちらは Springfield Mechanics の Rebecca Smalls です。お客さまの New York 出張に使うのに間に合うよう車をお戻しする予定です。②いつ出発するのか教えてください。

女性は"Let me know when you're leaving"と言う際、何を示唆していますか？
(A) 送別会を計画しなくてはならない。
(B) 車を返す期限が知りたい。
(C) 男性に同伴したいと思っている。

【解説】トーク1では、話し手は自分の車が壊れたことと、乗せてもらいたいことを伝えている。その直後に、いつ出発するのか教えてほしいと発言しているので、ターゲット文は「同行したい気持ち」を示している。よって、(C) が正解。トーク2では、聞き手が使う車を出張に間に合うよう返却すると述べている。聞き手の出発時期を尋ねているのは、車の納車期限を確認するためなので、(B) が正解。
正解：①(C) ②(B)

▶▶▶ SET 8

トーク1

男性：私は Troy Barnes と言いまして、オリエンテーション研修を指導します。質問があれば、遠慮せずに聞いてください。①私はここに15年以上いるので、お答えできるでしょう。

トーク2

男性：人事考課では、昇進を要求するつもりです。②ここに15年以上いますから。現在のところ、私のキャリアは少しも進展していないように感じます。

聞き手は"I've been here for more than 15 years"と言う際、何を意図していますか？
(A) 会社のことをよく知っている。
(B) 新しい場所で働きたいと思っている。
(C) もっと職責を負いたい。

【解説】トーク1のターゲット文の前後から、話し手はどんな質問にも答える自信があることが分かる。これは新人研修での発言なので、「会社に詳しい」ことを意味している。(A) が正解。トーク2では、ターゲット文の直前で話し手は「昇進を要求する」と言っている。「長い間働いてきたから責任ある職に就きたい」という意図なので、正解は (C) だ。(B) も文脈次第では正解となる。
正解：①(A) ②(C)

▶▶▶ SET 9

トーク1

女性：家具は少し古いし、その多くが店で展示品として使われていたものなのに、10パーセントしか割引してくれないのよ。①これは私が期待していた割引じゃないわ。先に他の家具店を見ましょう。

トーク2

女性：家具店の店長が合計75パーセントの割引をしてくれたの。②これは私が期待していたような割引じゃないわ。せいぜい次回家具購入時の割引券か何かくらいだと思っていたの。

話し手は"This isn't the kind of discount I was hoping for"と言う際、何を意図していますか？
(A) 交渉の長さに驚いている。
(B) 値段はもっと高いと予想していた。
(C) 店がもっと大きな割引を提供してくれるだろうと思った。

【解説】トーク1の前半から、話し手は10パーセントという割引率に不満であることが分かる。後半で、他の家具店を見ることを提案しているのは、より安い店を探すためだ。よって、ターゲット文は、話し手がもっと大きな割引を期待していたことを示している。(C) がこれに合致する。トーク2は逆パターン。話し手は、今回の購入に対する割引があるとは思っていなかったので、(B) が正解だ。
正解：①(C) ②(B)

▶▶▶ SET 10

トーク1

女性：まだ空港にいますが、Hammondさんが現れません。①もう1時間たちました。彼が来るとは思えないので、オフィスに向かいます。

トーク2

女性：先ほど電話したとき、保守管理係が配管を確認しにくるのを少し待つように言われました。②もう1時間たちましたが、誰もそれについて話をしてくれていません。最新の情報をお聞かせください。

話し手は "It's been an hour now" と言う際、何を示唆していますか？
(A) サービスに時間がかかり過ぎる。
(B) 来訪者は現れそうにない。
(C) 計画は回避すべきである。

【解説】トーク1では、ターゲット文の前にある発言から、話し手は1時間もHammond氏を待っていることが分かる。さらに、「彼が来るとは思えない」と述べていることから、(B) が正解。トーク2では、ターゲット文の an hour が直前の a few minutes と対比されている。数分で保守管理係が来るはずだったのに、1時間も待たされているということだ。よって、(A) が正解だ。
正解：① (B)　② (A)

▶▶▶ SET 11

トーク1

男性：Singh さんは少し遅れます。彼が到着したらすぐ、上の階へ案内して研修を始めてもらってください。①皆さんは会議室に集まっているので。

トーク2

男性：CEO が訪れるときはいつも、②全員会議室に集まります。彼はいつも、今後数カ月の彼の目標について全社員に話をします。そして、そこの責任者と共にオフィス内を見学するのです。

話し手はなぜ "Everyone's gathered in the meeting room" と言っていますか？
(A) 会社のポリシーを説明しているから。
(B) 従業員は来訪者を迎える準備ができている。
(C) お知らせが発表される。

【解説】トーク1では、遅れている研修講師が到着したら部屋に案内するよう話し手は聞き手に依頼している。ターゲット文の主語 Everyone は研修の参加者だ。参加者が会議室に集まっているということは、準備ができているということなので、(B) が正解。トーク2では、最初から最後まで CEO がどのように行動するかについて述べているので、(A) が正解。(C) は文脈次第では正解となる。
正解：① (B)　② (A)

▶▶▶ SET 12

トーク1

女性：あなたがどれだけ忙しいのかは分かっているし、1年の中でもあなたに出張へ行くお願いをするのに今が最適な時期でないことも理解しています。①他の誰にお願いできるでしょうか？ あなたは橋梁工学の経験を持つ社内で唯一の人物なのですから。

トーク2

女性：あなたが Simpson さんの退社時に引き継ぎをすべきだと挙げてくれた人たちにざっと目を通しましたが、誰も適任に思えません。②他に頼めそうな人はいますか？ 必要があれば、社外で探してもいいですよ。

話し手は "Who else could we ask" と言う際、何を示唆していますか？
(A) もっと宣伝をしたい。
(B) 適任者は一人しかいない。
(C) 候補者に不満がある。

【解説】トーク1では、ターゲット文の直後で、話し手は聞き手が「橋梁工学の経験を持つ社内で唯一の人」だと述べている。つまり、話し手は「依頼できる人はあなたをおいて他にいない」と暗に伝えているため、(B) が正解。トーク2では、文字通り「他に頼めそうな人はいますか」と質問をしている。その前では、引き継ぎ候補として挙げられた人々が適任ではないと述べているので、(C) が正解。
正解：① (B)　② (C)

Part 6のまとめ
ヒロ前田

Part 6はココが変わった!

問題数が増えた!
- 12問（3問×4セット）から16問（4問×4セット）になった
- 1セット当たりの設問数が3問から4問に増えた

レイアウトが変わった!
- これまで空所の真下に印刷されていた選択肢が、全て文書の外に移動した。問題を解く上でそれほど大きな影響はないと思われる

新しい問題形式が登場!
- 空所に「文」を入れる「文選択問題」が登場。1セットに1問出題される
- 文選択問題はストーリーを理解する力が問われる
- 1セット中残りの3問については、従来の問題が引き続き出題される

解説　問題数増で時間管理もアップデート

　問題数が増えたことで、パートとして要する時間が増えます。これまで「Part 6は○分で解く!」と時間管理の方針をきちんと立てていた人は、それを更新する必要があります。
　「1セット当たり2分、計8分」というのがボクの推奨するペースです。セットによっては他より時間がかかるものもあります。その場合、2分30秒ぐらいまではかけてもいいでしょう。ただし、全セットに2分半ずつはかけ過ぎです。Part 5、7とのバランスを考えると、Part 6は確実に10分以内で解くよう時間管理を徹底させましょう。

Part 6 攻略の基本

ここではPart 6の新形式、「文選択問題」の取り組み方についてお話しします。

● 文選択問題は最後に解く

文選択問題は4問中何問目に出題されるか分かりませんが、何問目にあっても最後に解くことを強くお勧めします。文選択問題は空所の近くを見るだけで解ける問題ではなく、全体のストーリーを見てから取り組んだ方が解きやすいからです。

文選択問題が途中にあったら解かずに通過しましょう。途中で解こうとすると、多くの場合、空所の前後で情報収集をしたり、選んだ選択肢について検証したりと「余計な読み」が発生します。そうなっては時間のロスも大きく、非効率的です。

● 目の付け所

文選択問題を解く際に、正解・不正解を判断する根拠として、目を付けるべき情報が存在します。その代表的なものが次の3つです。

①代名詞

例えば、あなたが正解ではないかと思っている選択肢が、

Those regulations will not apply to ...（それらの規則は…には適用されない）

という文だったとします。もしこの文が正解なら、空所の前にはThoseが指す何らかの規則が複数書かれているはずです。もしThoseの指すものが見当たらなければ、その選択肢を入れても話が通りません。

ターゲットの選択肢に these、those、that、we、he、she といった代名詞があれば、このような照合をする必要があります。

②副詞

「例えば」「しかし」「〜にも関わらず」「同様に」…といった言葉がターゲットの選択肢の中にあったら、空所の前にある情報の流れを確認します。空所にその選択肢を入れた後も、前後の流れが論理的に成立する必要があります。「例えば…」という表現を含む選択肢なら、空所の前が、例を挙げて説明する必要があるストーリーになっていなければ正解にはなり得ません。likewise、too、as well、also、unlike、for example、to the contrary ... といった表現に敏感になりましょう。

③助動詞

should、must のような助動詞も重要です。例えば、

Employees must submit the expense report by the end of the month.（従業員は月末までに経費明細を提出しなくてはならない）

という文がターゲットだとします。must には「〜しなくてはいけない」という義務の意味が込められていますが、それが正解であるならば、空所は従業員の義務が述べられるのにふさわしい場所になくてはなりません。空所の前後の情報でそのことを確認しましょう。

代名詞、副詞、助動詞は小さな情報ですが、文選択問題はこういった細部にこそ正誤の根拠があります。ですから、速読より精読の練習の方が効果的です。

Part 6 ドリル

1セット 2分
トータル 20分

空所に入れるのに最も適切な語句・文を選ぼう。

Questions 1-4 refer to the following letter.

Peabody's Surf & Ski
Shop 16 — Greendale Mall — East Greendale

May 16

Dear Mr. Lane Myer,

This letter is just a ------- that the skis you brought to us last month are ready for you to come and pick up. The boot binding was ------- repair and we had to have a new one sent from the manufacturer. The total for parts and labor came to $135. You get 10 percent discount as a special member, so please find the attached invoice for $121.50. -------. Although Peabody's does not have a late payment penalty, there is a storage fee for items held over a month. I encourage you to ------- the skis as soon as possible.
    1.   2.
                                                3.
        4.

Sincerely.

Rick Smitty

---

1. (A) reminder
   (B) reminding
   (C) remind
   (D) reminded

2. (A) worth
   (B) against
   (C) despite
   (D) beyond

3. (A) If you do not pay immediately, a late fee will be applied.
   (B) We will provide you with a competitive quote for repairs.
   (C) Please note, this is the second invoice you have received for this work.
   (D) We cannot begin the repairs without receiving payment in advance.

4. (A) deliver
   (B) retrieve
   (C) purchase
   (D) restore

Questions 5-8 refer to the following article.

Sales Down, Profits Up at Redding Corporation

The yearly financial report from Redding Corporation has shown that profits are ------- growing steadily. Interestingly, this has occurred at a time when sales figures are falling. This surprising ------- is a result of the new president's strong focus on increasing efficiency and cutting costs. An interesting side effect of the purely financial motivations is the improved environmental impact rating the company has received. The reduced waste and energy expenditure at the plants were highly praised by the minister for the environment, Daniel Clem. -------. A spokesperson for Redding Corporation stated that ------- they were happy with the result, the company would now be focusing on improving sales.

---

5. (A) very
   (B) still
   (C) once
   (D) seldom

6. (A) pleasure
   (B) addition
   (C) outcome
   (D) formation

7. (A) In a recent speech, he urged other companies to follow suit.
   (B) Time will tell whether or not his advice leads to a positive outcome.
   (C) He was critical of the company's effort to meet state standards.
   (D) He said that the boost to sales was quite unexpected.

8. (A) if
   (B) when
   (C) after
   (D) while

GO ON TO THE NEXT PAGE

Questions 9-12 refer to the following e-mail.

To: Maggie O'Reily <moreily@grandoaksresort.com>
From: Danny Kemp <dkemp@grandoaksresort.com>
Date: December 11
Subject: Staffing

Dear Ms. O'Reily,

It has been 18 months since we opened the Grand Oaks Resort in Bushwood. Visitor numbers are in line with ------- was predicted and we are experiencing adequate sales in all of our stores and restaurants. -------, I have one issue to which I would like to draw your attention.

-------. This is making it difficult to hire enough staff who can properly serve customers and it is affecting the resort's -------. I would like to suggest that we either start a comprehensive in-house training program or provide incentives for people to move here from the urban areas.

I look forward to hearing your thoughts on the issue.

Sincerely,

Danny Kemp
Manager — Grand Oaks Resort (Bushwood)

9. (A) what
   (B) whom
   (C) that
   (D) everyone

10. (A) As a result
    (B) Accordingly
    (C) On behalf of
    (D) Nevertheless

11. (A) We are about to start our winter campaign.
    (B) There is a shortage of qualified people in the area.
    (C) The resort will be welcoming a group of visiting politicians.
    (D) Some of the facilities are in urgent need of repairs.

12. (A) reputable
    (B) reputed
    (C) reputation
    (D) reputably

Questions 13-16 refer to the following advertisement.

Winter Employment Opportunity

------- . Why not head south? There are farms in California and New Mexico which desperately
  13.

need people to help pick fruit and vegetables in these winter months. Food and accommodation

------- in addition to financial incentives. Work five days a week and take the other two days to see
  14.

the sights and travel around the state.

Contracts are available for terms as short as one week and as long as six months. For further

details, check us out on the Web at www.caligrowers.com. ------- can learn more about our farms,
                                                                            15.

living conditions and even read testimonials from previous employees.

Don't miss this opportunity to build lasting memories and valuable friendships, while ------- a
                                                                                                                             16.

generous hourly wage.

---

13. (A) There are abundant job opportunities in the northern states.
    (B) If you are looking for people to work on your farm, we can help.
    (C) During Washington's long cold winter, there are few jobs for young adults.
    (D) Californian real estate prices are rising beyond expectations.

14. (A) are providing
    (B) are provided
    (C) were provided
    (D) have been providing

15. (A) We
    (B) They
    (C) Whoever
    (D) You

16. (A) earning
    (B) reflecting
    (C) desiring
    (D) admitting

GO ON TO THE NEXT PAGE

Questions 17-20 refer to the following e-mail.

To: Jennifer Zemeckis<jzemeckis@yoshiokahotels.com>
From: Taiki Yoshioka <tyoshioka@yoshiokahotels.com>
Date: June 6
Re: Language requirements

In recent years, we have been receiving larger and larger numbers of South American guests and it has come to the point where more than half of the island's visitors are Spanish speakers. In contrast, we ------- only two Spanish speakers at our most popular hotel. This is starting to
         17.
become an issue because guests are having difficulty ordering services and we are unable to provide ------- with their travel arrangements.
        18.

Alarmingly, our competitors are already putting great effort ------- improving the Spanish ability of
                                                              19.
their staff. ------- . To this end, I would like you to start teaching Spanish to our staff members for
             20.
one hour a day from July.

Best regards,

Taiki Yoshioka

---

17. (A) employ
    (B) are employed
    (C) have been employed
    (D) were employing

18. (A) assist
    (B) assisted
    (C) assistant
    (D) assistance

19. (A) over
    (B) through
    (C) into
    (D) without

20. (A) I doubt that this will provide them an advantage in the future.
    (B) We have to offer similar service to continue to enjoy our recent success.
    (C) You should carefully consider any positions they offer you.
    (D) We have been asked to help support them in this effort.

Questions 21-24 refer to the following memo.

TO: All employees
FROM: Sean Costello, Personnel Director
DATE: 16 August
SUBJECT: New graphic designer

I am happy to announce that we have hired a new graphic designer. On Monday, 14 August, Ms. Garfield ------- in her new position working with our documentary team. She has come to us from
    21.
JBL Productions in Canada, where she was a chief photographer for three years. I imagine that she will have a lot to learn here as her previous experience was ------- in advertising.
                                                  22.

To welcome her to the company, I have ------- a dinner party at Tiffany's Restaurant in the
                                             23.
Vandelay Hotel. It is this Friday from 7 P.M. ------- .
                                     24.

21. (A) started
    (B) is started
    (C) will start
    (D) had started

22. (A) yet
    (B) much less
    (C) nearly
    (D) mostly

23. (A) canceled
    (B) rejected
    (C) organized
    (D) attended

24. (A) Please suggest any topics which should be covered at the workshop.
    (B) If you will be unable to attend, please contact me as early as possible.
    (C) We should thank JBL Productions for their hospitality.
    (D) This project should be given particular attention.

GO ON TO THE NEXT PAGE

Questions 25-28 refer to the following information.

Job Title: Librarian

The purpose of this document is to summarize the responsibilities ------- with the position of
                                                                    25.
librarian at the Harper City Central Library. -------. Accordingly, you may be called upon to take on
                                               26.
tasks not specifically described in this document.

Generally speaking, librarians are expected to process books as they are loaned and returned. Books which have not been returned by the due date should be investigated. It may also be necessary to assist users with library facilities. -------, librarians are tasked with purchasing books
                                                                      27.
and preparing them for inclusion in the library catalog.

------- librarians are required to participate in one training course a year at a recognized institution.
28.
There are more conditions, which will be discussed at the interview.

25. (A) associated
    (B) association
    (C) associate
    (D) associating

26. (A) The position is not being advertised in newspapers or on the Internet.
    (B) Only the following tasks may be required of people employed as librarians.
    (C) Send applications to the chief librarian at chief@hcckibrary.com.
    (D) It should be noted that librarians are expected to be flexible in their role.

27. (A) Therefore
    (B) In contrast
    (C) Furthermore
    (D) On the contrary

28. (A) Both
    (B) All
    (C) Other
    (D) Several

Questions 29-32 refer to the following announcement.

The New South Wales Environmental Protection Council has an exciting announcement. World-renowned professor of marine biology, Dr. Steve Mitchel ------- as the keynote speaker at the World Environmental Conference in Sydney in May.
29.

In recent years, Dr. Mitchel has written a number of important articles on environmental protection, which have influenced governmental policy and public awareness. He ------- for his weekly radio show which has a following of over a million listeners.
30.

He will be speaking in depth about the ------- from his study into Australia's coastlines and his predictions for the next 50 years.
31.

-------. To register, contact the New South Wales Environmental Protection Council Planning Committee at 02-555-9898 or via e-mail at wecpc@nswepcouncil.com.
32.

29. (A) served
    (B) will serve
    (C) has served
    (D) serves

30. (A) knows
    (B) is knowing
    (C) is known
    (D) knew

31. (A) aims
    (B) grants
    (C) reductions
    (D) findings

32. (A) Tickets are expected to sell out very quickly.
    (B) Unfortunately, he has declined to attend.
    (C) Submit your research proposals to the professor directly.
    (D) If you would like to make a donation, please visit the Web site.

GO ON TO THE NEXT PAGE

Questions 33-36 refer to the following information.

------- . For years, we've been providing home delivery for customers whose private vehicles were
  33.
too small to carry home bulky items. It is a popular service and we have been able to offer it at
very little ------- cost. However, some customers have mentioned that it is not always -------.
           34.   35.
Unfortunately, some items can arrive very late in the day. This makes it hard for ------- to complete
                                                                                   36.
weekend home improvement projects.

From this month, Howard's Hardware is offering free use of its three delivery trucks to customers
to carry their goods home. Inquire at the service counter for details.

33. (A) After 50 years in business, Howard's Hardware is closing its doors.
    (B) Howard's Hardware is opening its first store in Gladstone.
    (C) For this month only, Howard's Hardware's home delivery service is free.
    (D) Howard's Hardware is offering a new service.

34. (A) additional
    (B) addition
    (C) additionally
    (D) add

35. (A) correct
    (B) fast
    (C) needed
    (D) provided

36. (A) me
    (B) him
    (C) them
    (D) us

Questions 37-40 refer to the following notice.

Waste Management

TelAmeri Corporation has conducted an internal review of its paper usage and found that all departments are creating excessive waste. ------- . We are not only spending too much on paper, but also on its disposal.
                                                                    37.

Please ------- more on multipage printing functions and use both sides of the page for large print
        38.
jobs. From today, each ------- will be issued a card to use when making copies so that we can
                         39.
keep track of individual usage. Finally, we have entered into an arrangement with a recycling company, which will pick up our paper waste twice a week. So, be sure to separate paper from other items when ------- things away.
                    40.

General Affairs Department

37. (A) This is bad for both the environment and the company's finances.
    (B) This is a wonderful achievement for a company of our size.
    (C) There does not appear to be any need to take action at this time.
    (D) Contact senior management if your budget will not cover the cost.

38. (A) reliability
    (B) reliably
    (C) reliable
    (D) rely

39. (A) client
    (B) student
    (C) employee
    (D) visitor

40. (A) storing
    (B) throwing
    (C) putting
    (D) keeping

Part 6 ドリルの解答・解説

問題文と訳

Questions 1-4 refer to the following letter.

Peabody's Surf & Ski
Shop 16 — Greendale Mall — East Greendale

May 16

Dear Mr. Lane Myer,

This letter is just a ___1.___ that ① the skis you brought to us last month are ready for you to come and pick up. The boot binding was ___2.___ repair and we had to have a new one sent from the manufacturer. The total for parts and labor came to $135. You get 10 percent discount as a special member, so please find the attached invoice for $121.50. ___3.___. ② Although Peabody's does not have a late payment penalty, there is a storage fee for items held over a month. I encourage you to ___4.___ the skis as soon as possible.

Sincerely.

Rick Smitty

問題 **1-4** は次の手紙に関するものです。

Peabody's Surf & Ski
店舗16—Greendale モール—East Greendale

5月16日

Lane Myer 様

この手紙は、先月当店に持ち込まれたスキー板を取りに来ていただく準備ができていることをお知らせするものです。ビンディングは修理がきかない状態だったので、新しいものを製造元から取り寄せなくてはなりませんでした。部品と工賃の合計額は135ドルです。お客さまには特別会員として10パーセントの割引があるので、添付されている121ドル50セントの請求明細をご確認ください。これは今回の作業に関してお客さまにお送りした2通目の請求明細である点にご留意ください。Peabody'sでは支払い遅延の罰金はございませんが、1カ月以上お預かりした品物には保管料をいただきます。できるだけ早くスキー板をお引き取りになることをお勧めします。

敬具

Rick Smitty

※訳中の青字部分は文選択問題の正解を表しています（以下、同）

□**boot binding**：ビンディング、バインディング　※スキー板にブーツを固定する器具　□**manufacturer**：製造元、メーカー　□**storage**：保管

112

選択肢と訳

1.
(A) reminder （名 お知らせ、思い出させるもの）
(B) reminding （他動 ～に思い出させる［現在分詞・動名詞］）
(C) remind （他動 ～に思い出させる）
(D) reminded （他動 ～に思い出させた［過去形・過去分詞］）

2.
(A) worth （形 ～の価値がある、名 価値）
(B) against （前 ～に反対して）
(C) despite （前 ～にもかかわらず）
(D) beyond （前 ～を超えて）

3. （NEW）
(A) If you do not pay immediately, a late fee will be applied. （すぐにお支払いいただかなければ、延滞料が適用されます）
(B) We will provide you with a competitive quote for repairs. （修理の相見積もりをお出しします）
(C) Please note, this is the second invoice you have received for this work. （これは今回の作業に関してお客さまにお送りした2通目の請求明細である点にご留意ください）
(D) We cannot begin the repairs without receiving payment in advance. （事前にお支払いをいただかないと修理を始めることができません）

□**late fee**：延滞料　□**be applied**：適用される
□**competitive quote**：相見積もり　□**invoice**：請求明細（書）、インボイス

4.
(A) deliver （他動 ～を届ける）
(B) retrieve （他動 ～を引き取る）
(C) purchase （他動 ～を購入する）
(D) restore （他動 ～を修復する）

解説

正解：(A)
文頭から空所までが主節で、空所の直後には接続詞thatが導く節が続いている。空所の直前には冠詞 a があるので、空所には名詞が入る。よって (A) が正解。a reminder that ~ は「~ということを思い出させるもの」という表現。「スキー板を取りに来ていただく準備ができているということを思い出させるもの」とは、つまり「スキー板を取りに来てほしいという催促」である。

正解：(D)
空所のある文の and 以降で、「新しいもの（＝ビンディング）を取り寄せなくてはならなかった」と述べている。文頭から空所直後の repair までが and 以降に矛盾なくつながるためには、「ビンディングは修理不可」であるべき。beyond repair は「修理を超えた状態」、すなわち「修理がきかない状態」なので、(D) が正解。「修理の価値がある」では and 以降と矛盾するので、(A) は不正解。

正解：(C)
①から、手紙の受取人はまだスキー板を取りに行っていないことが分かる。空所の直前の文は、請求明細を添付しているという内容で、空所の直後には「支払い遅延の罰金はないが、保管料をいただく」という文が続いている。よって、請求明細を送るのは2度目であることに注意を促す (C) が文脈に合う。遅延料は発生しないので (②)、(A) は不適切。すでに修理は完了しているので、(B) も (D) も不正解。

正解：(B)
文脈に合う意味の動詞を選ぶ語彙問題。修理済みのスキー板をまだ取りに来ていない手紙の受取人に対し、直前の②では「1カ月以上お預かりした品物には保管料をいただく」と述べている。(B) を空所に入れて「(従って) できるだけ早くスキー板を引き取ることを勧める」という文意にするのが適切。その他の選択肢を空所に入れても文脈に合った文にはならない。

【品詞記号の見方】
自動：自動詞　他動：他動詞　助：助動詞　形：形容詞　副：副詞　名：名詞　代：代名詞　接：接続詞

問題文と訳

Questions 5-8 refer to the following article.

Sales Down, Profits Up at Redding Corporation

①The yearly financial report from Redding Corporation has shown that profits are ---5.--- growing steadily. Interestingly, this has occurred at a time when sales figures are falling. This surprising ---6.--- is a ②result of the new president's strong focus on increasing efficiency and cutting costs. An interesting side effect of the purely financial motivations is the improved environmental impact rating the company has received. ③The reduced waste and energy expenditure at the plants were highly praised by the minister for the environment, Daniel Clem. ---7.---. A spokesperson for Redding Corporation stated that ---8.--- ④they were happy with the result, ⑤the company would now be focusing on improving sales.

問題 5-8 は次の記事に関するものです。

Redding Corporation、売り上げ落ちるも利益は増加

Redding Corporation の年次会計報告は、収益が引き続き順調に伸びていることを示している。興味深いことに、これは売り上げが減少している中でのことだ。この驚くべき成果は、新社長が効率アップとコスト削減を重視したことの結果である。その純粋に経済的な動機付けの興味深い影響の1つが、同社の環境影響評価が改善されたという点だ。工場での廃棄物とエネルギー消費量の削減は、環境大臣の Daniel Clem からも高く評価された。最近のスピーチの中で彼は、他の企業も見習うよう呼び掛けた。Redding Corporation の広報担当者は、結果に満足しているとはいえ、同社は今後、売り上げの改善に力を入れると述べた。

- □**steadily**：順調に　□**occur**：起こる、発生する　□**efficiency**：効率　□**side effect**：副作用、副次的な影響
- □**purely**：完全に、まったく　□**energy expenditure**：エネルギー消費（量）　□**spokesperson**：広報担当者

選択肢と訳

5.
(A) very （副非常に）
(B) still （副引き続き）
(C) once （副以前）
(D) seldom （副ほとんど〜ない）

6.
(A) pleasure （名喜び）
(B) addition （名追加）
(C) outcome （名成果）
(D) formation （名形成）

7. NEW
(A) In a recent speech, he urged other companies to follow suit.（最近のスピーチの中で彼は、他の企業も見習うよう呼び掛けた）
(B) Time will tell whether or not his advice leads to a positive outcome.（彼の助言が良い結果をもたらすかどうかは時がたてば分かる）
(C) He was critical of the company's effort to meet state standards.（彼は基準を満たそうという同社の取り組みに批判的だった）
(D) He said that the boost to sales was quite unexpected.（彼は売り上げ増加は実に意外だと述べた）

□**follow suit**：後に続く、見習う　□**time will tell 〜**：〜は時がたてば分かる　□**be critical of 〜**：〜に批判的である　□**boost**：増加、上昇

8.
(A) if （接もし）
(B) when （接〜するときに）
(C) after （接〜してから）
(D) while （接〜とはいえ）

解説

正解：(B)
be 動詞の are と現在分詞 growing の間に入り、growing を修飾する副詞を選ぶ語彙問題。「収益が引き続き伸びている」という意味になる (B) が正解。(A) very は steadily の直前に置いて「とても順調に収益が伸びている」とすることはできるが、growing を修飾することはできない。(C) や (D) を空所に入れても意味が通らないので不正解。

正解：(C)
This surprising に修飾され、文の主語になる名詞を選ぶ語彙問題。空所の前の①で、Redding Corporation は、売り上げが減少していても、収益が順調に伸びていることが述べられている。空所のある文が説明しているのは、収益の伸びという「この驚くべき成果」とするのが最も自然なので、正解は (C)。is の後ろの② result（結果）も答えを導くヒントになっている。

正解：(A)
空所の前の③では、Daniel Clem 環境大臣が、工場からの廃棄物とエネルギー消費量の削減を高く評価したことが述べられている。4つの選択肢の he あるいは his は Daniel Clem を指している。「Daniel Clem は、他の企業も見習うよう呼び掛けた」という文を空所に入れると文脈に合う。正解は (A)。助言や批判はしていないので、(B) と (C) は不適切。売り上げは減少しているので、(D) も不正解。

正解：(D)
that 以下に続く2つの節（④と⑤）をつなぐのに適切な接続詞を選ぶ問題。コンマの前にある④は「（売り上げが減少していても、会社の収益が伸びたという）結果に満足している」ことを意味している。コンマ以下の⑤は、「同社は今後、売り上げの改善に力を入れる」と述べられている。「結果に満足しているとはいえ」とすると、矛盾なくつながるので、正解は (D)。

問題文と訳

Questions 9-12 refer to the following e-mail.

To: Maggie O'Reily <moreily@grandoaksresort.com>
From: Danny Kemp <dkemp@grandoaksresort.com>
Date: December 11
Subject: Staffing

Dear Ms. O'Reily,

It has been 18 months since we opened the Grand Oaks Resort in Bushwood. Visitor numbers are in line with ___9.___ was predicted and ①we are experiencing adequate sales in all of our stores and restaurants. ___10.___, ②I have one issue to which I would like to draw your attention.

___11.___. ③This is making it difficult to hire enough staff who can properly serve customers and it is affecting the ④resort's ___12.___. I would like to suggest that we either start a comprehensive in-house training program or provide incentives for people to move here from the urban areas.

I look forward to hearing your thoughts on the issue.

Sincerely,

Danny Kemp
Manager — Grand Oaks Resort (Bushwood)

問題 9-12 は次のEメールに関するものです。

宛先：Maggie O'Reily <moreily@grandoaksresort.com>
送信者：Danny Kemp <dkemp@grandoaksresort.com>
日付：12月11日
件名：人員の配置

O'Reily 様

われわれが Bushwood に Grand Oaks Resortを開業してから18カ月たちます。来訪者数は予測通りですし、店舗やレストランは全て十分な売り上げを上げています。しかしながら、お考えいただきたい問題が1つあります。

この地域には適格な人材が不足しています。このことがお客さまにきちんと対応できるスタッフを十分に雇うことを困難にしており、当リゾートの評判にも影響しています。総合的な社内研修プログラムを始めるか、人々が都市部からこの地域に移住する気になるような動機を提供することを提案いたします。

この問題についてのお考えを聞かせていただければ幸いです。

敬具

Danny Kemp
支配人 — Grand Oaks Resort (Bushwood)

- **staffing**：人員（の配置）　　□**in line with ~**：～と合致して　　□**adequate**：十分な　　□**draw** *someone's* **attention**：～の注意を引く　　□**comprehensive**：総合的な　　□**in-house**：社内の　　□**incentive**：動機、奨励金

選択肢と訳

9. ※訳は省略
(A) what
(B) whom
(C) that
(D) everyone

解説

正解：(A)

前置詞 with の後ろには名詞に相当するものが置かれるので、空所から predicted までは名詞節でなければならない。関係代名詞の what は「~すること(もの)」という名詞節を導くことができる。what was predicted(予想されたこと)で文脈にも合うので正解は (A)。that も接続詞として名詞節を作ることはできるが、その場合 that 以下には主語と動詞のセットが必要。ここでは主語がないので (C) は不可。(B)、(D) は名詞節を導かないので不正解。

10.
(A) As a result（結果として）
(B) Accordingly（副 従って、その結果）
(C) On behalf of（~の代わりに、~を代表して）
(D) Nevertheless（副 しかしながら、それにもかかわらず）

正解：(D)

選択肢には、空所の前の文と空所以下の文を論理的に結ぶ副詞句 (A) と副詞の (B)、(D) がある。(C) は、後ろに名詞が必要な群前置詞。空所の直後はコンマで、名詞がないので (C) は不正解。空所の前が①「全ての店舗やレストランは、十分に売り上げを上げている」というポジティブな内容であるのに対し、空所の後には②「問題が1つある」というネガティブな内容が続く。①と②を矛盾なく結ぶ、逆接の副詞 (D) が正解。

---

11. NEW
(A) We are about to start our winter campaign.（われわれは冬季キャンペーンを開始しようとしているところです）
(B) There is a shortage of qualified people in the area.（この地域には適格な人材が不足しています）
(C) The resort will be welcoming a group of visiting politicians.（当リゾートは訪問中の政治家の一団をもてなす予定です）
(D) Some of the facilities are in urgent need of repairs.（一部の設備は緊急の修繕が必要です）

□**be about to ~**：まさに~しようとしている　□**qualified**：適任な、能力のある　□**visiting**：訪問中の、滞在中の

正解：(B)

空所の後ろで、③「このことが、お客さまにきちんと対応できる、十分な人数のスタッフを雇うことを困難にしている」と述べられている。文の主語 This (このこと) は、空所の内容を指している。This を、「この地域に適格な人材が不足していることが」と考えると意味が通るので、正解は (B)。

12.
(A) reputable（形 評判の良い）
(B) reputed（形 評判の良い、有名な）
(C) reputation（名 評判）
(D) reputably（副 評判良く）

正解：(C)

文法知識が試される品詞の問題。空所の直前には④ resort's がある。所有格の後ろには名詞が入るので、(C) 以外の選択肢は消去できる。このように、Part 6 には空所の近くにある情報から判断して短時間で解答できる品詞問題も出題される。短時間で解答できる問題は素早く解き、文脈を考えて解かなければならない問題に時間を多く使うことが重要。

問題文と訳

Questions 13-16 refer to the following advertisement.

Winter Employment Opportunity

___13.___ ①Why not head south? ②There are farms in California and New Mexico which desperately need people to help pick fruit and vegetables in these winter months. ③Food and accommodation ___14.___ in addition to financial incentives. ④Work five days a week and take the other two days to see the sights and travel around the state.

Contracts are available for terms as short as one week and as long as six months. ⑤For further details, check us out on the Web at www.caligrowers.com. ___15.___ ⑥can learn more about our farms, living conditions and even read testimonials from previous employees.

⑦Don't miss this opportunity to build lasting memories and valuable friendships, ⑧while ___16.___ a generous hourly wage.

問題 13-16 は次の広告に関するものです。

冬季の雇用機会

Washington の長くて寒い冬に、若者向けの仕事はほとんどありません。南を目指しませんか？ California や New Mexico には、こんな冬場にも果物や野菜の収穫を手伝ってくれる人を切実に必要としている農場がたくさんあります。金銭的な報奨に加え、食事と宿泊先が提供されます。週5日働いて、あとの2日は名所を見たり州内をあちこち回ってみましょう。

契約は1週間という短期間から6カ月という長期間のものまであります。さらなる詳細はウェブサイト www.caligrowers.com をご覧ください。私たちの農場と住環境についてもっと知ることができ、元従業員の感想を読むこともできます。

十分な時間給を稼ぎながら、長く残る思い出と貴重な友情を築くことができる、この機会をお見逃しなく。

□**why not ~？**：なぜ〜しないのか？、〜してみたらどうですか？　□**head**：進む、行く　□**desperately**：必死に、切実に　□**financial incentive**：金銭的な報奨　□**sights**：名所、見どころ　□**contract**：契約　□**term**：期間　□**living conditions**：生活環境、生活状態　□**testimonials**：利用者の声、感想　□**hourly wage**：時間給

選択肢と訳

13. NEW
(A) There are abundant job opportunities in the northern states.（北部の州には豊富な雇用の機会があります）
(B) If you are looking for people to work on your farm, we can help.（あなたが農場で働く人を探しているのなら、私たちがお役に立てます）
(C) During Washington's long cold winter, there are few jobs for young adults.（Washington の長くて寒い冬に、若者向けの仕事はほとんどありません）
(D) Californian real estate prices are rising beyond expectations.（California の不動産価格は予想以上に高騰しています）

□**abundant**：豊富な、十分な　□**young adult**：若者、ヤングアダルト

14. ※訳は省略
(A) are providing
(B) are provided
(C) were provided
(D) have been providing

15.
(A) We（代 われわれ）
(B) They（代 彼ら）
(C) Whoever（代 誰が～でも）
(D) You（代 あなた）

16.
(A) earning（他動 ～を稼ぐ［現在分詞］）
(B) reflecting（自動／他動 熟考する、～を熟考する［現在分詞］）
(C) desiring（自動／他動 望む、～を切望する［現在分詞］）
(D) admitting（自動／他動 余地がある、～を認める［現在分詞］）

解説

正解：(C)
空所の後ろには、①「南を目指しませんか」と勧誘する文と、②「California や New Mexico にはこのような冬場でも人手を必要としている農場がある」という文がある。空所には、「このような冬場」を「Washington の長くて寒い冬」だと特定し、「若者向けの仕事はほとんどない」と述べている (C) が適切。その他の選択肢は「このような冬場」を特定せず、空所の後の文脈にも合わないので不適切。

正解：(B)
主語の③ Food and accommodation（食事と宿泊先）は、提供されるものなので、空所に入る動詞は受動態が適切。受動態は (B) と (C) なので、次に時制を考える。空所のある文の前の文②では現在形の動詞が使われており、後ろの文④でも「週に5日働く」という労働条件が現在形で述べられている。空所のある文で述べられているのも労働条件なので、食事と宿泊先が「提供される」という現在形の受動態 (B) が正解。

正解：(D)
適切な代名詞を選ぶ問題。空所の前の文⑤は命令文で、「さらなる詳細は、ウェブサイトをご覧ください」と読み手に促している。空所を含む文には、⑥「農場と住環境についてもっと知ることができ、元従業員の感想を読むこともできる」と、ウェブサイト上で知り得る情報が書かれている。ウェブサイトを見るのは読み手なので、正解は (D)。

正解：(A)
適切な意味を選ぶ語彙問題。コンマの前の節⑦は、「長く残る思い出と貴重な友情を築くことのできるこの機会をお見逃しなく」という否定命令文。コンマの後ろ⑧には、「～しながら」という意味の接続詞と「十分な時間給」という名詞句が空所を挟んでいる。「十分な時間給を稼ぎながら」とすると文意が通るので、(A) が正解。

問題文と訳

Questions 17-20 refer to the following e-mail.

To: Jennifer Zemeckis<jzemeckis@yoshiokahotels.com>
From: Taiki Yoshioka <tyoshioka@yoshiokahotels.com>
Date: June 6
Re: Language requirements

In recent years, we have been receiving larger and larger numbers of South American guests and ①it has come to the point where more than half of the island's visitors are Spanish speakers. ②In contrast, we ----**17.**---- only two Spanish speakers at our most popular hotel. ③This is starting to become an issue because guests are having difficulty ordering services and we are unable to provide ----**18.**---- with their travel arrangements.

Alarmingly, our competitors are already putting great effort ----**19.**---- ④improving the Spanish ability of their staff. ----**20.**----. ⑤To this end, I would like you to start teaching Spanish to our staff members for one hour a day from July.

Best regards,

Taiki Yoshioka

問題 17-20 は次のEメールに関するものです。

宛先：Jennifer Zemeckis<jzemeckis @yoshiokahotels.com>
送信者：Taiki Yoshioka <tyoshioka@yoshiokahotels.com>
日付：6月6日
件名：語学の必要性

近年、ますます大勢の南米からのお客さまを迎えており、島を訪れる人の半数以上がスペイン語話者という状況になっています。その一方で、わが社では、最も人気のあるホテルにおいても、スペイン語を話せる人を2人しか雇用していません。お客さまがサービスを頼むのに苦労されたり、お客さまのご旅行の手配をお手伝いすることができなかったりしていて、このことは問題になり始めています。

憂慮すべきことに、競合他社はすでに、従業員のスペイン語力向上に熱心に取り組んでいます。このところの成功を引き続き享受するためには、われわれも同等のサービスを提供しなくてはなりません。そのために、あなたに7月から1日1時間、スタッフへのスペイン語の指導を始めていただきたいと思います。

敬具

Taiki Yoshioka

□**requirement**：要件、必要性　　□**it comes to the point where ～**：～という局面に達する　　□**in contrast**：それに対して、その一方で　　□**alarmingly**：驚くほどに、憂慮すべきことに　　□**to this end**：そのため、その目的を達成するため

選択肢と訳

17． ※訳は省略
(A) employ
(B) are employed
(C) have been employed
(D) were employing

18．
(A) assist （自動／他動 力を貸す、〜を支援する）
(B) assisted （形 援助された、補助付きの）
(C) assistant （名 助手）
(D) assistance （名 助け、補助）

19． ※訳は省略
(A) over
(B) through
(C) into
(D) without

20． NEW
(A) I doubt that this will provide them an advantage in the future. （これが将来、彼らに利益をもたらすとは思いません）
(B) We have to offer similar service to continue to enjoy our recent success. （このところの成功を引き続き享受するためには、われわれも同等のサービスを提供しなくてはなりません）
(C) You should carefully consider any positions they offer you. （あなたは彼らが提供するあらゆる地位を慎重に検討すべきです）
(D) We have been asked to help support them in this effort. （私たちはこの取り組みで彼らを支援するよう依頼されています）

解説

正解：(A)
動詞の形を問う問題。空所の後ろに動詞 employ（〜を雇用する）の目的語となる only two Spanish speakers（スペイン語話者を2人だけ）があるので、受動態の (B) と (C) を消去できる。空所のある文②は In contrast（それに対して）という副詞句で始まっているが、それとは対照的な内容になっていると推測できる前の文①も、②の内容を「This（このこと）」と指している後ろの③も、現在形。空所にも現在形が適切なので、正解は (A)。

正解：(D)
空所の前の他動詞 provide（〜を提供する）の後ろには目的語となる名詞が必要。よって、空所には名詞の (C) か (D) が入る。ホテル側が旅行の手配で客に提供するのは「助手」ではなく「助け」なので正解は (C)。このように、同じ品詞の選択肢が複数存在する品詞問題では、文法知識で候補を絞り込んでから、語彙の知識で正解を選ぶという2段階のアプローチが有効だ。

正解：(C)
put effort into 〜（〜するよう努力する、〜に取り組む）を知っていれば、素早く (C) を選べる。もし知らなくても、put 〜 into ... から「〜を…につぎ込む」とイメージできれば、空所後の④「従業員のスペイン語力を向上させること」をヒントに正解を選ぶことができる。put 〜 over ... は「〜を…の上に置く」、put 〜 through ... は「〜を…の中に通す」を意味するので、(A) と (B) は不正解。(D) without は「〜なしで」なので、これも不正解。

正解：(B)
空所の後ろにある⑤の文は、To this end（そのために）で始まり、「7月から1日1時間、スタッフへのスペイン語指導を始めてほしい」と依頼する内容が続いている。空所には前の文とつながり、「達成すべき目的」に該当するような内容の文が入る。「このところの成功を引き続き享受するために、競合相手と同様のサービスを提供しなくてはならない」とすると文脈に合うので、(B)が正解。

問題文と訳

Questions 21-24 refer to the following memo.

TO: All employees
FROM: Sean Costello, Personnel Director
DATE: ①16 August
SUBJECT: New graphic designer

I am happy to announce that we have hired a new graphic designer. ②On Monday, 14 August, Ms. Garfield ---21.--- in her new position working with our documentary team. She has come to us from JBL Productions in Canada, where she was a chief photographer for three years. ③I imagine that she will have a lot to learn here as her previous experience was ---22.--- in advertising.

④To welcome her to the company, I have ---23.--- a dinner party at Tiffany's Restaurant in the Vandelay Hotel. ⑤It is this Friday from 7 P.M. ---24.---.

問題 21-24 は次の連絡メモに関するものです。

宛先：全従業員
発信者：Sean Costello、人事部長
日付：8月16日
件名：新しいグラフィック・デザイナー

新しいグラフィック・デザイナーを採用したことをお知らせします。8月14日の月曜日に、Garfield さんはわが社のドキュメンタリー班での仕事を始めました。彼女は、Canada の JBL Productions から転職してきました。彼女は同社でチーフ・カメラマンを3年間勤めました。彼女の前職での経験は主に広告分野でのものだったので、ここで学ぶことがたくさんあるだろうと想像します。

彼女を歓迎するため、Vandelay Hotel の Tiffany's Restaurant での夕食会を企画しました。今週金曜日の午後7時からです。参加できなくなる場合には、できるだけ早く私に連絡してください。

選択肢と訳

21. ※訳は省略
(A) started
(B) is started
(C) will start
(D) had started

22.
(A) yet（副 まだ）
(B) much less（まして～でない）
(C) nearly（副 ほとんど）
(D) mostly（副 主に）

23.
(A) canceled（他動 ～を中止する［過去分詞］）
(B) rejected（他動 ～を却下する［過去分詞］）
(C) organized（他動 ～を企画する［過去分詞］）
(D) attended（他動 ～に参加する［過去分詞］）

24. NEW
(A) Please suggest any topics which should be covered at the workshop.（研修で取り上げられるべき課題を提案してください）
(B) If you will be unable to attend, please contact me as early as possible.（参加できなくなる場合には、できるだけ早く私に連絡してください）
(C) We should thank JBL Productions for their hospitality.（私たちは JBL Productions の手厚いもてなしに感謝すべきです）
(D) This project should be given particular attention.（このプロジェクトは特に注目されるべきです）

□**cover**：～を取り上げる、～を取り扱う
□**hospitality**：手厚いもてなし、歓待

解説

正解：(A)
動詞の形を問う問題。メモの上部①から、このメモが書かれたのは 8月16日だと分かる。空所を含む文②は「8月14日の月曜日に」という書き出しなので、過去のことを述べていることになる。従って、過去形の (A) が正解。過去完了形（had ＋過去分詞）は、過去のある時点から見て、それ以前に起こったことを述べる場合に用いられるので、(D)は不正解。

正解：(D)
空所のある文③中の she は、新しく採用されたグラフィック・デザイナーの Garfield さんを指す。「彼女の経験は主に広告分野でのものなので、ここで学ぶことが多くある」で文意が通るので、(D)が正解。(A) yet は否定文で「まだ～（ない）」、(B) much less は否定語句に続けて「なおさら～ない」、(C) nearly は「ほとんど」を意味し、nearly complete（「完全に近い」＝完全ではない）のように何かに対して少し欠けている様子を表す。

正解：(C)
空所のある文は「彼女を歓迎するために」（④）という書き出し。「夕食会を企画した」とすれば文意が通るので、(C)が正解。a dinner party（夕食会）を指す It（それ）で始まる次の文⑤に「それは今週の金曜日の午後7時からだ」とあることからも、夕食会の企画は中止も却下もされていないことが分かる。従って、(A)と(B)は不正解。⑤から夕食会はこれから開かれるので、(D)も不正解。

正解：(B)
空所の前の文⑤は「それ（＝夕食会）は今週の金曜日の午後7時からだ」という内容。文脈に合うのは、「もし参加できなくなったら、できるだけ早く連絡してくれ」という (B)。メモの締めくくりの文としても適切だ。この文書では、(A) の workshop（研修）と (D) の project については述べられていない（メモの読み手が夕食会の企画者であれば project と呼べるが、実際は違うので不可）。また、(C) の JBL Productions は第1段落に登場する会社だが、同社による「もてなし」も触れられていない。

Part 6

問題文と訳

Questions 25-28 refer to the following information.

Job Title: Librarian

The purpose of this document is to summarize the responsibilities ---25--- with the position of librarian at the Harper City Central Library. ---26---. ①Accordingly, you may be called upon to take on tasks not specifically described in this document.

Generally speaking, librarians are expected to process books as they are loaned and returned. Books which have not been returned by the due date should be investigated. ②It may also be necessary to assist users with library facilities. ---27---, ③librarians are tasked with purchasing books and preparing them for inclusion in the library catalog.

---28---, ④librarians are required to participate in one training course a year at a recognized institution. There are more conditions, which will be discussed at the interview.

問題 25-28 は次の情報に関するものです。

職名：司書

この文書の目的は、Harper City 中央図書館の司書に関連する職責を要約することです。注意すべきは、司書は自身の役割において柔軟であることが求められるという点です。従って、この文書に特に記載されていない業務を引き受けるよう要請される可能性もあります。

一般的に、司書は貸し出されたり返却されたりする本を処理することを期待されます。期日までに返却されていない本は調べられなくてはなりません。図書館の設備について利用者を助ける必要もあるかもしれません。さらに、司書は本を購入したり、その本を図書目録に加える準備をしたりといった任務も負います。

全ての司書は、広く認められている機関で、年に1つ研修コースを受講することが求められています。他にも条件はありますが、それについては面接の際に話し合われます。

☐**librarian**：図書館員、司書　☐**be called upon to ～**：～することを要請される　☐**take on ～**：～を引き受ける
☐**specifically**：特に、具体的に　☐**generally speaking**：一般的には、大体は　☐**due date**：期日、締め切り
☐**investigate**：～を調査する　☐**be tasked with ～**：～の任務を負う、～を任される　☐**inclusion**：含めること、組み入れ　☐**recognized**：広く認められている　☐**institution**：機関

選択肢と訳

25.
(A) associated（他動 ～を関連付ける［過去分詞］）
(B) association（名 関連）
(C) associate（他動 ～を関連付ける）
(D) associating（他動 ～を関連付ける［現在分詞・動名詞］）

26. NEW
(A) The position is not being advertised in newspapers or on the Internet.（その職は新聞でもインターネットでも告知されていません）
(B) Only the following tasks may be required of people employed as librarians.（次の業務だけが司書として採用された人々に求められます）
(C) Send applications to the chief librarian at chief@hcckibrary.com.（願書は chief@hcckibrary.com. の図書館長まで送ってください）
(D) It should be noted that librarians are expected to be flexible in their role.（注意すべきは、司書は自身の役割において柔軟であることが求められるという点です）

□**chief librarian**：図書館長　□**flexible**：柔軟な、融通のきく

27.
(A) Therefore（副 従って）
(B) In contrast（それに対して）
(C) Furthermore（副 さらに）
(D) On the contrary（それどころか）

28.
(A) Both（形 両方の）
(B) All（形 全ての）
(C) Other（形 他の）
(D) Several（形 何人かの）

解説

正解：(A)
空所には直前にある名詞の responsibilities（職責）を修飾することができる(A) associatedか (D) associating が適切。職責は、「関連付ける」という行為を起こす側ではなく、受ける側なので、受動の意味を表す過去分詞の (A) が正解。「司書職に関連付けられている職責」で意味が通る。現在分詞の (D) は、「関連付けている」という能動の意味を表す。「司書職に関連付けている職責」では意味が通らず不正解。

正解：(D)
空所の直後の文①は Accordingly（従って）という接続副詞で始まっている。空所にはAccordingly以下の文と矛盾しないでつながる文が入る。「この文書に特に記載されていない業務を引き受けるよう要請される可能性もある」という文と矛盾しないでつながる文は、「司書は役割において柔軟であることが求められる」なので、正解は(D)。他の選択肢を空所に入れると、Accordingly の前後が「理由と結論」の関係にならないため不適切。

正解：(C)
選択肢には、2つの文を結ぶ接続副詞や副詞句が並んでいる。空所の前の文②では、「図書館の設備について利用者を助ける必要もあるかもしれない」と司書の業務が説明されている。空所の後ろ③では、「司書は本を購入したり、その本を図書目録に加える準備をしたりという任務も負う」という別の業務が説明されている。この2つを結ぶことができるのは「さらに」なので、(C)が正解。

正解：(B)
選択肢には、空所の直後にある名詞 librarians（司書）を修飾できる語が並んでいる。空所の後ろの④で述べられているのは、「1つの研修コースを受講することが求められている」という司書全員に関係する情報だ。2つのもの・人について用いる (A)、「数個の・数人の」という意味を表す (D)、「他の」の意味で用いる (C) は不適切。「全ての」を表す (B)が正解。

問題文と訳

Questions 29-32 refer to the following announcement.

The New South Wales Environmental Protection Council has an exciting announcement. World-renowned professor of marine biology, Dr. Steve Mitchel ---29.--- as the keynote speaker at the World Environmental Conference in Sydney ①in May.

In recent years, Dr. Mitchel has written a number of important articles on environmental protection, which have influenced governmental policy and public awareness. He ---30.--- ②for his weekly radio show which has a following of over a million listeners.

③He will be speaking in depth about the ---31.--- from his study into Australia's coastlines and his predictions for the next 50 years.

---32.---. ④To register, contact the New South Wales Environmental Protection Council Planning Committee at 02-555-9898 or via e-mail at wecpc@nswepcouncil.com.

問題 29-32 は次のお知らせに関するものです。

New South Wales 環境保全評議会からの素晴らしいお知らせです。5月に Sydney で開かれる世界環境会議で、世界的に著名な海洋生物学教授の Steve Mitchel 博士が基調講演の講演者を務めてくださいます。

近年、Mitchel 博士は環境保護に関するいくつかの重要な記事を執筆していますが、それらは政府の政策や大衆の意識を動かしてきました。彼は毎週放送されているラジオ番組で知られており、それには100万人を超えるリスナーの支持を受けています。

博士は Australia の海岸線地帯に関する自身の研究の成果と、今後50年の予測について掘り下げて話をしてくれることでしょう。

チケットはすぐに売り切れることが予想されます。お申し込みは、02-555-9898 にお電話をいただくか、wecpc@nswepcouncil.com に E メールをいただくかの方法で、New South Wales 環境保全評議会実行員会までご連絡ください。

☐**environmental protection**：環境保全、環境保護　☐**council**：評議会、審議会　☐**world-renowned**：世界的に著名な　☐**marine biology**：海洋生物学　☐**keynote speaker**：基調講演の講演者　☐**public awareness**：国民の意識、大衆の意識　☐**have a following of ～**：～の支持を受けている　☐**in depth**：掘り下げて、徹底的に　☐**coastline**：海岸線、海岸線地帯　☐**prediction**：予測、予想　☐**register**：登録する、申し込む　☐**planning committee**：実行委員会　☐**via**：～によって、～を介して

選択肢と訳

29． ※訳は省略
(A) served
(B) will serve
(C) has served
(D) serves

30． ※訳は省略
(A) knows
(B) is knowing
(C) is known
(D) knew

31．
(A) aims （名目標）
(B) grants （名助成金）
(C) reductions （名削減）
(D) findings （名研究結果）

□**grant**：助成金　□**finding**：研究結果、調査結果

32． NEW
(A) Tickets are expected to sell out very quickly.
（チケットはすぐに売り切れることが予想されます）
(B) Unfortunately, he has declined to attend.（残念ながら、彼は出席を辞退しました）
(C) Submit your research proposals to the professor directly.（研究案は直接教授に提出してください）
(D) If you would like to make a donation, please visit the Web site.（寄付をなさりたい場合はウェブサイトをご覧ください）

□**decline to ～**：～するのを断る、～するのを辞退する

解説

正解：(B)

時制を問う問題。空所のある文の文末には、①in May（5月に）という時を表す情報がある。「Steve Mitchel 博士が基調講演の講演者を務める」5月が、過去の5月ならば (A)、未来の5月ならば (B) が適切。3段落目の③He will be speaking …の主語 He は Steve Mitchel 博士を指し、ここで基調講演の内容、テーマが説明されていることから、講演は未来の5月でなければ文脈に合わないので、(B) が正解。

正解：(C)

動詞の形を問う問題。②「100万人を超えるリスナーの支持を受けている毎週放送のラジオ番組により」彼は「知られている」という受動態の形が適切なので、(C) が正解。for 以下は、知られている理由。知る対象となる目的語が必要な能動態の (A) (B) (D) は不適切。

正解：(D)

空所のある文③の「Australiaの海岸線地帯に関する彼自身の研究からの」が修飾し、「掘り下げて話をする」対象として適切なのは「研究結果」なので、(D) が正解。(A) aims は前置詞 from ではなく、of または in と共に「～の目標」を表すので不適切。(B) と (C) を空所に入れても文意が通らないので、いずれも不正解。

正解：(A)

空所の後ろには、④「申し込むためには、電話かメールで連絡してください」という文が続いている。チケットはすぐに売り切れることが予想され、そのチケットを申し込むために連絡するというつながりが適切なので、正解は (A)。その他の選択肢は文脈に合わないので不適切。

問題文と訳

Questions 33-36 refer to the following information.

___33___. ①For years, we've been providing home delivery for customers whose private vehicles were too small to carry home bulky items. ②It is a popular service and we have been able to offer it ③at very little ___34___ cost. However, ④some customers have mentioned that it is not always ___35___. ⑤Unfortunately, some items can arrive very late in the day. This makes it hard for ___36___ to complete weekend home improvement projects.

⑥From this month, Howard's Hardware is offering free use of its three delivery trucks to customers to carry their goods home. Inquire at the service counter for details.

問題 33-36 は次の案内に関するものです。

Howard's Hardware は新しいサービスの提供を始めます。かさばる商品を持ち帰るにはお車が小さいというお客さまのために、私たちは長年宅配を行っています。人気のあるサービスで、ほんのわずかな追加料金で提供することができています。しかしながら、必ずしも迅速ではないとおっしゃるお客さまもいらっしゃいました。残念ながら、商品の中には遅めの時間に届くこともあります。これではお客さまが週末の日曜大工プロジェクトを完成させるのも困難です。

今月から、Howard's Hardware では、商品をご自宅まで運ばれるお客さまに、店の3台の配達トラックを無料でお使いいただけるよう提供いたします。詳しくはサービスカウンターでお尋ねください。

☐**home delivery**：宅配　☐**bulky**：かさばる、大きい　☐**home improvement**：日曜大工、家の修繕　☐**inquire**：尋ねる、聞く　☐**for details**：詳しくは、詳細は

選択肢と訳

33. NEW

(A) After 50 years in business, Howard's Hardware is closing its doors.（創業から50年、Howard's Hardware は閉店します）
(B) Howard's Hardware is opening its first store in Gladstone.（Howard's Hardware は Gladstone で初の店舗を開店します）
(C) For this month only, Howard's Hardware's home delivery service is free.（今月の間だけ、Howard's Hardware の宅配サービスは無料です）
(D) Howard's Hardware is offering a new service.（Howard's Hardware は新しいサービスの提供を始めます）

□**hardware**：金物、工具　□**close *one's* doors**：閉店する、操業を止める

34.
(A) additional（形 追加の）
(B) addition（名 追加）
(C) additionally（副 さらに）
(D) add（他動 〜を加える）

□**additional cost**：追加料金

35.
(A) correct（形 正しい）
(B) fast（形 迅速な）
(C) needed（形 必要とされる）
(D) provided（形 与えられた）

36.
(A) me（代 私に）
(B) him（代 彼に）
(C) them（代 彼らに）
(D) us（代 私たちに）

解説

正解：(D)

空所以降では、①「かさばる商品のために宅配サービスを行ってきた」や⑤「品物が届くのが遅くなることがある」など、宅配サービスについて述べられている。さらに⑥では「今月から配達トラックを無料で使用できるようにする」と宣言されている。文書の冒頭に来るものとして適切なのは、文書全体のトピックである「新しいサービスを提供する」という文なので、正解は (D)。文書の最初の文が空所になっている場合は、他の問題を全て解いてから解答すべきだ。最初から解こうとすると、不必要に長い時間がかかってしまう恐れがある。

正解：(A)

適切な品詞の語を選ぶ品詞問題。空所の近くから判断して答えることができる。空所の前には、前置詞 at と副詞 very と副詞 little があり、空所の後ろには名詞 cost がある。cost が名詞であると判断できるのは、at で始まる前置詞句（③）の最後の語だからだ。空所にはcostを修飾する形容詞が入る。正解は形容詞の(A)。very little（ほんのわずかに）は、additionalを修飾している。

正解：(B)

空所のある文④のthat節中のitは、文②の主語Itと同様に、home delivery（宅配）を指している。空所のある文の後ろは、⑤「残念ながら、いくつかの商品は非常に遅く到着することがある」という意味の文。この前後の情報をつなぐことができるのは「宅配は必ずしも迅速ではない」なので、正解は (B)。他の選択肢は文法的には問題ないが、文脈に合わず不正解。

正解：(C)

空所のある文の前には、④「宅配が必ずしも迅速ではないと言う顧客もいる」ことと、⑤「いくつかの商品は非常に遅く到着することがある」ということが述べられている。空所のある文の主語This（このこと）とは、「商品が遅く到着すること」。この宅配の遅れが困難にしているのは、「顧客がする週末の日曜大工プロジェクト」なので、空所には some customers の代名詞である (C) themを入れるのが適切。

問題文と訳

Questions 37-40 refer to the following notice.

Waste Management

①TelAmeri Corporation has conducted an internal review of its paper usage and found that all departments are creating excessive waste. ---37---. ②We are not only spending too much on paper, but also on its disposal.

③Please ---38--- more on multipage printing functions and use both sides of the page for large print jobs. ④From today, each ---39--- will be issued a card to use when making copies so that we can keep track of individual usage. Finally, ⑤we have entered into an arrangement with a recycling company, which will pick up our paper waste twice a week. So, be sure to separate paper from other items when ---40--- things away.

⑥General Affairs Department

問題 37-40 は次のお知らせに関するものです。

無駄の抑制

TelAmeri Corporation で紙の使用に関する内部調査を実施したところ、どの部署も度を越えた無駄を出していることが判明しました。このことは環境にも当社の財務状況にも良くありません。紙だけでなくその廃棄にもお金を使い過ぎています。

複数ページ印刷機能をもっと活用し、大量の印刷作業には両面印刷を使うようにしてください。本日より、個人の使用状況を追跡できるよう、各従業員にはコピーを取る際に使うカードが支給されます。最後に、週に2回紙ごみを取りに来てくれるリサイクル会社との提携を始めました。ですから、物を捨てるときには、紙をその他のものと分別するようにしてください。

総務部

□**conduct**：〜を実施する、〜を行う　□**internal**：内部の　□**review**：調査、点検　□**usage**：使用、利用
□**excessive**：必要以上の、度を超えた　□**disposal**：廃棄、処分　□**issue**：〜を発行する　□**keep track of 〜**：〜を追跡する、〜を記録する　□**enter into 〜**：〜を始める、〜に取り掛かる

130

選択肢と訳

37. NEW

(A) This is bad for both the environment and the company's finances.（このことは環境にも当社の財務状況にも良くありません）
(B) This is a wonderful achievement for a company of our size.（私たちのような規模の企業にとって、これは素晴らしい成果です）
(C) There does not appear to be any need to take action at this time.（現時点で行動を起こす必要があるようには見えません）
(D) Contact senior management if your budget will not cover the cost.（その費用を予算で賄えない場合は上層部に連絡してください）

□**achievement**：成果、業績　□**take action**：行動を起こす、措置を講じる　□**at this time**：現時点で、現段階で
□**senior management**：上層部

解説

正解：(A)

空所の前には、①「内部調査で度を越えた紙の無駄を出していることが判明した」とあり、空所の後ろには、②「紙だけでなく、廃棄にも浪費している」という文がある。2つの文の間に入れても、文脈上矛盾しない (A) が正解。空所の前で「成果」について述べられていないので、(B) は不正解。第2段落では今後講じられる措置が述べられているので、(C) も不可。「その費用」が何を指すのか不明なので、(D) も不適切。

38.
(A) reliability（名 信頼性）
(B) reliably（副 確実に）
(C) reliable（形 信頼できる）
(D) rely（自動 頼る、当てにする）

正解：(D)

空所を含む文③は、丁寧さを添える Please が付いた命令文。命令文は動詞の原形で始めるので、(D) が正解。rely は自動詞なので、前置詞なしで目的語を続けることができない。rely on ～ の形で「～に頼る」を表す。

39.
(A) client（名 顧客）
(B) student（名 学生）
(C) employee（名 従業員）
(D) visitor（名 来場者）

正解：(C)

「総務部」（⑥）によって書かれているこのお知らせは、①「TelAmeri Corporation のどの部署も度を越えた無駄を出している」という紙使用の問題を提起する文で始まっている。空所のある文④は、「コピーを取る際のカードが支給される」という問題解決法の1つを述べている。文の主語である空所には、カードが支給される人、つまり TelAmeri Corporation の「従業員」を入れるのが適切なので、(C) が正解。

40.
(A) storing（他動 ～を保管する［現在分詞］）
(B) throwing（他動 ～を保管する［現在分詞］）
(C) putting（他動 ～を置く［現在分詞］）
(D) keeping（自動／他動 ～のままでいる、～を維持する［現在分詞］）

□**throw ～ away**：～を捨てる

正解：(B)

空所のある文は So（だから）で始まるので、その前の文の結論が書かれているはず。前の文では、⑤「リサイクル会社が週に2回紙ごみを取りに来る」と述べられている。その結論として適切なのは、紙ごみが回収されるように、「物を捨てるときには、紙をその他のものと分別するように」なので、(B) が正解。throw ～ away あるいは、throw away ～ は、「～を捨てる」という意味の動詞句。正解以外の選択肢も「store ～ away（～をしまっておく）」「put ～ away（～を片付ける）」「keep ～ away（～を遠ざける）」という動詞句。

Part 7のまとめ
ヒロ前田

Part 7はココが変わった!

問題数が増えた
- パート全体の問題数が48問から54問になった
- 「シングルパッセージ」は28問から29問（9セットから10セット）に微増。10セットの内訳は、設問2問が4セット、設問3問が3セット、設問4問が3セット。5問の設問が付いたセットは、シングルパッセージからは消滅した
- 「ダブルパッセージ」は2文書と3文書から成る「マルチプルパッセージ」と呼ばれることに。2文書は2セット（設問は各5問）。3文書は3セット（設問は各5問）

新しい形式が複数登場
- ターゲットとなる文を挿入すべき場所を選ぶ「位置選択問題」、意図問題を設問に含む「チャット系」、3文書がセットになった「トリプルパッセージ」が登場

より自然な英語を読む機会が増える
- 「チャット系」に登場する携帯メールやオンラインチャットなどのやりとりでは、これまでのリーディングセクションには登場しなかった口語的な表現も使われる。書かれた会話のようなものなので、これまでのPart 7の文書と比べて、読みやすいと感じる受験者が多いはず

解説 問題数は増えた、でも実態は…

　6問増えたインパクトは意外に小さいものかもしれません。増えた問題の大部分は「トリプルパッセージ」の同義語問題になっている可能性が高いからです。同義語問題なら、読解問題より短い時間で解けるはずですね。
　シングルパッセージは1セット増えて10セットになりましたが、そのうちの2セットがチャット系だと聞けば気が楽になりませんか？　解きにくかった5問付き文書もなくなりました。1セット当たりの負荷は下がった印象です。ダブルパッセージは、難易度なども特に変化はないようです。

Part 7 攻略の基本

●「時間管理」が重要

「Part 5とPart 6に計18～20分、Part 7に55～57分」というのが推奨モデルです。その場合、Part 7は1問当たり1分で解く計算になりますが、「1問1分」と意識するのではなく、ブロックで考えるべきです。シングルパッセージなら29問なので、29～30分です。ただし、チャット系の問題に1問1分はかけ過ぎなので、実際は25分辺りを目安とするのが妥当です。ダブルパッセージは10問だから10分、トリプルパッセージは15問だから15分、Part 7全体で50分という計算ですが、これで時間が余るとは限りません。トリプルパッセージも後ろへ行くと面倒くさい問題や、長い文書など時間がかかるものがあり、ペースが落ちることが予測されます。

時間管理については自分なりの型を確立することが大切です。「リーディングセクションはまずPart 7から解く」「Part 7では最後のトリプルパッセージから解く」…などいろいろなパターンがあります。型を自分のものにするには、模試などを利用して何回か練習するのが一番です。

● 速く精読する

Part 7では「文書は飛ばさずに全部読む」というのが、新形式導入以降特に妥協できない大前提となっています。上で述べた時間は文書を読むことだけに費やせる時間ではありません。実際には考える時間、解答する時間も含まれているのですから、英文をできるだけ速く読むことは鉄則です。

「もっと速く読めるようになるにはどうすればいいですか？」という質問をよく受けます。そういう人は、「英文を速く読むには何らかの『技術』があって、読むのが速い人たちはそれを使っているに違いない」と思っているのかもしれませんが、それは勘違いです。技術ではなく、普段から英語をたくさん読んでいるから、その結果速くなるだけ、というのがボクの持論です。

速く読むために「やってはいけないこと」なら、もっと具体的なアドバイスができます。

①きれいな日本語に訳さない

「日本語に訳すな」というのをあらゆるレベルの人に押し付けるつもりはありません。英語を処理する際、頭に日本語が浮かぶのはある程度仕方がないことです。「きれいな日本語」に訳すのをやめましょう。

②文の途中で行ったり来たりしない

関係代名詞に出会うと「〜するところの○○は…」のように、行ったり来たりして解釈しようとする人がいます。英語は文の頭から処理する癖をつけましょう。

③単語単位で処理しない

例えば長めのこんな文。
I'm writing this letter to let you know that we have reviewed your résumé and have decided to offer you ...

これを理解するのに、単語ごとに処理していては時間がいくらあっても足りません。英文をたくさん読んでいる人は、意味のかたまり（チャンク）ごとに内容を理解していきます。例えばこんな風に。

I'm writing this letter/ to let you know/ that we have reviewed your résumé/ and have decided to offer you ...

これができるようになれば、スピードが上がるはずです。ただし、Part 7で本当に必要なのは「速い精読」です。いくら読むのが速くても、正確な読解がなければミスをします。思い出してください。残り時間が30分以上あるときに解いた問題は全問正解ですか？　時間があっても間違えるなら、速く読んでも間違えますよ。Part 7で「なんとなく答えを選ぶ」ことがあるなら、精読ができていない証拠です。ぜひ、英文を丁寧に読んで理解する練習を増やしてください。精読練習を繰り返せばスピードが上がります。それが「速い精読」です。

「位置選択問題」はこんな問題！

1回のテストで2問出題される
- 設問3〜4問付きのシングルパッセージで出題される
- そのセットの最後の設問として出る

「場所」を問う問題
- 設問で示されているターゲット文を「文書のどこかに入れるとしたらどこがベストか？」を問う

文書も設問も特徴的だから一目瞭然
- 文書には1〜4の番号を振られた空所が存在する
- In which of the positions marked [1], [2], [3], and [4] does the following sentence best belong? という問いの下にターゲット文が印刷されている。選択肢には空所の場所を示す数字が並ぶ

解説　空所に慣れよう

　Part 7の文書に空所があるというのは初めてのことなので気になるかもしれません。慣れるしかありませんが、読んでいる間は空所のことはなるべく忘れ、ストーリーの把握に集中してください。他の問題では、その設問が何番目にあるかがヒントを探す際の手がかりになることが多いですが、位置選択問題は常に最後にあるので、その手がかりがありません。ストーリーの理解こそが最大の手がかりです。

解説　文書は細部まで丁寧に読む

　位置選択問題は英文ライティング（レター、Eメール、エッセーなど）の練習をしたことがある人には有利です。接続副詞、代名詞などの細部に注意を払い、丁寧に読むことが重要だからです。残念ながら、日本の学校での英語教育では、段落の作り方、接続詞や接続副詞の使い方といったロジックの組み立て方を十分に学べません。不安がある人には精読の練習をお勧めします。問題集の英文（スクリプト）、ウェブのニュース記事など、英文があればどこででもできます。

「位置選択問題」攻略の基本

● 解くのは最後、文書は全部読む
　手前の設問を解く過程で文書を読んでいると、「もしかしてこれが最後の位置選択問題の正解かもしれない」と感じる空所を通るかもしれません。このときにやってはいけないのが、すぐにターゲット文を確認しに行き、その空所に入るかどうかを検証するという行為です。途中で行ったり来たりするのは時間のロスが大きく危険です。位置問題は「最後に解く」という姿勢でOKです。「文書を読む前にターゲット文に目を通しておく」という人もいます。自分に合う解き方かどうか試してみる価値はありますが、個人的には、「どうせ全部読まなくてはいけないのだから、ターゲット文は最終問題を解くときに読めばいい」というスタンスです。

● 正解の場所を選ぶ目の付け所
　位置選択問題で正解を選ぶ際のヒントをいくつか挙げておきます。こういう細部への注意力は、普段から精読をしていれば養われます。

① 比較／対照の関係
　正解となる空所の近くには、ターゲット文と対照的な情報が存在することがよくあります。例えば、ターゲット文は「今期のいすの売り上げが20パーセントアップした」という内容で、ある空所の近くに「スチール製テーブルの売り上げは35パーセントダウンした」という情報があるとします。その空所にターゲット文を入れることで、いすの売り上げが好調だったのに対し、スチール製テーブルの売り上げは不振だったという比較が成立し、正解！…というパターンです。

② 接続副詞
　空所の直後、またはターゲット文の中の接続副詞も要注意です。例えば、ターゲット文の中に接続副詞 therefore（だから）があるとします。
　Therefore, the sales of chairs have risen by 20 percent.（だから、いすの売り上げは20パーセント伸びた）
　この場合、正解となる空所の前には、売上増の原因となる事象が書かれていなければなりません。これは大きなヒントとなり得ます。

③ 並列の関係
　あるテーマに基づき、複数の例が挙げられている文書において、ターゲット文はその例の1つだというケースがあります。その場合は、ターゲット文がその他の例と並列の関係を成立させることができる空所が正解です。

④ ターゲット文中の代名詞・副詞・助動詞
　ターゲット文中の代名詞・副詞・助動詞もヒントになる重要な情報です。
- **副詞**　例）even、as well、likewise、also、～, too　など
　ターゲット文中にこれらの表現があれば、正解の空所の前には、その類似情報が確実に存在します。
- **助動詞**　例）should、must　など
　ターゲット文中の助動詞がターゲット文が属する段落のヒントをくれる場合があります。ターゲット文が You should submit ～（～を提出しなくてはなりません）という形を取っているとします。その場合、読み手に対して「～しなさい」という情報を集めた段落があり、ターゲット文はその段落の一部である可能性が高いでしょう。
- **代名詞**　例）these、that　など
　例えば、These rules ...（これらの規則は…）で始まるターゲット文があるとします。正解の空所の前では、複数の規則について述べられているはずです。

Part 7　①位置選択問題　ドリル

1セット 5分
トータル 25分

次の文書を読んで問題に答えよう。

Questions 1-4 refer to the following Web page.

http://www.films4u.com/faq

Welcome to FILMS 4 U
The World's Best Online Movie Service!

FILMS 4U

| HOME | FAQ | TESTIMONIALS | NEW RELEASES |

FILMS 4 U Frequently Asked Questions

What are the details of the free trial?
You get access to our entire movie library for a period of 28 days from the moment you register on the Web site. — [1] —. If you would like to continue, there is nothing more to do — you will be billed from your second month.

What selection of movies is available?
There are thousands of titles available — too many to list. — [2] —. We have films as new as six months old as well as classic films up to 30 years old.

Can more than one member of my family use the service?
There are service plans available that will allow you to have up to three people watching simultaneously. — [3] —. You can increase the number of users at any time by logging on to the Web site and accessing your account information.

Do I need a special television?
You do not need a special television. In fact, you do not need a television at all. You can watch FILMS 4 U movies on your mobile phone, computer and most major video game machines. Many modern televisions do support our service, but you may also connect your computer to your television if you want to watch films on a big screen. — [4] —.

1. For whom is the Web page intended?
   (A) Newly hired sales staff
   (B) Customer support operators
   (C) Installers of specialized devices
   (D) People considering subscribing to a service

2. How long is the free membership period?
   (A) Four weeks
   (B) Five weeks
   (C) Six weeks
   (D) Seven weeks

3. What is suggested about the service?
   (A) The only payment method is a credit card.
   (B) Different membership levels are available.
   (C) Users must buy a device from FILMS 4 U.
   (D) There is a waiting period for connection.

4. In which of the positions marked [1], [2], [3], and [4] does the following sentence best belong?

   "If you are no longer interested in viewing films from our catalog after that, you may cancel your subscription."

   (A) [1]
   (B) [2]
   (C) [3]
   (D) [4]

① 位置選択問題

GO ON TO THE NEXT PAGE

Questions 5-8 refer to the following e-mail.

To:	Phil Graham <pgraham@gardengreen.com>
From:	Stacy Greene <sgreene@gardengreen.com>
Date:	June 11
Subject:	Business Trip June 19 - June 22

Dear Phil:

Let me congratulate you on an amazing first year. Your performance this year has been excellent and your coworkers and supervisors have had nothing but kind things to say about you.

Ordinarily, we would not ask a relatively inexperienced employee to go on a business trip of this nature, but we're making an exception. — [1] —. As this will be your first business trip for the company, I think it is important to explain some of the requirements.

— [2] —. You are required to submit an expense report within a week of your return to Victoria. This must include receipts for your accommodations and meals. — [3] —. If you need to rent a car, you must choose the least expensive available vehicle for your needs. Fuel and other expenses must also be reported and supported by receipts from the respective sellers. Let me stress that you will not be reimbursed for any purchases for which you cannot produce a receipt.

— [4] —. We have already spoken about the goals of your trip and the written summary, which is due on the day of your return.

Sincerely,

Stacy Greene
General Manager — Garden Green

5. What is indicated about Mr. Graham?
   (A) He does not live in Victoria.
   (B) He will use his own vehicle.
   (C) He has been evaluated highly.
   (D) He is a manager of Garden Green.

6. What is suggested about the company?
   (A) It specializes in imported goods.
   (B) It is looking for more local suppliers.
   (C) It provides employees with company vehicles.
   (D) It chooses experienced employees for important trips.

7. When is the deadline for a written summary of Mr. Graham's trip?
   (A) On June 11
   (B) On June 19
   (C) On June 22
   (D) On June 29

8. In which of the positions marked [1], [2], [3], and [4] does the following sentence best belong?

   "Any tickets for public transport should be standard fare and the time, date and reason for your travel should be fully documented."

   (A) [1]
   (B) [2]
   (C) [3]
   (D) [4]

① 位置選択問題

GO ON TO THE NEXT PAGE

Questions 9-12 refer to the following information.

Working and Cooperating Effectively

These days, the business world is very competitive. Many employees try to stand out as individuals, but modern employers evaluate employees' collaborative efforts even more highly. — [1] —.

It is often difficult to work in teams because many people tend to compete for the attention of upper management. On the other hand, it is very difficult to achieve excellent results on our own. — [2] —. Usually, however, it is through teamwork that most businesses succeed.

This can only happen when you are aware of each other's projects, so good communication is necessary. Offer help to those who need it, ask for help from others and thank them in front of team members. — [3] —. People like to feel appreciated, and by sharing work, we are given many opportunities to express gratitude.

— [4] —. Remember that planning is of key importance. Keep a schedule of upcoming events and refer to it from time to time so that you are never surprised by a deadline. Every day, make a list of things that need to be done and check them off as you complete them. With effective time management, you will likely find that you have more free time every day.

9. According to the information, what is more important to employers?
   (A) Experience in a variety of positions
   (B) The ability to cooperate with others
   (C) A candidate's academic history
   (D) Finding ways to attract new customers

10. What is mentioned as an effective work practice?
    (A) Working early in the morning
    (B) Taking occasional breaks
    (C) Completing large jobs first
    (D) Keeping coworkers informed

11. What advice is NOT provided in the information?
    (A) Having a flexible schedule
    (B) Offering assistance
    (C) Making a things-to-do list
    (D) Showing appreciation

12. In which of the positions marked [1], [2], [3], and [4] does the following sentence best belong?

    "Aside from sharing tasks, there are several other things you can do to get your work done on time."

    (A) [1]
    (B) [2]
    (C) [3]
    (D) [4]

Questions 13-16 refer to the following advertisement.

Lockheed Suits and Formalwear

Get the right fit with a tailor-made suit from Lockheed Suits!

Don't trust your image to just anyone. Your sense of personal style should be reflected in the clothes you wear. — [1] —. There are items of clothing you choose off the rack, and there are items that should be as individual as you are. Owning a Lockheed suit has been a sign of financial and career success among the people of Chicago for more than 30 years. — [2] —.

Visit us on the Web at www.lockheedsafw.com, where you will see samples of our work, testimonials, and our full design selection. There is a huge range of options available including pocket shapes, coat length, and lining color. For out-of-town residents, we have even started an online ordering system, whereby you can input your measurements and requirements and have a suit shipped anywhere in the country at no extra cost. — [3] —. Having your signature or monogram stitched into the lining inside the lapel is a classy touch that our expert sewers can accomplish for only $50 more. — [4] —.

---

13. What is most likely true about Lockheed Suits?

(A) It is based in Chicago.
(B) It employs famous designers.
(C) It is a family-owned business.
(D) It keeps records of clients' measurements.

14. What is NOT mentioned as being available on the Web site?

(A) Work samples
(B) Customer reviews
(C) Style choices
(D) Store locations

15. According to the advertisement, what service does Lockheed Suits provide for an additional fee?

(A) Domestic shipping
(B) Monogram stitching
(C) Colored lining
(D) Fashion consulting

16. In which of the positions marked [1], [2], [3], and [4] does the following sentence best belong?

"Nevertheless, a tailor-made suit that fits perfectly can cost less than one from a major design house."

(A) [1]
(B) [2]
(C) [3]
(D) [4]

GO ON TO THE NEXT PAGE

Questions 17-20 refer to the following article.

Drummond is Drumming up Business

September 1—The first stages of Drummond City's push to attract greater visitor numbers and generate revenue for local businesses are already going ahead. Over the past three years, discussions and planning meetings have been held at City Hall with many officials making trips to major tourist destinations such as Paris, Rome, and New York to learn what it is that makes these places attractive to travelers.

A number of attributes were identified and debated by a committee initially headed by Anthony Caldwell. Mr. Caldwell had to leave the committee to take up his political campaign. — [1] —. Nevertheless, the committee's proposals are still being taken very seriously, the first of which is the publicly subsidized restoration of the Lennon Building on William Street. During his campaign for the position of mayor of Drummond City, Mr. Caldwell indicated that significant funds would be spent on this cause. This resulted in an overwhelming political victory, and according to his supporters, he intends to live up to the promises he made. — [2] —.

Other targets for beautification include the riverfront area along Harding Street and the old sandstone buildings in Hansen Street and Douglass Street. — [3] —.

— [4] —. In addition to these projects, there are other changes on their way to Drummond City. There will be new ordinances forcing companies to keep the streets clean as well as incentives for projects that enhance the city's cultural allure.

17. What is the article mainly about?
  (A) Proposals to improve the appearance of a city.
  (B) Choosing members to serve on a committee.
  (C) The cost of upgrading local infrastructure.
  (D) Planning a musical festival to attract guests.

18. What is suggested about the Lennon Building?
  (A) It was one of the first buildings in Drummond City.
  (B) It is a popular destination among tourists.
  (C) Its reconstruction may be carried out with public funds.
  (D) It has been chosen as a venue for committee meetings.

19. What is implied about Mr. Caldwell?
  (A) He has worked in other cities.
  (B) He is mayor of Drummond City.
  (C) He is opposed to increased spending.
  (D) He was invited to see European cities.

20. In which of the positions marked [1], [2], [3], and [4] does the following sentence best belong?

"These locations have historical significance and natural charm that will make them popular with visitors."

  (A) [1]
  (B) [2]
  (C) [3]
  (D) [4]

Part 7 ①位置選択問題 ドリルの解答・解説

問題文と訳

Questions 1-4 refer to the following ① Web page.

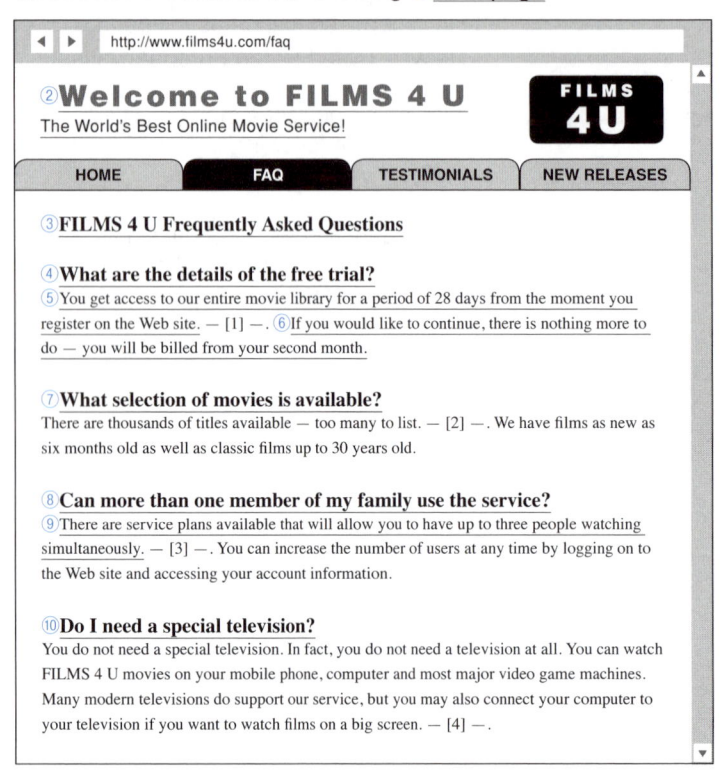

---

http://www.films4u.com/faq

② **Welcome to FILMS 4 U**
The World's Best Online Movie Service!

FILMS 4U

| HOME | FAQ | TESTIMONIALS | NEW RELEASES |

③ FILMS 4 U Frequently Asked Questions

④ What are the details of the free trial?
⑤ You get access to our entire movie library for a period of 28 days from the moment you register on the Web site. — [1] —. ⑥ If you would like to continue, there is nothing more to do — you will be billed from your second month.

⑦ What selection of movies is available?
There are thousands of titles available — too many to list. — [2] —. We have films as new as six months old as well as classic films up to 30 years old.

⑧ Can more than one member of my family use the service?
⑨ There are service plans available that will allow you to have up to three people watching simultaneously. — [3] —. You can increase the number of users at any time by logging on to the Web site and accessing your account information.

⑩ Do I need a special television?
You do not need a special television. In fact, you do not need a television at all. You can watch FILMS 4 U movies on your mobile phone, computer and most major video game machines. Many modern televisions do support our service, but you may also connect your computer to your television if you want to watch films on a big screen. — [4] —.

問題 1-4 は次のウェブページに関するものです。

---

http://www.films4u.com/faq
FILMS 4 U へようこそ
世界一のオンライン映画サービスです！

| ホーム | よくあるご質問 | お客さまの声 | 新作 |

FILMS 4 U よくあるご質問

無料お試しの詳細は？
ウェブサイトでご登録いただいた瞬間から28日間、当社の全映画ライブラリーをご利用いただけます。その後、当社のカタログの映画を観ることにもうご興味がなければ、視聴を中止することも可能です。継続を希望される場合には、それ以上していただくことは何もありません。2カ月目から請求書が送られます。

どんな映画のセレクションがありますか？
数千タイトルをご利用いただけます——列挙するには多過ぎるほどです。6カ月前の新作から30年前の名画までそろえています。

家族内で複数人がサービスを利用できますか？
同時に3人まで視聴できるサービスプランがあります。ウェブサイトにログオンしてアカウント情報にアクセスすれば、利用者の数はいつでも増やすことができます。

特別なテレビが必要ですか？
特別なテレビは必要ありません。実際には、テレビさえ必要ありません。FILMS 4 U の映画は、携帯電話、パソコン、そしてほとんどの主要なテレビゲーム機で視聴できます。多くの最新のテレビが当社のサービスに対応していますが、大画面で映画を観たい場合に、パソコンをテレビに接続することもできます

※訳中の青字部分は位置選択問題の正解を表しています（以下、同）

- **for a period of 〜**：〜の間
- **be billed**：請求される、請求書を送られる
- **list**：〜のリストを作る、〜を列挙する
- **simultaneously**：同時に
- **log on to 〜**：〜にログオンする

選択肢と訳

1.
For whom is the Web page intended?（誰のためのウェブページですか？）
(A) Newly hired sales staff（新しく採用された販売スタッフ）
(B) Customer support operators（顧客サポートのオペレーター）
(C) Installers of specialized devices（特別な機器の設置業者）
(D) People considering subscribing to a service
（サービスの申し込みを検討している人々）

□**installer**：設置業者　□**subscribe to**：〜に申し込む

2.
How long is the free membership period?（無料会員期間の長さはどのくらいですか？）
(A) Four weeks（4週間）
(B) Five weeks（5週間）
(C) Six weeks（6週間）
(D) Seven weeks（7週間）

3.
What is suggested about the service?（サービスについて何が分かりますか？）
(A) The only payment method is a credit card.（唯一の支払い方法はクレジットカードである）
(B) Different membership levels are available.
（異なる会員レベルが利用できる）
(C) Users must buy a device from FILMS 4 U.（ユーザーは FILMS 4 U から機材を購入しなくてはならない）
(D) There is a waiting period for connection.（接続を待つ期間がある）

4. NEW
In which of the positions marked [1], [2], [3], and [4] does the following sentence best belong?（[1]、[2]、[3]、[4]と記載された箇所のうち、次の文が入るのに最もふさわしいのはどれですか？）

"If you are no longer interested in viewing films from our catalog after that, you may cancel your subscription."（その後、当社のカタログの映画を観ることにもう興味がなければ、視聴を中止することも可能です）

(A) [1]　　　(C) [3]
(B) [2]　　　(D) [4]

解説

正解：(D)
指示文の①と本文の②から、この文書は、オンライン映画サービスを提供する FILMS 4 U のウェブページであり、表示されている画面は、FAQ のタブの色が他と違っていることと、画面上部の見出し③から、「よくあるご質問」のページだと分かる。太字で書かれた④、⑦、⑧、⑩の見出しは、映画サービスに関心を持った人がよく尋ねる質問だ。これらの理由からこのページは、サービスの申し込みを検討している人々のためのページだと判断できるので、正解は(D)。

正解：(A)
設問中の free membership（無料会員）がキーワード。答えのヒントはウェブページの④「無料お試しの詳細は？」にあるはずだ。⑤から、「28日間」無料で試すことができると分かる。28日間を4週間と言い換えた (A) が正解。TOEIC には、複雑な計算をしなければ解答できない問題は出題されないが、このように単純な置き換えが必要な場合は多い。

正解：(B)
サービスについては⑧「家族内で複数人がサービスを利用できますか？」の下に記載されている。「同時に3人まで視聴できるサービスプランがある」（⑨）とあることから、異なる会員レベルのサービスがあり、利用可能だと分かる。正解は (B)。

正解：(A)
新形式の位置選択問題。ターゲット文は、「その後、視聴を中止することが可能」という内容。ヒントになっているのは「その後」だ。この文を[1]に入れると、⑤「28日間、全映画ライブラリーにアクセスできる」に自然につながり、⑥「継続したければ、それ以上すべきことは何もない」という後ろの文と情報を対比させることができる。正解は (A)。

問題文と訳

Questions 5-8 refer to the following e-mail.

---

①To: Phil Graham <pgraham@gardengreen.com>
②From: Stacy Greene <sgreene@gardengreen.com>
Date: June 11
Subject: ③Business Trip June 19 - June 22

Dear Phil:

Let me congratulate you on an amazing first year. ④Your performance this year has been excellent and your coworkers and supervisors have had nothing but kind things to say about you.

⑤Ordinarily, we would not ask a relatively inexperienced employee to go on a business trip of this nature, but we're making an exception. — [1] —. As this will be your first business trip for the company, I think it is important to explain some of the requirements.

— [2] —. ⑥You are required to submit an expense report within a week of your return to Victoria. This must include receipts for your accommodations and meals. — [3] —. If you need to rent a car, you must choose the least expensive available vehicle for your needs. Fuel and other expenses must also be reported and supported by receipts from the respective sellers. Let me stress that you will not be reimbursed for any purchases for which you cannot produce a receipt.

— [4] —. ⑦We have already spoken about the goals of your trip and the written summary, which is due on the day of your return.

Sincerely,

⑧Stacy Greene

General Manager — Garden Green

問題 5-8 は次の E メールに関するものです。

宛先： Phil Graham <pgraham@gardengreen.com>
送信者： Stacy Greene <sgreene@gardengreen.com>
日付： 6月11日
件名： 6月19日～22日の出張

Phil へ

あなたの素晴らしい最初の1年にお祝いを言わせてください。今年のあなたの仕事ぶりは優秀で、同僚や上司があなたについて口にするのは好意的なことばかりです。

通常わが社は、比較的経験の浅い社員にこのような性質の出張に行くことはお願いしないのですが、特例を設けます。これはあなたの当社での初出張になるので、いくつかの要件について説明することが重要だと思います。

Victoria に戻ったら1週間以内に、経費報告書を提出してください。これには宿泊や食事の領収証を付ける必要があります。公共交通機関の乗車券は標準運賃で、時間、日付、移動の理由が全て記載されていなければなりません。もし車を借りる必要があれば、あなたのニーズに合い、利用できる中で一番安い車を選ばなくてはなりません。燃料やその他の経費も報告の必要があり、それぞれの業者からの領収証で裏付けられなくてはなりません。領収証のない購入については払い戻しを受けられないということを強調させてください。

出張の目的と、出張から戻る日が締め切りとなっている書面による概要報告については、すでにお話ししました。

敬具

Stacy Greene
本部長、Garden Green

□**congratulate ~ on ...**：～に…のことでお祝いを言う　□**supervisor**：監督者、上司　□**have nothing but ~**：～しかない、～ばかりである　□**ordinarily**：通常は、普段は　□**inexperienced**：経験の浅い　□**nature**：性質　□**make an exception**：例外を認める、特例を設ける　□**expense**：経費　□**receipt**：領収証、受領書　□**respective**：それぞれの　□**be reimbursed for ~**：～を払い戻される　□**general manager**：本部長

146

選択肢と訳

5.
What is indicated about Mr. Graham?(Graham さんについて何が示されていますか?)
(A) He does not live in Victoria. (Victoria には住んでいない)
(B) He will use his own vehicle. (自分の車を使うだろう)
(C) He has been evaluated highly. (高く評価されている)
(D) He is a manager of Garden Green. (Garden Green の部長である)

6.
What is suggested about the company?(その会社について何が分かりますか?)
(A) It specializes in imported goods. (輸入品を専門に扱う)
(B) It is looking for more local suppliers. (もっと地元の納入業者を探している)
(C) It provides employees with company vehicles. (従業員に社用車を提供する)
(D) It chooses experienced employees for important trips. (重要な出張には経験のある従業員を選ぶ)

7.
When is the deadline for a written summary of Mr. Graham's trip?(Graham さんの出張の書面による概要報告の締切はいつですか?)
(A) On June 11 (6月11日)
(B) On June 19 (6月19日)
(C) On June 22 (6月22日)
(D) On June 29 (6月29日)

8. NEW
In which of the positions marked [1], [2], [3], and [4] does the following sentence best belong?([1]、[2]、[3]、[4]と記載された箇所のうち、次の文が入るのに最もふさわしいのはどれですか?)

"Any tickets for public transport should be standard fare and the time, date and reason for your travel should be fully documented." (公共交通機関の乗車券は標準運賃で、時間、日付、移動の理由が全て記載されていなければなりません)

(A) [1]
(B) [2]
(C) [3]
(D) [4]

解説

正解: (C)
①から、設問文の Mr. Graham は E メールの受信者の Phil Graham 氏であり、メッセージの中では you(あなた)で表されていると分かる。第1段落の④で書き手は、「あなたの今年の仕事ぶりは優秀で、同僚や上司があなたについて口にするのは好意的なことばかりだ」と述べている。つまり、Graham 氏 は高く評価されているので、正解は (C)。(A) に関する情報は書かれていないが、「書かれていない」ということを確認するには時間がかかるので、迷ったらすぐに (B) 以降をチェックするべき。

正解: (D)
①と②のメールアドレスから、受信者の Phil Graham と送信者の Stacy Greene は同じ組織に属しており、⑧から、Greene 氏は、Garden Green の本部長だと分かる。Greene 氏は、⑤で「通常わが社は、比較的経験の浅い社員にこのような性質の出張へ行くことは依頼しない」と述べている。すなわち、会社は重要な出張には経験のある社員を選ぶことを暗示しているので、正解は (D)。

正解: (C)
設問中の written summary(書面による概要報告)は、⑦に登場し、その締め切りは「出張から戻る日である」と書かれている。E メールの件名③に、出張の期間は6月19日から6月22日までと示されているので、(C)「6月22日」が正解。

正解: (C)
ターゲット文は、「公共交通機関の乗車券は標準運賃で、利用日時と理由が記載されているべきである」という交通費の精算についての注意事項だ。出張中の経費に関する情報は、第3段落にまとめられている(⑥)。段落内には空所が2カ所あるが、[3]に問題文を入れると、報告書に含める他の情報(宿泊、食事代およびレンタカーに関する費用など)と公共交通機関の情報を並列させることができる。従って、正解は(C)。

問題文と訳

Questions 9-12 refer to the following information.

---

①Working and Cooperating Effectively

These days, the business world is very competitive. ②Many employees try to stand out as individuals, but modern employers evaluate employees' collaborative efforts even more highly. — [1] —.

It is often difficult to work in teams because many people tend to compete for the attention of upper management. On the other hand, it is very difficult to achieve excellent results on our own. — [2] —. Usually, however, ③it is through teamwork that most businesses succeed.

④This can only happen when you are aware of each other's projects, so good communication is necessary. ⑤Offer help to those who need it, ask for help from others and ⑥thank them in front of team members. — [3] —. People like to feel appreciated, and by sharing work, we are given many opportunities to express gratitude.

— [4] —. Remember that planning is of key importance. ⑦Keep a schedule of upcoming events and refer to it from time to time so that you are never surprised by a deadline. Every day, ⑧make a list of things that need to be done and check them off as you complete them. With effective time management, you will likely find that you have more free time every day.

問題 9-12 は次の情報に関するものです。

成果が出る協働

近年、ビジネスの世界は非常に競争が激しくなっています。多くの従業員は、個人として目立とうとしますが、現代の雇用主は従業員たちの協働努力をより高く評価します。

チームの中で働くのはしばしば困難なことです。多くの人が上層部の注目を引こうと競い合うからです。一方で、自分一人で素晴らしい成果を挙げるのは非常に困難です。しかしながら通常、ほとんどの企業はチームワークを通じて成功を収めます。

チームワークはお互いのプロジェクトをよく分かっていなければ実現しないことなので、十分な意思疎通が必要です。必要としている人には手助けを申し出、他者に助けを求め、チームのメンバーたちの前で感謝をしましょう。人は感謝されていると感じることを好むものです。そして仕事を共有することで、感謝の意を表す機会が多く得られます。

作業を共有すること以外で、仕事を期限内に済ませるためにできることが他にもいくつかあります。計画することは極めて重要だということをお忘れなく。今後のイベントを予定表に書き、時々それに注意を向けるようにすれば、締め切りに驚くことは決してないでしょう。毎日、やらなくてはいけないことのリストを作り、やり終えたら完了の印を入れましょう。時間をうまく管理することで、毎日もっと自由な時間を持てるようになります。

□**stand out**：目立つ、人目を引く　□**upper management**：上層部　□**gratitude**：感謝（の気持ち）　□**of key importance**：極めて重要で　□**keep a schedule of ~**：~を予定表に書く　□**upcoming**：近づきつつある、間もなく訪れる　□**refer to ~**：~に注意を向ける　□**from time to time**：時々　□**check ~ off**：~にチェック済みの印を入れる、~に完了のチェックを入れる

選択肢と訳

9.
According to the information, what is more important to employers?（情報によると、雇用主にとってより重要なのは何ですか？）
(A) Experience in a variety of positions（さまざまな職務での経験）
(B) The ability to cooperate with others（他者と協力する能力）
(C) A candidate's academic history（候補者の学歴）
(D) Finding ways to attract new customers（新規客を引きつける方法を見つけること）

10.
What is mentioned as an effective work practice?（成果が出る仕事の仕方として何が述べられていますか？）
(A) Working early in the morning（朝早くに働くこと）
(B) Taking occasional breaks（時々休憩すること）
(C) Completing large jobs first（大きい仕事から片付けること）
(D) Keeping coworkers informed（同僚に常に情報を与えること）

□**work practice**：仕事の習慣、仕事の仕方
□**occasional**：時折の、たまの　□**keep ~ informed**：~に報告する、~に情報提供する

11.
What advice is NOT provided in the information?（情報に含まれていないのはどの助言ですか？）
(A) Having a flexible schedule（融通のきくスケジュールを組むこと）
(B) Offering assistance（他の人たちに支援を申し出ること）
(C) Making a things-to-do list（やることのリストを作ること）
(D) Showing appreciation（感謝を示すこと）

□**things-to-do list**：やることのリスト

12. NEW
In which of the positions marked [1], [2], [3], and [4] does the following sentence best belong?（[1]、[2]、[3]、[4]と記載された箇所のうち、次の文が入るのに最もふさわしいのはどれですか？）

"Aside from sharing tasks, there are several other things you can do to get your work done on time."（作業を共有すること以外で、仕事を期限内に済ませるためにできることが他にもいくつかあります？）

(A) [1]　　(C) [3]
(B) [2]　　**(D) [4]**

□**aside from ~**：~は別として

解説

正解：(B)
この情報のタイトルは、①の「成果が出る協働」だ。第1段落の②で、「多くの従業員は個人として目立とうとするが、現代の雇用主は、従業員たちの協働しようとする努力をより高く評価する」と述べられている。つまり、この情報によれば、雇用主は他者と協力できる従業員の能力がより重要だと考えているので、(B) が正解。

正解：(D)
③で、「多くの企業は従業員のチームワークを通じて成功する」と述べている。続く第3段落④では、「チームワークはお互いのプロジェクトがよく分かっていなければ実現しないので、十分な意思疎通が必要だ」と記述している。これを「同僚に常に情報を与えること」と言い換えた(D) が正解。

正解：(A)
この情報の中で述べられていない助言を選ぶ NOT 問題。助言は命令文の形で示されることが多い。(B) は⑤の「必要としている人に手助けを申し出なさい」で、(C) は⑧の「しなければならないことのリストを作りましょう」で、(D) は⑥の「チーム・メンバーの前で感謝しなさい」でそれぞれ述べられている。スケジュールについての助言は、⑦に「今後のイベントを予定表に書く」とあるが、(A) は述べられていない。

正解：(D)
ターゲット文にある「作業を共有すること以外で」と、「遅れることなく仕事を済ませるためにできるいくつかの他のこと」がヒント。ターゲット文の前には「作業を共有すること」が書かれ、後ろには「いくつかのこと」が書かれているはずだ。[4]の前には「作業を共有すること」、後ろには遅れることなく仕事を済ませるためにできるいくつかのことが述べられているので、(D) が正解。

Part 7　① 位置選択問題

問題文と訳

Questions 13-16 refer to the following advertisement.

Lockheed Suits and Formalwear

① *Get the right fit with a tailor-made suit from Lockheed Suits!*

Don't trust your image to just anyone. Your sense of personal style should be reflected in the clothes you wear. — [1] —. There are items of clothing you choose off the rack, and there are items that should be as individual as you are. ②Owning a Lockheed suit has been a sign of financial and career success among the people of Chicago for more than 30 years. — [2] —.

Visit us on the Web at www.lockheedsafw.com, where you will ③see samples of our work, ④testimonials, and our ⑤full design selection. There is a huge range of options available including pocket shapes, coat length, and lining color. For out-of-town residents, we have even started an online ordering system, whereby you can input your measurements and requirements and have a suit shipped anywhere in the country at no extra cost. — [3] —. ⑥Having your signature or monogram stitched into the lining inside the lapel is a classy touch that our expert sewers can accomplish for only $50 more. — [4] —.

問題 **13-16** は次の広告に関するものです。

Lockheed Suits and Formalwear

Lockheed Suits のオーダーメード・スーツでジャストフィット！

あなたのイメージは誰にでも任せていいものではありません。あなたのファッションセンスはあなたが着る服に表れます。既製品から選ぶ服もあれば、あなたそのもののような個性的な服もあるべきです。Lockheed のスーツを所有することは、Chicago の人々の間では30年以上にわたって、経済的・職業的な成功の証しとなっています。それでいながら、ぴったり合うオーダーメードのスーツが、大手デザイン・ブランドのものより安いこともあるのです。

当店のウェブサイト www.lockheedsafw.com を訪れていただけば、当店の製品のサンプル、お客さまの声、全デザイン集をご覧いただけます。ポケットの形、コートの丈、裏地の色といった非常に多くのオプションがございます。町の外にお住まいの方々のために、寸法と必要事項を入力いただけば全国どこへでも追加料金なしでお送りする、オンラインでの注文システムも始めました。お名前またはモノグラムを襟の内側の裏地に刺しゅうすることで高級な仕上がりになります。当店の熟練の職人がわずか50ドルの追加料金で仕上げます。

☐ **fit**：(服などが) ぴったり合っていること　☐ **tailor-made**：オーダーメードの　☐ **trust ~ to …**：~を…に任せる　☐ **style**：ファッション　☐ **be reflected in ~**：~に反映される、~に表れる　☐ **choose ~ off the rack**：~を既製品から選ぶ　☐ **testimonials**：お客さまの声　☐ **lining**：裏地　☐ **out-of-town**：町の外からの、市外の　☐ **whereby**：(それによって) ~するところの　☐ **measurement**：寸法、サイズ　☐ **at no extra cost**：追加料金なしで　☐ **monogram**：モノグラム ※イニシャルなどの文字を図案化したもの　☐ **stitch into ~**：~を縫い込む　☐ **lapel**：(下) 襟　☐ **classy**：高級な、一流の　☐ **sewer**：裁縫をする人、仕立て職人　☐ **accomplish**：~を仕上げる

150

選択肢と訳

13.
What is most likely true about Lockheed Suits?
(Lockheed Suits について最も正しいと思われるものは何ですか？)
(A) It is based in Chicago. (Chicago を本拠としている)
(B) It employs famous designers. (有名なデザイナーを採用している)
(C) It is a family-owned business. (同族経営企業である)
(D) It keeps records of clients' measurements. (顧客のサイズの記録を残している)

□**be based in ～**：～を本拠としている　□**family-owned business**：同族経営企業、ファミリー企業

14.
What is NOT mentioned as being available on the Web site? (ウェブサイトで見られるものとして述べられていないのは何ですか？)
(A) Work samples（製品の見本）
(B) Customer reviews（顧客のレビュー）
(C) Style choices（スタイルの選択肢）
(D) Store locations（店の場所）

15.
According to the advertisement, what service does Lockheed Suits provide for an additional fee?（広告によれば、Lockheed Suitsは追加料金でどんなサービスを提供しますか？）
(A) Domestic shipping（国内発送）
(B) Monogram stitching（モノグラムの刺しゅう）
(C) Colored lining（色付きの裏地）
(D) Fashion consulting（ファッションの相談）

16. NEW
In which of the positions marked [1], [2], [3], and [4] does the following sentence best belong? ([1]、[2]、[3]、[4] と記載された箇所のうち、次の文が入るのに最もふさわしいのはどれですか？)

"Nevertheless, a tailor-made suit that fits perfectly can cost less than one from a major design house."
(それでいながら、ぴったり合うオーダーメードのスーツが、大手デザイン・ブランドのものより安いこともあるのです)

(A) [1]　　　　　(C) [3]
(B) [2]　　　　(D) [4]

□**house**：企業、ブランド

解説

正解：(A)
店名の下にある①から、Lockheed Suits and Formalwear がオーダーメード・スーツを作る店だと分かる。②の「Chicagoの人々の間では、30年以上にわたって、Lockheedのスーツを所有することが経済的・職業的な成功の証し」との記述から、Lockheed Suits and Formalwear はChicagoにある店だと推測できる。正解は (A)。

正解：(D)
ウェブサイトに関する情報は、第2段落にある。ウェブサイトで見ることができるのは、③「製品のサンプル」、④「お客さまの声」、⑤「全デザイン集」の3つだ。③のサンプルは (A) に該当し、④は (B) に、⑤は (C) にそれぞれ当てはまる。ウェブサイトで見られるものとして述べられていないのは店の場所なので、正解は (D)。

正解：(B)
設問文の an additional fee（追加料金）がヒント。only $50 more（わずか50ドルの追加料金）を含む⑥に、「名前かモノグラムを襟の内側の裏地に刺しゅうすることで高級な仕上がりになり、わずか50ドルの追加料金で当店の熟練の職人がそれを仕上げます」と書かれている。正解は「モノグラムの刺しゅう」で (B)。

正解：(B)
ターゲット文の Nevertheless（それにもかかわらず）がヒント。Nevertheless 以降の「オーダーメードのスーツが安いこともある」という文とは意味が対比する文が前にあるはず。[2]の前の文は、オーダーメードの「Lockheedのスーツを所有することが経済的・職業的な成功の証し」、すなわち、「オーダーメードは高いはず」ということを示唆しており、ターゲット文の内容とは対照的である。よって、文を入れるのに最も適した位置は[2]、つまり正解は (B)。

問題文と訳

Questions 17-20 refer to the following article.

Drummond is Drumming up Business

September 1—The first stages of Drummond City's push to attract greater visitor numbers and generate revenue for local businesses are already going ahead. ①Over the past three years, discussions and planning meetings have been held at City Hall with many officials making trips to major tourist destinations such as Paris, Rome, and New York to learn what it is that makes these places attractive to travelers.

②A number of attributes were identified and debated by a committee initially headed by Anthony Caldwell. ③Mr. Caldwell had to leave the committee to take up his political campaign. — [1] —. Nevertheless, the committee's proposals are still being taken very seriously, ④the first of which is the publicly subsidized restoration of the Lennon Building on William Street. ⑤During his campaign for the position of mayor of Drummond City, Mr. Caldwell indicated that significant funds would be spent on this cause. ⑥This resulted in an overwhelming political victory, and according to his supporters, he intends to live up to the promises he made. — [2] —.

⑦Other targets for beautification include the riverfront area along Harding Street and the old sandstone buildings in Hansen Street and Douglass Street. — [3] —.

— [4] —. In addition to these projects, there are other changes on their way to Drummond City. There will be new ordinances forcing companies to keep the streets clean as well as incentives for projects that enhance the city's cultural allure.

問題 17-20 は次の記事に関するものです。

Drummond市 が事業を拡大中

9月1日―より多くの観光客を引きつけて地元企業の収益を生み出すための、Drummond City の取り組みの第1段階はすでに進行中だ。過去3年にわたって、市役所では討論会や企画会議が開かれ、何が旅行者にとって魅力的な土地にするのかを学ぶため、多くの職員が Paris、Rome、New York といった有名な観光目的地を訪れた。

当初 Anthony Caldwell が率いていた委員会により、多くの特徴が特定され議論された。Caldwell 氏は自身の政治運動に着手するため、委員会を去らなくてはならなかった。しかしながら、委員会の提言は現在も非常に真摯に受け止められており、その1つ目となるのが、William Street にある Lennon Building の公的補助を受けた修復である。Drummond City の市長職を目指す選挙運動の期間中、Caldwell 氏は多額の資金がこの目的に投入されることを表明した。これが圧倒的な政治的勝利をもたらしたが、支持者によれば、Caldwell 氏は自分がした約束を果たすつもりでいるという。

その他の美化の対象には、Harding Street 沿いの河岸地区と、Hansen Street と Douglass Street の古い砂岩ビル群がある。これらの場所は、訪問者が好みそうな歴史的意義と自然の魅力を備えている。

これらのプロジェクトに加え、Drummond City には他にも変化が訪れようとしている。通りをきれいに保つことを企業に義務付ける新条例と、市の文化的魅力を向上させるプロジェクトに対する奨励金が制定される。

□**drum up**：～を拡大する　□**push**：活動、行動　□**generate**：～を生み出す　□**revenue**：収益、収入　□**tourist destination**：観光目的地、観光スポット　□**attribute**：特質、特性　□**be identified**：特定される　□**committee**：委員会　□**take up ～**：～に着手する、～に取り組む　□**subsidized**：補助を受けている　□**restoration**：修復、復旧　□**significant**：大幅の、かなりの　□**cause**：理由、大義　□**overwhelming**：圧倒的な　□**live up to ～**：(約束を)果たす　□**beautification**：美化　□**riverfront**：河岸(の)　□**sandstone**：砂岩　□**ordinance**：条例　□**incentive**：報奨金、奨励金　□**enhance**：～を向上させる、～を増進させる　□**allure**：魅力

選択肢と訳

17.
What is the article mainly about?（主に何に関する記事ですか？）

(A) Proposals to improve the appearance of a city.（市の景観を改善する提案）
(B) Choosing members to serve on a committee.（委員会の一員として働くメンバーの選出）
(C) The cost of upgrading local infrastructure.（地元地域のインフラを向上させる費用）
(D) Planning a musical festival to attract guests.（客を集めるための音楽祭の計画）

□**serve on ～**：～の一員として働く
□**infrastructure**：基盤、インフラ

18.
What is suggested about the Lennon Building?（Lennon Building についてどんなことが分かりますか？）
(A) It was one of the first buildings in Drummond City.（Drummond City の初めてのビルの1つ）
(B) It is a popular destination among tourists.（旅行者に人気のある観光スポット）
(C) Its reconstruction may be carried out with public funds.（その修復は公的資金で行われる可能性がある）
(D) It has been chosen as a venue for committee meetings.（委員会の会合の会場に選ばれた）

□**venue**：開催地、会場

19.
What is implied about Mr. Caldwell?（Caldwell さんについて何が示唆されていますか？）
(A) He has worked in other cities.（別の市で働いたことがある）
(B) He is mayor of Drummond City.（Drummond City の市長である）
(C) He is opposed to increased spending.（支出の増加に反対している）
(D) He was invited to see European cities.（ヨーロッパの都市の視察に招待された）

20. NEW
In which of the positions marked [1], [2], [3], and [4] does the following sentence best belong?（[1]、[2]、[3]、[4] と記載された箇所のうち、次の文が入るのに最もふさわしいのはどれですか？）

"These locations have historical significance and natural charm that will make them popular with visitors."（これらの場所は、訪問者が好みそうな歴史的意義と自然の魅力を備えている）

(A) [1]
(B) [2]
(C) [3]
(D) [4]

解説

正解：(A)
第1段落の①では、観光客を引きつけるため、「Drummond City が取り組みを続けている」ことが書かれ、第2段落ではビルの修復について述べられている。第3段落では、そのビル以外の美化対象が挙げられ、第4段落では道をきれいに保つことや市の文化的魅力を向上させるプロジェクトが書かれている。これらのヒントから、この記事は市の景観を改善する提案に関する記事だと分かるので、正解は (A)。

正解：(C)
Lennon Building については、第2段落の④で述べられている。which の先行詞は the committee's proposals（委員会の提言）だ。「委員会の提言の1つ目がWilliam Street にある Lennon Building の公的補助を受けた修復だ」と書かれているので、ビルの修復が公的資金で行われる可能性があると分かる。正解は (C)。

正解：(B)
第2段落の②には、Caldwell 氏は「初期に委員会を率いた」と記述されている。それに続く③には、Caldwell 氏が政治運動に着手するため委員会を去ったこと、⑤と⑥には、Caldwell 氏が Drummond 市長を目指す選挙運動中に、ビルの修復に資金投入を約束し、政治的勝利を果たしたことが書かれている。これにより現在 Caldwell 氏は Drummond City の市長だと考えられるので、正解は (B)。

□**above-mentioned**：前述の

正解：(C)
ターゲット文にある These locations が決定的なヒント。直前に複数の場所が述べられているのは[3]だ。⑦で、「美化の対象」として、河岸地区と砂岩ビル群が述べられており、それらについて、ターゲット文が説明を加えている。よって、[3]の位置にターゲット文を入れると情報の流れが自然になるため、(C) が正解。なお、[4]は異なる段落にあり、別のトピックを扱っているため不適切だ。

「チャット系」はこんな形式！

1回のテストに2セット出題される
- シングルパッセージに2セット登場する。設問は2問と4問のパターンがある
- 設問2問のパターンでは2人の間のやりとりで、設問4問のパターンは3人以上の人々の間のやりとり
- 意図問題が1セットに1問出題される

見た目が特徴的
- デザインは、スマホ、タブレット、パソコンの画面を思わせるものから罫線で囲んだだけのシンプルなものまでバリエーションがある。発言者の名前、発言の時刻が記されているので認識しやすい
- 文書は携帯メールやオンラインチャットのやりとり

以前よりカジュアルな英語も登場
- これまでのリーディングセクションにはあまり登場しなかった、口語的な表現やフラグメント（「断片」。完全な文の形を成していない発言）も登場する

解説　落としてはいけないサービス問題！

　スマートフォンやタブレットを思わせる画面など親しみが持てるデザインの効果もあってか、実際に受験した人たちの感想も、「解きやすい」「簡単」いうものが多いようです。内容も、長文読解という感覚は薄く、文字化された会話という感覚なので読みやすいはずです。それだけに落としてはいけない問題であるとも言えます。

解説　意図問題がある

　Part 7ではこの「チャット系」で意図問題が出題されます。発言の意図・動機を問う問題であることは、Part 3、4と同じです。設問に発言者の名前と時刻が入っている点、when xx says ... の says が writes になっている点が、リスニングセクションと異なります。Part 7独自のフォーマットです。

「チャット系」攻略の基本

● 飛ばさずにチャットを全部読む

　テキスト量が少ないもの（設問が2問のもの）は、チャットの最初から最後まで一気に読み、読み終えてから2問連続で解くのがお勧めです。内容を問う問題1問と意図問題1問しかない場合に、設問に関係ありそうな場所のみを読むのはお勧めできません。複数の場所に散らばっているヒントを統合して解かなくてはいけない問題もあるからです。結果論として「ココだけを読めば解けた」ということはあるにしても、そういうアプローチは、新形式ではマイナス面が大きいと思ってください。

　テキスト量が多いもの（設問が4問のもの）もチャット全体を読む必要があるという点は同じです。ただ、情報を記憶に留めるのが難しくなるので、「一気」に読めない人は次のような解き方を試してみてください。
1問目の設問を頭に入れ、そのヒントを見つけるためにチャットを頭から読む（たとえ序盤に設問の主語が登場しないとしても）
　↓
ヒントらしきものが見つかったら、そこを少し通り過ぎるところまで読んで解答する
　↓
2問目の設問を頭に入れて、そのヒントを少し通り過ぎるところまで読んで解答する
…この繰り返しです。例えば意図問題の設問に「午後3時58分に…」と書いてあったら、今解いた問題のヒントから3時58分の発言までの間にある情報を飛ばして読みたくなるかもしれません。でも、その間のやりとりも必ず全部読んでください。3時58分の発言にそのヒントがあるわけではありません。ヒントとなる情報は、3時58分より前から始まっているはずです。

● 意図問題は丁寧に

　このチャット系の意図問題では、日常でよく使われる口語表現（慣用表現に近いようなものまで）がターゲット文として出題される可能性がPart 3、4よりも高めです。さらに、Part 3、4の意図問題より、不正解の選択肢を消去しにくい傾向があります。例えば、次のような問題と選択肢のセットです。

　At 10:45 A.M., what does Mr. Maeda mean when he writes, "大丈夫"?（午前10時45分に、Maedaさんが書いている「大丈夫」は何を意図していますか？）
　(A) 体調が良い。
　(B) お金を十分に持っている。
　(C) 時間に間に合う。
　(D) 申し出を断っている。

Part 3、4の意図問題では、選択肢の中の大抵2つは、ターゲット文を文字通り解釈したようなあからさまな「ニセモノ」でした（P. 14-15の「たまらん」の例を思い出してください）。でも上の選択肢には、一瞬で排除できそうなものが見当たりません。ただし、チャットを丁寧に読みさえすれば解ける問題です。丁寧さは要求されるものの、決して難しいものではないということを忘れないで取り組んでください。

Part 7 ②チャット系 ドリル

1セット / トータル 20分　次の文書を読んで内容に関する問題に答えよう。

Questions 21-22 refer to the following text-message chain.

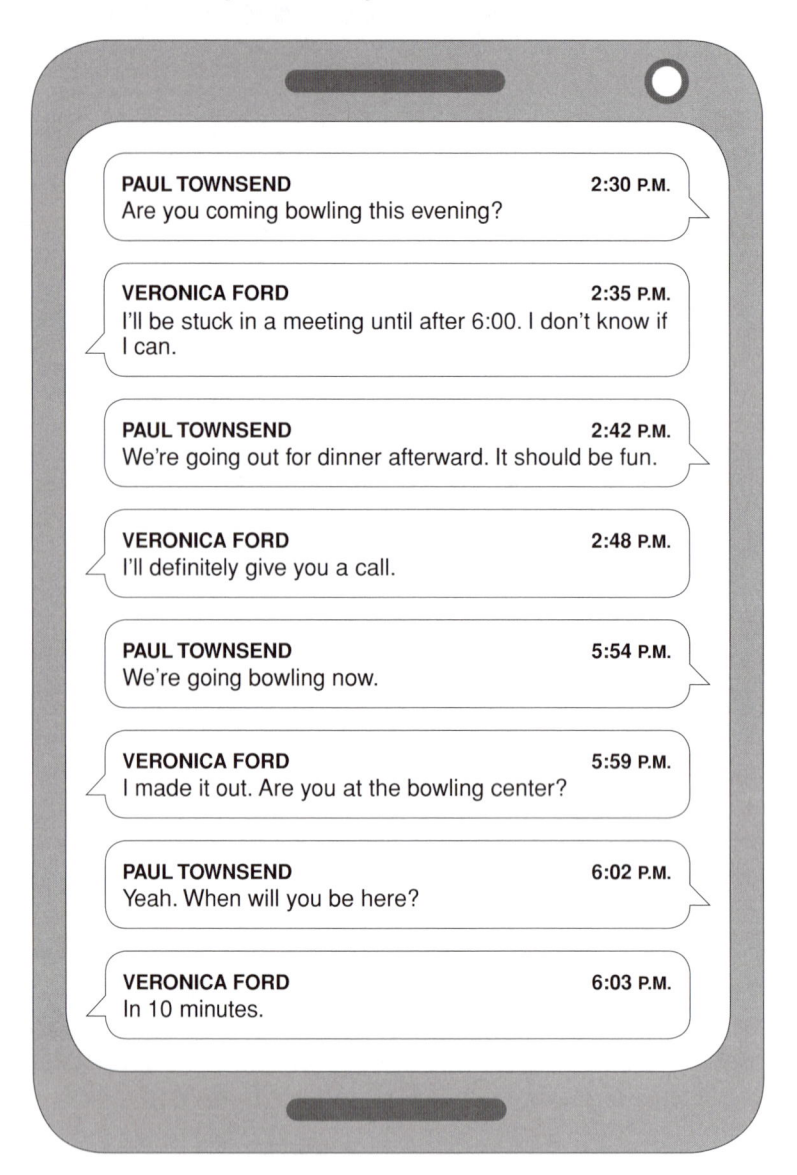

PAUL TOWNSEND　　　　　　　　　　　　　　2:30 P.M.
Are you coming bowling this evening?

VERONICA FORD　　　　　　　　　　　　　　2:35 P.M.
I'll be stuck in a meeting until after 6:00. I don't know if I can.

PAUL TOWNSEND　　　　　　　　　　　　　　2:42 P.M.
We're going out for dinner afterward. It should be fun.

VERONICA FORD　　　　　　　　　　　　　　2:48 P.M.
I'll definitely give you a call.

PAUL TOWNSEND　　　　　　　　　　　　　　5:54 P.M.
We're going bowling now.

VERONICA FORD　　　　　　　　　　　　　　5:59 P.M.
I made it out. Are you at the bowling center?

PAUL TOWNSEND　　　　　　　　　　　　　　6:02 P.M.
Yeah. When will you be here?

VERONICA FORD　　　　　　　　　　　　　　6:03 P.M.
In 10 minutes.

---

21. Why did Mr. Townsend send the text message?

(A) To invite a colleague to a gathering
(B) To schedule a meeting
(C) To request assistance with some work
(D) To recommend a restaurant

22. At 5:59 P.M., what does Ms. Ford mean when she writes, "I made it out"?

(A) She has filled out a form.
(B) She has drawn up an invoice.
(C) She was able to understand a message.
(D) She has left a meeting.

Questions 23-24 refer to the following text messages.

WI YING WANG   3:12 P.M.

Did you hear that Mr. Gavin is coming back from his trip to London early?

COLE HOLDEN   3:14 P.M.

No! When is he back?

WI YING WANG   3:15 P.M.

Tomorrow. Apparently, the clients signed immediately and he doesn't need to do any more work there.

COLE HOLDEN   3:15 P.M.

How about that!

WI YING WANG   3:16 P.M.

Yeah! I know. I'm so glad. We really need him to help with our latest ad campaign.

COLE HOLDEN   3:25 P.M.

Are you going to meet him at the airport tomorrow morning?

WI YING WANG   3:30 P.M.

I don't think so. He gets in really early. He'll just take a taxi, I'm sure.

COLE HOLDEN   3:31 P.M.

OK, let me know if you need me to go. I don't mind.

---

23. What is mentioned about Mr. Gavin?
(A) He will return from a trip ahead of schedule.
(B) He works in the London office.
(C) He is a company president.
(D) He has requested a pickup.

24. At 3:15 P.M., why does Mr. Holden write, "How about that"?
(A) He would like to hear an opinion.
(B) He is pleasantly surprised.
(C) He is making a suggestion.
(D) He will demonstrate a tool.

GO ON TO THE NEXT PAGE

Questions 25-26 refer to the following text messages.

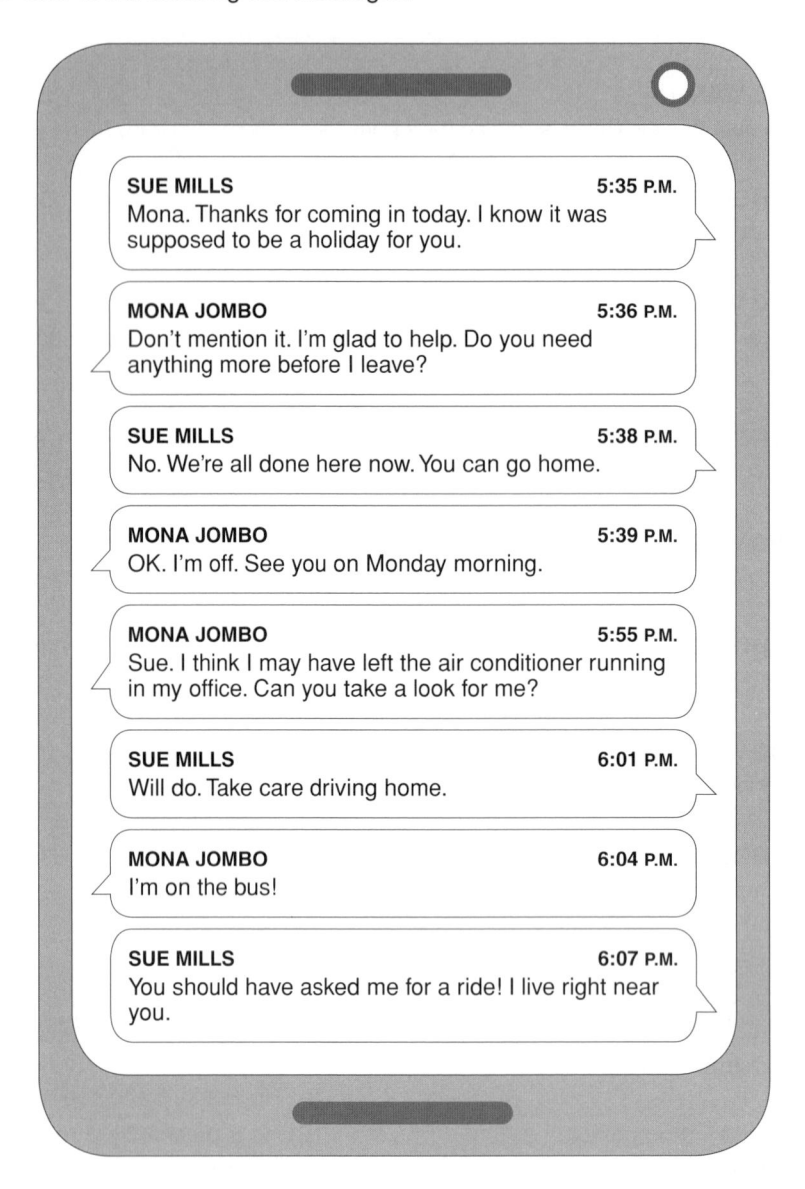

SUE MILLS — 5:35 P.M.
Mona. Thanks for coming in today. I know it was supposed to be a holiday for you.

MONA JOMBO — 5:36 P.M.
Don't mention it. I'm glad to help. Do you need anything more before I leave?

SUE MILLS — 5:38 P.M.
No. We're all done here now. You can go home.

MONA JOMBO — 5:39 P.M.
OK. I'm off. See you on Monday morning.

MONA JOMBO — 5:55 P.M.
Sue. I think I may have left the air conditioner running in my office. Can you take a look for me?

SUE MILLS — 6:01 P.M.
Will do. Take care driving home.

MONA JOMBO — 6:04 P.M.
I'm on the bus!

SUE MILLS — 6:07 P.M.
You should have asked me for a ride! I live right near you.

---

25. At 5:39 P.M., what does Ms. Jombo mean when she writes, "I'm off"?

(A) She is on holiday.
(B) She is about to leave.
(C) She has gotten off a bus.
(D) She does not have any work scheduled.

26. What is implied about Ms. Mills?

(A) She is in charge of building maintenance.
(B) She has known Ms. Jombo for a long time.
(C) She drives to work.
(D) She will work extra hours tonight.

Questions 27-28 refer to the following text-message chain.

LIAM HILLS   9:50 A.M.

I'll be back in the office in about 20 minutes. I've been at the advertising agency watching the promotional video we commissioned.

IBU KANZAKI   9:51 A.M.

How did you find it?

LIAM HILLS   9:53 A.M.

It was well done, but a bit too long. I don't think they focused on the functions enough.

IBU KANZAKI   9:53 A.M.

OK. Did you give them some pointers?

LIAM HILLS   9:54 A.M.

Not yet. I'm bringing a copy back to the office for everyone to look at. I want to hear a range of opinions before we change anything.

IBU KANZAKI   9:59 A.M.

Good idea. Shall I arrange a meeting in the conference room or something?

LIAM HILLS   10:02 A.M.

Would you? That'd be great. Around 11:00.

IBU KANZAKI   10:03 A.M.

No problem.

---

27. At 9:51 A.M., why does Ms. Kanzaki write, "How did you find it"?

(A) She wonders how Mr. Hills got to an office.
(B) She assumed that a device had been misplaced.
(C) She is interested in Mr. Hills' opinion of a video.
(D) She is glad that a lost item has been located.

28. What will staff members most likely do at 11:00 A.M.?

(A) Choose a promotional agency
(B) Evaluate some advertising
(C) Attend a performance review
(D) Discuss recent sales figures

Questions 29-32 refer to the following online chat discussion.

Walter Gibson [1:20 P.M.]:		Has anyone seen a brown briefcase lying around? A guest named Helga Brent claims to have left it in the lobby.
Judy Bradbury [1:21 P.M.]:		I'm in the lobby now and I can't see it anywhere. Can you give me any more information?
Walter Gibson [1:21 P.M.]:		Apparently, she was sitting in one of the armchairs. But she also went to the restaurant as well as the restrooms so it could be anywhere. She's returning from the station to pick it up. Judy, can you check the bathrooms next?
Alia Kahn [1:22 P.M.]:		Is there any chance she left it in her room? If you give me the room number, I'll go and check.
Walter Gibson [1:22 P.M.]:		Thanks, Alia. It was 804.
Krishna Rao [1:25 P.M.]:		I'm checking the restaurant now. But it doesn't seem to be here.
Alia Kahn [1:28 P.M.]:		Found it. It was in the closet. There was a used towel over it. I'll bring it down to the lobby now. I hope she makes her train.
Walter Gibson [1:30 P.M.]:		Great news! Good work, Alia. Hurry down, she doesn't have much time.
Krishna Rao [1:32 P.M.]:		Well spotted, Alia!
Walter Gibson [1:35 P.M.]:		Judy isn't reading these messages. I'd better go and tell her to stop looking.

29. Where do the writers most likely work?
(A) In a furniture store
(B) In a hotel
(C) In a train station
(D) In a storage facility

30. What does Mr. Gibson write about Ms. Brent?
(A) She has left her phone behind.
(B) She is a member of the staff.
(C) She forgot to leave her contact details.
(D) She is on her way back.

31. At 1:25 P.M., what does Mr. Rao mean when he writes, "it doesn't seem to be here"?
(A) He cannot find what he is looking for.
(B) Some damage has been repaired perfectly.
(C) An event appears to have been rescheduled.
(D) A location is not marked on a map.

32. What will Mr. Gibson most likely do next?
(A) Clean a closet
(B) Go to the bathrooms
(C) Cancel a reservation
(D) Organize a meeting

Questions 33-36 refer to the following online chat.

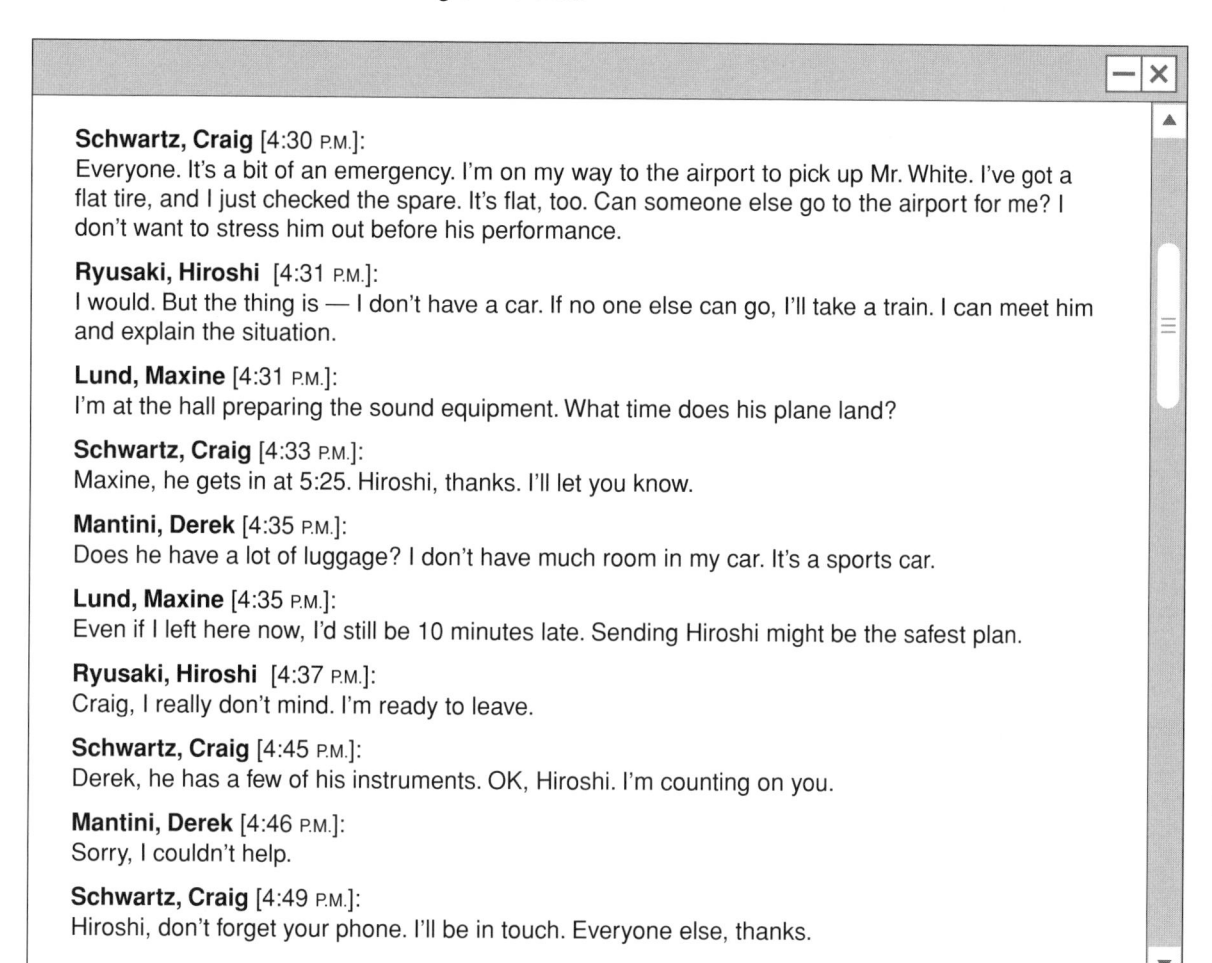

Schwartz, Craig [4:30 P.M.]:
Everyone. It's a bit of an emergency. I'm on my way to the airport to pick up Mr. White. I've got a flat tire, and I just checked the spare. It's flat, too. Can someone else go to the airport for me? I don't want to stress him out before his performance.

Ryusaki, Hiroshi [4:31 P.M.]:
I would. But the thing is — I don't have a car. If no one else can go, I'll take a train. I can meet him and explain the situation.

Lund, Maxine [4:31 P.M.]:
I'm at the hall preparing the sound equipment. What time does his plane land?

Schwartz, Craig [4:33 P.M.]:
Maxine, he gets in at 5:25. Hiroshi, thanks. I'll let you know.

Mantini, Derek [4:35 P.M.]:
Does he have a lot of luggage? I don't have much room in my car. It's a sports car.

Lund, Maxine [4:35 P.M.]:
Even if I left here now, I'd still be 10 minutes late. Sending Hiroshi might be the safest plan.

Ryusaki, Hiroshi [4:37 P.M.]:
Craig, I really don't mind. I'm ready to leave.

Schwartz, Craig [4:45 P.M.]:
Derek, he has a few of his instruments. OK, Hiroshi. I'm counting on you.

Mantini, Derek [4:46 P.M.]:
Sorry, I couldn't help.

Schwartz, Craig [4:49 P.M.]:
Hiroshi, don't forget your phone. I'll be in touch. Everyone else, thanks.

---

33. Why did Mr. Schwartz start the chat?
    (A) To correct an error
    (B) To provide an update
    (C) To seek assistance
    (D) To praise a colleague

34. Who most likely is Mr. White?
    (A) An important contributor
    (B) A product reviewer
    (C) A returning colleague
    (D) A visiting musician

35. At 4:33 P.M., what does Mr. Schwartz imply when he writes, "I'll let you know"?
    (A) An arrival time may change.
    (B) He can answer a question when he has more time.
    (C) He will wait to see if there is a better offer.
    (D) There is some confidential information to share.

36. Who will most likely meet Mr. White at the airport?
    (A) Hiroshi Ryusaki
    (B) Maxine Lund
    (C) Craig Schwartz
    (D) Derek Mantini

GO ON TO THE NEXT PAGE

Questions 37-40 refer to the following online chat discussion.

Greg Black [9:20 A.M.]:		Does anyone have time to give me a hand setting up the tent?
Ang Bae [9:21 A.M.]:		Sorry Greg, I'm at the supplier getting all the beverages. I won't be there for another hour.
Adele Vuko [9:22 A.M.]:		I'm running a little behind schedule myself. One of the food warmers is broken and I've had to rent one for the day. I'll call you when I get there.
Greg Black [9:22 A.M.]:		OK, thanks, guys. Lachlan, how about you?
Lachlan Trieu [9:25 A.M.]:		Sorry about the delay. Sure. I had to pick up a few of the waiters on the way to the client, but we'll be there well before 10 o'clock. With all of us there, it won't take any time at all.
Greg Black [9:30 A.M.]:		That's a relief. I'll start unpacking the truck while I'm waiting for you to get here.
Adele Vuko [9:32 A.M.]:		We have plenty of time yet. Guests won't arrive until 11 A.M.
Greg Black [9:34 A.M.]:		You're right. It's only 9:30 now, but I'm just a bit anxious after last time.
Adele Vuko [9:36 A.M.]:		Don't remind me.

37. What kind of business do the writers most likely work for?
(A) An interior decorator
(B) A catering firm
(C) A financial institution
(D) A tour company

38. What does Mr. Black write that he will do?
(A) Redesign a floor plan
(B) Contact a business associate
(C) Unload equipment from a vehicle
(D) Write a review of a service

39. What time will the visitors arrive?
(A) At 9:30 A.M.
(B) At 10:00 A.M.
(C) At 11:00 A.M.
(D) At 11:30 A.M.

40. At 9:36 A.M., what does Ms. Vuko imply when she writes, "Don't remind me"?
(A) She knows what she has to do.
(B) Another staff member is responsible.
(C) She is not required to attend an event.
(D) A previous job did not go smoothly.

Questions 41-44 refer to the following online chat.

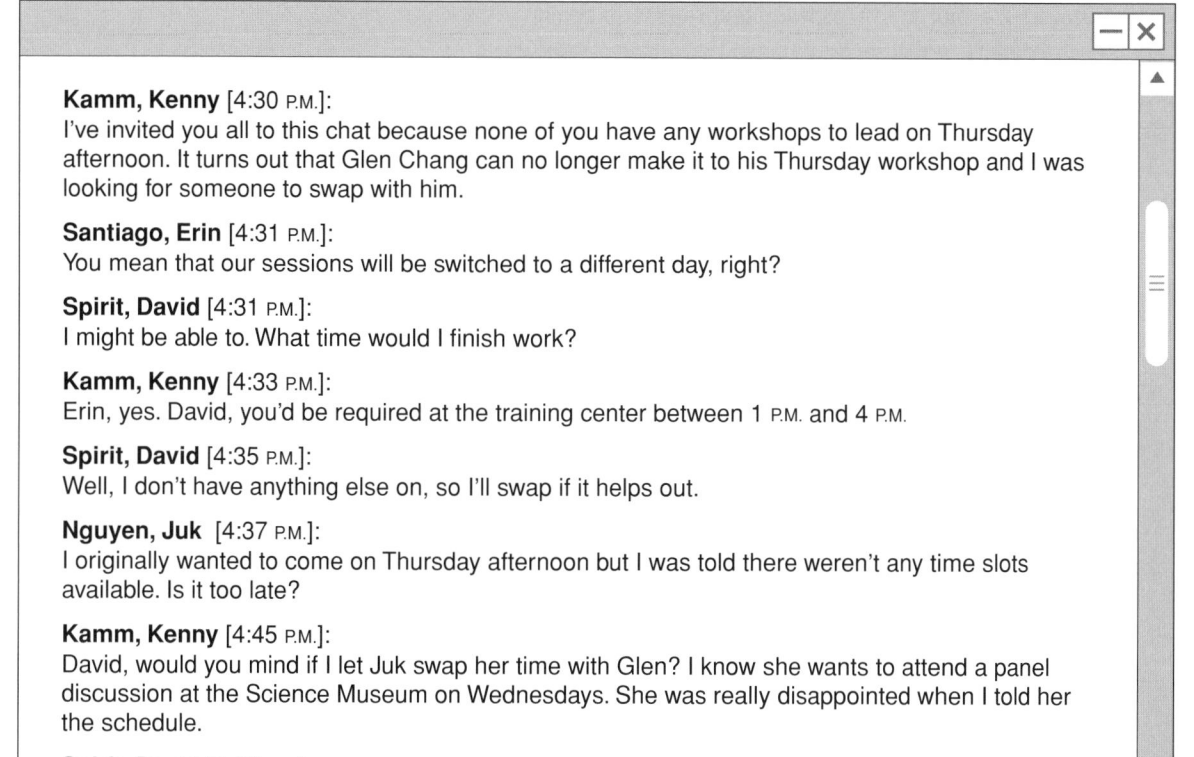

Kamm, Kenny [4:30 P.M.]:
I've invited you all to this chat because none of you have any workshops to lead on Thursday afternoon. It turns out that Glen Chang can no longer make it to his Thursday workshop and I was looking for someone to swap with him.

Santiago, Erin [4:31 P.M.]:
You mean that our sessions will be switched to a different day, right?

Spirit, David [4:31 P.M.]:
I might be able to. What time would I finish work?

Kamm, Kenny [4:33 P.M.]:
Erin, yes. David, you'd be required at the training center between 1 P.M. and 4 P.M.

Spirit, David [4:35 P.M.]:
Well, I don't have anything else on, so I'll swap if it helps out.

Nguyen, Juk [4:37 P.M.]:
I originally wanted to come on Thursday afternoon but I was told there weren't any time slots available. Is it too late?

Kamm, Kenny [4:45 P.M.]:
David, would you mind if I let Juk swap her time with Glen? I know she wants to attend a panel discussion at the Science Museum on Wednesdays. She was really disappointed when I told her the schedule.

Spirit, David [4:46 P.M.]:
Of course. I'm glad things worked out, Juk.

Chang, Glen [4:49 P.M.]:
Thanks everyone. I really appreciate this!

---

41. What is Mr. Kamm most likely in charge of?
   (A) A training program
   (B) A panel discussion
   (C) A recruitment event
   (D) A research project

42. What does Mr. Spirit write about his Thursday schedule?
   (A) He needs to check with a supervisor.
   (B) He is free in the afternoon.
   (C) He will take time off.
   (D) He cannot change it.

43. Who will most likely take the Thursday time slot?
   (A) Glen Chang
   (B) Erin Santiago
   (C) David Spirit
   (D) Juk Nguyen

44. At 4:45 P.M., why does Mr. Kamm write, "She was really disappointed when I told her the schedule"?
   (A) Ms. Nguyen was forced to change her plans.
   (B) Ms. Nguyen was asked to work late at night.
   (C) Ms. Nguyen's workload was too heavy.
   (D) Ms. Nguyen's travel time was made longer.

Part 7 ②チャット系　ドリルの解答・解説

問題文

Questions 21-22 refer to the following text-message chain.

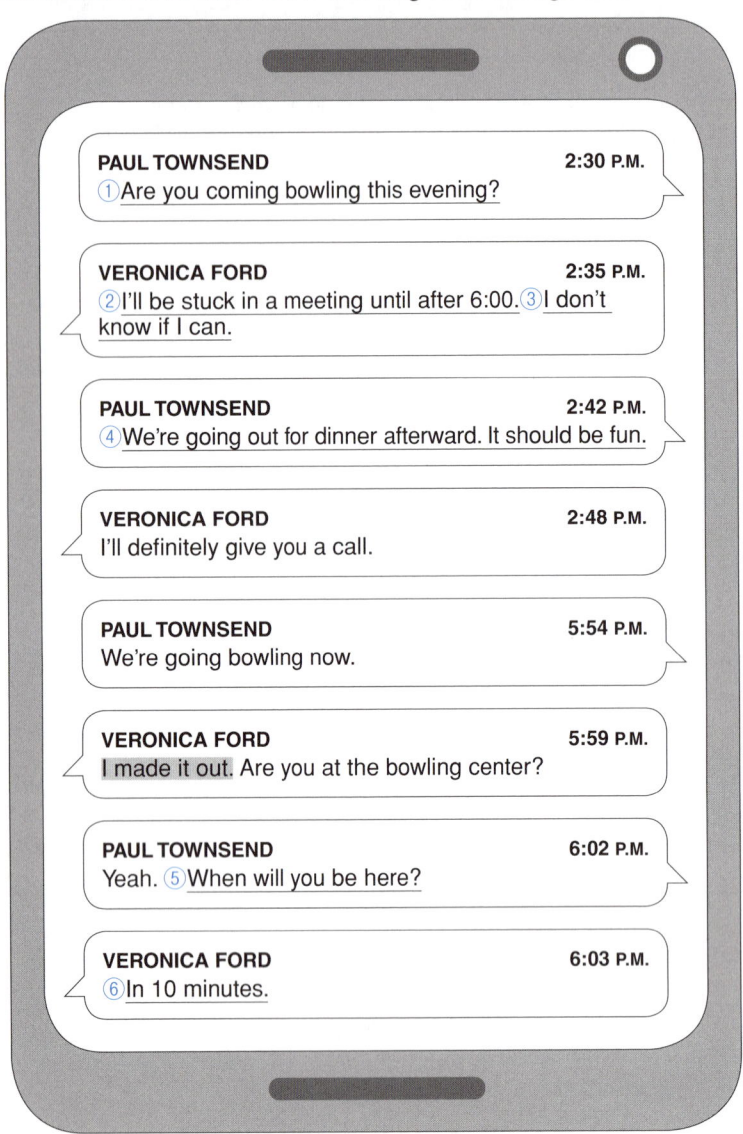

PAUL TOWNSEND　　　　　　　　　　　2:30 P.M.
①Are you coming bowling this evening?

VERONICA FORD　　　　　　　　　　　2:35 P.M.
②I'll be stuck in a meeting until after 6:00. ③I don't know if I can.

PAUL TOWNSEND　　　　　　　　　　　2:42 P.M.
④We're going out for dinner afterward. It should be fun.

VERONICA FORD　　　　　　　　　　　2:48 P.M.
I'll definitely give you a call.

PAUL TOWNSEND　　　　　　　　　　　5:54 P.M.
We're going bowling now.

VERONICA FORD　　　　　　　　　　　5:59 P.M.
I made it out. Are you at the bowling center?

PAUL TOWNSEND　　　　　　　　　　　6:02 P.M.
Yeah. ⑤When will you be here?

VERONICA FORD　　　　　　　　　　　6:03 P.M.
⑥In 10 minutes.

訳

問題 21-22 は次のメッセージのやりとりに関するものです。

PAUL TOWNSEND 今夜のボウリングに来る？	午後2時30分
VERONICA FORD 6時過ぎまで会議で身動きが取れないの。行けるかどうか分からない。	午後2時35分
PAUL TOWNSEND その後で食事に行くんだ。楽しいよ。	午後2時42分
VERONICA FORD 絶対に電話するわ。	午後2時48分
PAUL TOWNSEND 僕らはボウリングに出発するよ。	午後5時54分
VERONICA FORD 出られたわ。ボウリング場にいるの？	午後5時59分
PAUL TOWNSEND うん。君はこっちにいつ着く？	午後6時2分
VERONICA FORD 10分後。	午後6時3分

☐ **be stuck in 〜**：〜で身動きできない、〜から抜け出せない　☐ **make it out**：何とか切り抜ける

選択肢と訳

21.
Why did Mr. Townsend send the text message?
(Townsend さんはなぜこのメッセージを送ったのですか？)
(A) To invite a colleague to a gathering（同僚を集まりに招くため）
(B) To schedule a meeting（ミーティングの予定を入れるため）
(C) To request assistance with some work（仕事の手助けを依頼するため）
(D) To recommend a restaurant（レストランを薦めるため）

☐ **gathering**：集まり

22. NEW
At 5:59 P.M., what does Ms. Ford mean when she writes, "I made it out"?（午後5時59分に、Ford さんが書いている "I made it out" は何を意図していますか？）
(A) She has filled out a form.（用紙に記入した）
(B) She has drawn up an invoice.（送り状を作成した）
(C) She was able to understand a message.（メッセージを理解することができた）
(D) She has left a meeting.（会議を後にした）

解説

正解：(A)

Townsend 氏は①で「今夜のボウリングに来る？」と Ford 氏に尋ねている。③「行けるかどうか分からない」と返す Ford 氏に対し、④でボウリングの後で食事に行くことを告げ、「楽しいよ」とさらに誘っている。正解は (A)。

正解：(D)

Ford 氏は午後2時35分の時点では「6時過ぎまで会議から抜け出せない」（②）と書いている。5時59分に Townsend 氏にメッセージを送った後の⑤と⑥のやりとりから、Ford 氏は、すでに会議から解放され、10分後には Townsend 氏のいるところに着くことができる状況にあると分かる。正解は (D)。make it out はさまざまな異なる意味を持つ表現だが、ここでは「（難局や窮地などから）何とか出る・抜け出す」という意味。

> 問題文

Questions 23-24 refer to the following text messages.

WI YING WANG 3:12 P.M.
①Did you hear that Mr. Gavin is coming back from his trip to London early?

COLE HOLDEN 3:14 P.M.
No! When is he back?

WI YING WANG 3:15 P.M.
Tomorrow. Apparently, the clients signed immediately and he doesn't need to do any more work there.

COLE HOLDEN 3:15 P.M.
How about that!

WI YING WANG 3:16 P.M.
②Yeah! I know. I'm so glad. ③We really need him to help with our latest ad campaign.

COLE HOLDEN 3:25 P.M.
Are you going to meet him at the airport tomorrow morning?

WI YING WANG 3:30 P.M.
I don't think so. He gets in really early. He'll just take a taxi, I'm sure.

COLE HOLDEN 3:31 P.M.
OK, let me know if you need me to go. I don't mind.

訳

問題 23-24 は次のテキストメッセージに関するものです。

WI YING WANG 　　　　　　　　　　　　　　　　　　　　午後3時12分
Gavin さんが London から早く帰ってくるって聞いた？

COLE HOLDEN 　　　　　　　　　　　　　　　　　　　　午後3時14分
聞いてない！　いつ戻るの？

WI YING WANG 　　　　　　　　　　　　　　　　　　　　午後3時15分
明日。どうやらクライアントがすぐに署名してくれたから、もうあちらで仕事する必要がないらしいわ。

COLE HOLDEN 　　　　　　　　　　　　　　　　　　　　午後3時15分
やったー！

WI YING WANG 　　　　　　　　　　　　　　　　　　　　午後3時16分
そうよね！　私もうれしい。私たち、どうしても彼に最新の宣伝キャンペーンを手伝ってもらわなきゃいけないものね。

COLE HOLDEN 　　　　　　　　　　　　　　　　　　　　午後3時25分
君は明日の朝、空港で彼を出迎えるの？

WI YING WANG 　　　　　　　　　　　　　　　　　　　　午後3時30分
それはないと思う。すごく早い時間に着くのよ。タクシーに乗るでしょう、きっと。

COLE HOLDEN 　　　　　　　　　　　　　　　　　　　　午後3時31分
そうか、僕に行ってほしかったら知らせて。僕は構わないから。

□**apparently**：どうやら〜らしい　　□**How about that!**：これは驚いた！、やったー！

選択肢と訳

23.
What is mentioned about Mr. Gavin?（Gavin さんについて何が述べられていますか？）
(A) He will return from a trip ahead of schedule.（予定より早く旅から戻ってくる）
(B) He works in the London office.（Londonのオフィスで働いている）
(C) He is a company president.（会社社長である）
(D) He has requested a pickup.（お迎えを頼んだ）

□**pickup**：出迎え、迎え

24. NEW
At 3:15 P.M., why does Mr. Holden write, "How about that"?（午後3時15分に、Holden さんはなぜ "How about that" と書いているのですか？）
(A) He would like to hear an opinion.（意見を聞きたいから）
(B) He is pleasantly surprised.（うれしい驚きを感じているから）
(C) He is making a suggestion.（提案をしているから）
(D) He will demonstrate a tool.（道具の実演をする）

解説

正解：(A)

①に Gavin 氏が London から「早く」戻ってくるとある。early を ahead of schedule（予定より早く）と言い換えた (A) がこれと一致する。(B)、(C) については言及がない。終盤で Wang 氏が Gavin 氏は空港でタクシーに乗るだろうと書いているので、(D) も不適。

正解：(B)

ターゲット文の How about that! は、「これは驚いた！」「すごい！」のような感嘆を表す表現だが、それを知らなくても、この発言に対する Wang さんの反応から解答できる。Wang さんは②で Holden さんに同意し、「私もうれしい」と書いている。さらに③で、Gavin 氏が戻ってくることが、歓迎すべきことである理由も述べられている。よって Holden 氏の反応は、うれしい驚きの感情であることが分かる。正解は (B)。設問だけを読むと、(A) と (C) も正解の候補に見えてしまうため、チャット本文の中でターゲット文がどのように使われているかを確認する必要がある。

問題文

Questions 25-26 refer to the following text messages.

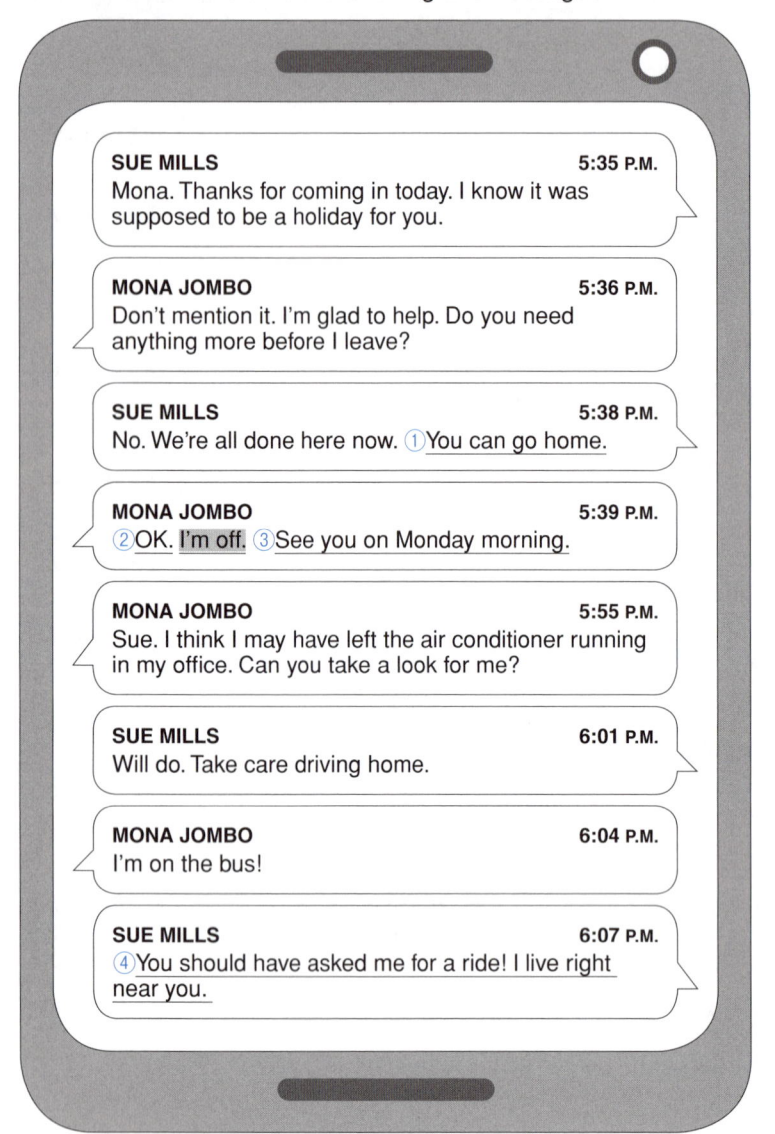

SUE MILLS — 5:35 P.M.
Mona. Thanks for coming in today. I know it was supposed to be a holiday for you.

MONA JOMBO — 5:36 P.M.
Don't mention it. I'm glad to help. Do you need anything more before I leave?

SUE MILLS — 5:38 P.M.
No. We're all done here now. ①You can go home.

MONA JOMBO — 5:39 P.M.
②OK. I'm off. ③See you on Monday morning.

MONA JOMBO — 5:55 P.M.
Sue. I think I may have left the air conditioner running in my office. Can you take a look for me?

SUE MILLS — 6:01 P.M.
Will do. Take care driving home.

MONA JOMBO — 6:04 P.M.
I'm on the bus!

SUE MILLS — 6:07 P.M.
④You should have asked me for a ride! I live right near you.

訳

問題 25-26 は次のテキストメッセージに関するものです。

SUE MILLS Mona。今日は出社してくれてありがとう。あなたにとっては休みの日だったのに。	午後5時35分
MONA JOMBO どういたしまして。お役に立ててうれしいです。帰る前に、他にご用はありますか?	午後5時36分
SUE MILLS いいえ。ここはもう終わったわ。帰っても大丈夫よ。	午後5時38分
MONA JOMBO 分かりました。帰ります。では月曜の朝に。	午後5時39分
MONA JOMBO Sue。オフィスのエアコンをつけっぱなしにしてきたかもしれません。確認してもらえますか?	午後5時55分
SUE MILLS 分かったわ。家まで気を付けて運転してね。	午後6時01分
MONA JOMBO バスに乗ってます!	午後6時04分
SUE MILLS 車で送るように言ってくれればよかったのに! 私はあなたのすぐ近くに住んでるんだから。	午後6時07分

□**come in**:出社する、仕事に出る　□**take a look**:見てみる　□**ask ~ for a ride**:~に車で送ってくれるよう頼む

選択肢と訳

25. NEW

At 5:39 P.M., what does Ms. Jombo mean when she writes, "I'm off"?(午後5時39分に、Jombo さんが書いている "I'm off" は何を意図していますか?)
(A) She is on holiday.(休暇中である)
(B) She is about to leave.(出発するところだ)
(C) She has gotten off a bus.(バスを降りた)
(D) She does not have any work scheduled.(何の仕事も予定されていない)

26.

What is implied about Ms. Mills?(Mills さんについて何が示唆されていますか?)
(A) She is in charge of building maintenance.(ビルのメンテナンスを担当している)
(B) She has known Ms. Jombo for a long time.(Jombo さんを長年知っている)
(C) She drives to work.(車で通勤している)
(D) She will work extra hours tonight.(今夜は残業をする)

解説

正解:(B)

直前の Mills 氏のメッセージ①を見ると、Mills 氏は Jombo 氏に「帰っても大丈夫」と告げている。それに対する応答②「分かりました」と③「では月曜の朝に」というあいさつに挟まれていることから、I'm off は、「帰る」という宣言だと理解するのがこの文脈では最も自然である。正解は (B)。

正解:(C)

Mills 氏は Jombo 氏からオフィスのエアコンを確認するよう頼まれてはいるが、メンテナンスの仕事をしているという言及はないので (A) は不適。また、(B) の2人の関係の長さを裏付ける情報もない。(D) に関する言及もないので不適。Mills 氏は④で、バスの中から連絡してきた Jombo 氏に、「車で送るように言ってくれればよかったのに」と書いている。つまり Mills 氏は勤務先には車で来ているということなので、(C) が正解。

問題文

Questions 27-28 refer to the following text-message chain.

LIAM HILLS　　　　　　　　　　　　　　　　　　　　　　　　　　　　　　　　　9:50 A.M.
I'll be back in the office in about 20 minutes. ①I've been at the advertising agency watching the promotional video we commissioned.

IBU KANZAKI　　　　　　　　　　　　　　　　　　　　　　　　　　　　　　　　　9:51 A.M.
How did you find it?

LIAM HILLS　　　　　　　　　　　　　　　　　　　　　　　　　　　　　　　　　9:53 A.M.
②It was well done, but a bit too long. I don't think they focused on the functions enough.

IBU KANZAKI　　　　　　　　　　　　　　　　　　　　　　　　　　　　　　　　　9:53 A.M.
OK. Did you give them some pointers?

LIAM HILLS　　　　　　　　　　　　　　　　　　　　　　　　　　　　　　　　　9:54 A.M.
③Not yet. I'm bringing a copy back to the office for everyone to look at. I want to hear a range of opinions before we change anything.

IBU KANZAKI　　　　　　　　　　　　　　　　　　　　　　　　　　　　　　　　　9:59 A.M.
④Good idea. Shall I arrange a meeting in the conference room or something?

LIAM HILLS　　　　　　　　　　　　　　　　　　　　　　　　　　　　　　　　　10:02 A.M.
⑤Would you? That'd be great. Around 11:00.

IBU KANZAKI　　　　　　　　　　　　　　　　　　　　　　　　　　　　　　　　　10:03 A.M.
No problem.

訳

問題 27-28 は次のメッセージのやりとりに関するものです。

LIAM HILLS	午前9時50分
あと20分ぐらいでオフィスに戻るよ。広告代理店でうちが発注したプロモーションビデオを見ていたんだ。	
IBU KANZAKI	**午前9時51分**
どうだった？	
LIAM HILLS	**午前9時53分**
よくできていたけど、ちょっと長過ぎる。機能に十分重点を置いてるように思えないな。	
IBU KANZAKI	**午前9時53分**
なるほど。彼らに何か助言をしたの？	
LIAM HILLS	**午前9時54分**
まだしてない。みんなが見られるようにコピーを持って帰るよ。何か変更する前に、幅広い意見を聞きたいんだ。	
IBU KANZAKI	**午前9時59分**
いい考えだわ。会議室でミーティングとか、何か手配しましょうか？	
LIAM HILLS	**午前10時02分**
そうしてくれる？　それはありがたい。11時ごろかな。	
IBU KANZAKI	**午前10時03分**
分かったわ。	

□commission：～を依頼する、～を発注する　□pointer：助言

選択肢と訳

27. NEW

At 9:51 A.M., why does Ms. Kanzaki write, "How did you find it"?（午前9時51分に Kanzaki さんが書いている "How did you find it" は何を意味していますか？）
(A) She wonders how Mr. Hills got to an office.（Hills さんがどうやって広告代理店に行ったのか疑問に思っている）
(B) She assumed that a device had been misplaced.（機材が置き忘れられたと思っていた）
(C) She is interested in Mr. Hills' opinion of a video.（ビデオについての Hills さんの意見に関心がある）
(D) She is glad that a lost item has been located.（紛失物が見つかったことを喜んでいる）

28.

What will staff members most likely do at 11:00 A.M.?（午前11時にスタッフは何をする可能性が高いか？）
(A) Choose a promotional agency（販促の代理店を選ぶ）
(B) Evaluate some advertising（宣伝を評価する）
(C) Attend a performance review（人事考課に出席する）
(D) Discuss recent sales figures（最近の売り上げについて議論する）

□performance review：人事考課、勤務評定

解説

正解：(C)

Kanzaki 氏の Hills 氏に対する質問、How did you find it? の意図を問う問題。通常、これは感想を尋ねるときの表現だ。①「広告代理店で発注したプロモーションビデオを見ていた」という Hills 氏のメッセージの直後に送信されているので、この場合、ビデオの感想を尋ねていると分かる。Hills 氏は質問に対する答えとして、②で自分の感想を述べている。よって、正解は (C)。なお、(A)、(B)、(C) は find を「～を見つける」と解釈した場合に魅力的な選択肢だが、このチャットではその意味で用いられていない。

正解：(B)

「午前11時」は Hills 氏のメッセージ⑤に登場するので、何の時刻なのかをそれより前にある情報で判断する。Hills 氏は③で、ビデオを持ち帰って、社内の人々の意見を聞こうと思っていることを明かしている。Kanzaki 氏は④でそれに賛同し、「会議室でミーティングとか、何か手配をしましょうか？」と申し出ている。「午前11時（ごろ）」は Hills 氏の会議の開始希望時刻だ。その会議では「（ビデオについて）幅広い意見を聞く（hear a range of opinions）」（③）ので、これを「宣伝を評価する（Evaluate some advertising）」と言い換えた (B) が正解。

問題文と訳

Questions 29-32 refer to the following online chat discussion.

👤 **Walter Gibson** [1:20 P.M.]:	Has anyone seen a brown briefcase lying around? ①A guest named Helga Brent claims to have left it in the ②lobby.
Judy Bradbury [1:21 P.M.]:	I'm in the lobby now and I can't see it anywhere. Can you give me any more information?
👤 **Walter Gibson** [1:21 P.M.]:	Apparently, she was sitting in one of the armchairs. But she also went to ③the restaurant as well as ④the restrooms so it could be anywhere. ⑤She's returning from the station to pick it up. ⑥Judy, can you check the bathrooms next?
Alia Kahn [1:22 P.M.]:	Is there any chance she left it ⑦in her room? ⑧If you give me the room number, I'll go and check.
👤 **Walter Gibson** [1:22 P.M.]:	Thanks, Alia. It was 804.
Krishna Rao [1:25 P.M.]:	⑨I'm checking the restaurant now. But it doesn't seem to be here.
Alia Kahn [1:28 P.M.]:	Found it. It was ⑩in the closet. There was a ⑪used towel over it. I'll bring it down to the lobby now. I hope she makes her train.
👤 **Walter Gibson** [1:30 P.M.]:	Great news! Good work, Alia. Hurry down, she doesn't have much time.
Krishna Rao [1:32 P.M.]:	Well spotted, Alia!
👤 **Walter Gibson** [1:35 P.M.]:	Judy isn't reading these messages. ⑫I'd better go and tell her to stop looking.

[SEND]

問題 **29-32** は次のオンライン・チャットでの話し合いによるものです。

👤 **Walter Gibson** [午後1時20分]:	誰か茶色のブリーフケースがその辺にあるのを見た？ Helga Brent様というお客さまがロビーに置き忘れたとおっしゃっているんだ。
Judy Bradbury [午後1時21分]:	今ロビーにいるけど、どこにも見当たらないわ。何かもっと情報をくれない？
👤 **Walter Gibson** [午後1時21分]:	彼女は肘掛けいすの1つに座っていたらしい。でも化粧室やレストランにも行ってるから、どこもあり得るね。お客さまはそれを取りに、駅から引き返しているんだ。Judy、次に化粧室を探してくれる？
Alia Kahn [午後1時22分]:	客室に忘れた可能性はない？ 部屋番号を教えてもらえれば、私が行って見てくるわ。
👤 **Walter Gibson** [午後1時22分]:	ありがとう、Alia。804号室だ。
Krishna Rao [午後1時25分]:	今レストランを見ているよ。でもここにはなさそうだ。
Alia Kahn [午後1時28分]:	見つけたわ。クロゼットの中にあった。使用済みのタオルが覆っていたの。今、ロビーに持って行くわ。お客さまが列車に間に合うといいけど。
👤 **Walter Gibson** [午後1時30分]:	素晴らしいニュースだ！ お手柄だね、Alia。急いで持ってきて、お客さまにはお時間があまりないから。
Krishna Rao [午後1時32分]:	よく見つけたね、Alia！
👤 **Walter Gibson** [午後1時35分]:	Judyはメッセージを読んでいないな。探すのをやめるよう、彼女に言いに行った方がよさそうだね。

[送信]

□**lie around**：その辺にある　□**armchair**：肘掛けいす

172

選択肢と訳

29.
Where do the writers most likely work?（書き手たちはどこで働いていると思われますか？）
(A) In a furniture store（家具店で）
(B) In a hotel （ホテルで）
(C) In a train station（電車の駅で）
(D) In a storage facility（保管施設で）

解説

正解：(B)
チャットのあちこちに散らばるヒントから、書き手の勤め先を推測する。②の「ロビー」、③の「レストラン」、④の「化粧室」、⑦の「彼女の部屋」、⑧の中の「部屋番号」、⑩の「クロゼット」、⑪の「使用済みタオル」というヒントから、書き手たちはホテルで働いていると推測できる。正解は(B)。

30.
What does Mr. Gibson write about Ms. Brent?（Gibson さんは Brent さんについて何と言っていますか？）
(A) She has left her phone behind.（彼女は電話を置き忘れた）
(B) She is a member of the staff.（彼女はスタッフの一員である）
(C) She forgot to leave her contact details.（彼女は連絡先を残すのを忘れた）
(D) She is on her way back.（彼女は戻って来る途中である）

□ **contact detail**：連絡先

正解：(D)
Gibson 氏は Brent 氏について最初の発言①で、「Helga Brent 様というお客さんが、ロビーにそれを置き忘れたと言っている」と述べている。「それ」とは、a brown briefcase（茶色のブリーフケース）だ。Gibson 氏は 2 回目の発言の⑤で Brent 氏を She（彼女）で指し、「彼女はそれを取りに、駅から引き返している」と書いている。これを「戻ってくる途中」と表した (D) が正解。

---

31. NEW
At 1:25 P.M., what does Mr. Rao mean when he writes, "it doesn't seem to be here"?（1 時 25 分に、Rao さんが書いている "it doesn't seem to be here" は何を意図していますか？）
(A) He cannot find what he is looking for.（探しているものが見つからない）
(B) Some damage has been repaired perfectly.（損傷が完全に修復された）
(C) An event appears to have been rescheduled.（イベントが予定変更になったらしい）
(D) A location is not marked on a map.（ある場所が地図に載っていない）

正解：(A)
書き手の意図を問う問題のヒントは、ターゲット文の前後にあることが多い。ターゲット文の前の⑨で Rao 氏は、「今レストランを見ている」と書いている。それに続けて、「でも、それはここにないみたいだ」と述べている。it（それ）とは、Brent 氏の忘れ物の「茶色のブリーフケース」だ。つまり、「探しているブリーフケースをレストランで見つけられない」ということを表しているので、正解は (A)。

32.
What will Mr. Gibson most likely do next?（Gibson さんは次に何をすると考えられますか？）
(A) Clean a closet（クロゼットを片付ける）
(B) Go to the bathrooms（化粧室へ行く）
(C) Cancel a reservation（予約を取り消す）
(D) Organize a meeting（会議を計画する）

正解：(B)
Gibson 氏は⑥で、「Judy、次に化粧室を探してくれないか」と依頼している。探しているブリーフケースが見つかり、問題が解決した後、Gibson 氏は⑫「Judy はメッセージを読んでいない。探すのをやめるよう彼女に言いに行った方がいい」と書いている。Gibson 氏は Judy がいるであろう化粧室へ向かうと考えられるので、正解は (B)。

問題文と訳

Questions 33-36 refer to the following online chat discussion.

Schwartz, Craig [4:30 P.M.]:
Everyone. ①It's a bit of an emergency. I'm on my way to the airport to pick up Mr. White. I've got a flat tire, and I just checked the spare. It's flat, too. ②Can someone else go to the airport for me? ③I don't want to stress him out before his performance.

Ryusaki, Hiroshi [4:31 P.M.]:
④I would. But the thing is — I don't have a car. If no one else can go, I'll take a train. I can meet him and explain the situation.

Lund, Maxine [4:31 P.M.]:
I'm at the hall ⑤preparing the sound equipment. What time does his plane land?

Schwartz, Craig [4:33 P.M.]:
Maxine, he gets in at 5:25. ⑥Hiroshi, thanks. I'll let you know.

Mantini, Derek [4:35 P.M.]:
Does he have a lot of luggage? I don't have much room in my car. It's a sports car.

Lund, Maxine [4:35 P.M.]:
Even if I left here now, I'd still be 10 minutes late. ⑦Sending Hiroshi might be the safest plan.

Ryusaki, Hiroshi [4:37 P.M.]:
Craig, I really don't mind. I'm ready to leave.

Schwartz, Craig [4:45 P.M.]:
Derek, ⑧he has a few of his instruments. ⑨OK, Hiroshi. I'm counting on you.

Mantini, Derek [4:46 P.M.]:
Sorry, I couldn't help.

Schwartz, Craig [4:49 P.M.]:
Hiroshi, don't forget your phone. I'll be in touch. Everyone else, thanks.

問題 33-36 は次のオンライン・チャットでの話し合いによるものです。

Schwartz, Craig［午後4時30分］：
みんな。ちょっと緊急事態なんだ。空港まで White さんを迎えに行く途中なんだけど。タイヤがパンクしたからスペアタイヤを見てみたんだ。それもぺしゃんこなんだよ。誰か僕の代わりに空港に行ってもらえない？ 演奏前に彼をいらいらさせたくないんだ。

Ryusaki, Hiroshi［午後4時31分］：
僕が行ってもいいんだけど。でも実は――車がないんだ。もし他に誰も行けなければ、電車で行くよ。僕が彼に会って事情を説明すればいい。

Lund, Maxine［午後4時31分］：
私はホールで音響機器の準備中。彼の飛行機は何時に着くの？

Schwartz, Craig［午後4時33分］：
Maxine、彼は5時25分に着く。Hiroshi、ありがとう。連絡するよ。

Mantini, Derek［午後4時35分］：
彼には荷物がたくさんあるのかな？ 僕の車はあまりスペースがないんだ。スポーツカーだから。

Lund, Maxine［午後4時35分］：
私が今ここを出たとしても10分の遅刻よ。Hiroshi に行ってもらうのが一番の安全策かも。

Ryusaki, Hiroshi［午後4時37分］：
Craig、僕は本当に構わないよ。出る準備はできてる。

Schwartz, Craig［午後4時45分］：
Derek、彼はいくつか楽器を持ってる。分かった、Hiroshi。頼むよ。

Mantini, Derek［午後4時46分］：
役に立てなくて残念。

Schwartz, Craig［午後4時49分］：
Hiroshi、電話を忘れないで。連絡するから。他のみんな、ありがとう。

□**get a flat tire**：タイヤがパンクする　□**stress ～ out**：～をいらいらさせる　□**the thing is**：実は

選択肢と訳

33.
Why did Mr. Schwartz start the chat?（Schwartz 氏はなぜこのチャットを始めたのですか？）
(A) To correct an error（間違いを訂正するため）
(B) To provide an update（最新情報を提供するため）
(C) To seek assistance（助けを求めるため）
(D) To praise a colleague（同僚をたたえるため）

34.
Who most likely is Mr. White?（White さんとは誰である可能性が高いか？）
(A) An important contributor（重要な寄付者）
(B) A product reviewer（製品評論家）
(C) A returning colleague（復帰する同僚）
(D) A visiting musician（訪れるミュージシャン）

□**contributor**：寄付者、貢献者　□**reviewer**：批評家、評論家

35. NEW
At 4：33 P.M., what does Mr. Schwartz imply when he writes, "I'll let you know"?（午後4時33分に、Schwartz さんが書いている "I'll let you know" は、何を意図していますか？）
(A) An arrival time may change.（到着時間が変わるかもしれない）
(B) He can answer a question when he has more time.（もっと時間があれば彼は質問に答えることができる）
(C) He will wait to see if there is a better offer.（もっと良い申し出があるか待ってみる）
(D) There is some confidential information to share.（共有すべき内密の情報がある）

□**confidential**：秘密の、内密の

36.
Who will most likely meet Mr. White at the airport?（White さんと空港で会うのは、誰だと考えられますか？）
(A) Hiroshi Ryusaki
(B) Maxine Lund
(C) Craig Schwartz
(D) Derek Mantini

解説

正解：(C)
Schwartz 氏は最初の発言の①で、「緊急事態だ」と告げてから、White 氏を空港に迎えに行く途中でタイヤがパンクし、スペアタイヤもパンクしているという事態を報告している。そして②で、「誰か代わりに空港に行ってもらえないか」と読み手に依頼している。Schwartz 氏は読み手たちに助けを求めるためにチャットを始めたので、正解は (C)。

正解：(D)
Schwartz 氏は③で White 氏に関して、「彼を演奏前にいらいらさせたくない」と述べている。Lund さんは⑤で、「音響機器を準備している」と書いている。Schwartz 氏は⑧で、「彼（White 氏）は楽器を持っている」と記述している。これらのヒントから、White 氏は演奏のためにこの地を訪れようとしているミュージシャンだと推測できるので、正解は (D)。

正解：(C)
Schwartz 氏の②の依頼に対して、Hiroshi Ryusaki 氏は④で、「行ってもいいが、車がない。他に誰も行けなければ電車で行く」と答えている。Schwartz 氏は⑥で Ryusaki 氏に I'll let you know.（連絡する）と述べ、その後もチャットを続けて、車で空港に行ける人を探している。つまり、Schwartz 氏は、Ryusaki 氏よりもっと良い申し出があるかどうか待つことを意図しているので、正解は (C)。

正解：(A)
Lund 氏が⑦で、「Hiroshiに行ってもらうのが一番の安全策」と述べたのに対し、Ryusaki 氏は「構わない」と答えている。Schwartz 氏は⑨で、Ryusaki 氏に「Hiroshi。頼む」と書いているので、空港で White 氏と会うのは (A) Hiroshi Ryusaki である。

Part 7　②チャット系

問題文と訳

Questions 37-40 refer to the following online chat discussion.

👤 **Greg Black** [9:20 A.M.]:		Does anyone have time to give me a hand ①setting up the tent?
Ang Bae [9:21 A.M.]:		Sorry Greg, ②I'm at the supplier getting all the beverages. I won't be there for another hour.
Adele Vuko [9:22 A.M.]:		I'm running a little behind schedule myself. ③One of the food warmers is broken and I've had to rent one for the day. I'll call you when I get there.
👤 **Greg Black** [9:22 A.M.]:		OK, thanks, guys. Lachlan, how about you?
Lachlan Trieu [9:25 A.M.]:		Sorry about the delay. Sure. I had to ④pick up a few of the waiters on the way to the client, but we'll be there well before 10 o'clock. With all of us there, it won't take any time at all.
👤 **Greg Black** [9:30 A.M.]:		That's a relief. ⑤I'll start unpacking the truck while I'm waiting for you to get here.
Adele Vuko [9:32 A.M.]:		We have plenty of time yet. ⑥Guests won't arrive until 11 A.M.
👤 **Greg Black** [9:34 A.M.]:		You're right. ⑦It's only 9:30 now, but ⑧I'm just a bit anxious after last time.
Adele Vuko [9:36 A.M.]:		Don't remind me.

問題 **37-40** は次のオンライン・チャットでの話し合いによるものです。

👤 **Greg Black** [午前9時20分]:	誰かテントの設営を手伝ってくれる時間はある？
Ang Bae [午前9時21分]:	ごめん Greg、飲み物の手配で納入業者にいるんだ。あと1時間はそっちへ行けない。
Adele Vuko [午前9時22分]:	私も少し予定より遅れているの。料理の保温器が1台故障していて、今日1日、1台借りないといけなくなったの。そっちに着いたら電話する。
👤 **Greg Black** [午前9時22分]:	分かった、ありがとう、みんな。Lachlan、君はどう？
Lachlan Trieu [午前9時25分]:	遅くなってごめん。もちろんいいよ。クライアントのところへ向かう途中で、ウエーターの人たちを車で拾わなくちゃならなかったんだけど、10時前にはそっちへ着く。僕ら全員いれば、時間は全然かからないよ。
👤 **Greg Black** [午前9時30分]:	それは安心だ。みんなが着くのを待つ間に、僕はトラックの荷ほどきを始めるとしよう。
Adele Vuko [午前9時32分]:	まだ十分な時間があるわね。お客さんたちは午前11時まで到着しないだろうし。
👤 **Greg Black** [午前9時34分]:	そうだね。今はまだ9時半だけど、前回のことがあって、僕はちょっと心配なんだ。
Adele Vuko [午前9時36分]:	思い出させないでよ。

☐ **well before**：〜よりずっと前に ☐ **That's a relief.**：「安心した」、「良かった」 ☐ **unpack**：〜の荷ほどきをする

選択肢と訳

37.
What kind of business do the writers most likely work for?（書き手たちが働いているのはどのような企業であると考えられますか？）
(A) An interior decorator（室内装飾業者）
(B) A catering firm（仕出し会社）
(C) A financial institution（金融機関）
(D) A tour company（旅行会社）

38.
What does Mr. Black write that he will do?（Blackさんは何をすると書いていますか？）
(A) Redesign a floor plan（間取りを設計し直す）
(B) Contact a business associate（仕事の関係者に連絡を取る）
(C) Unload equipment from a vehicle（機材を車から降ろす）
(D) Write a review of a service（サービスにレビューを書く）

□**floor plan**：間取り、見取り図　□**business associate**：仕事関係者　□**unload**：(荷物など) を降ろす

39.
What time will the visitors arrive?（客が到着するのは何時ですか？）
(A) At 9:30 A.M.（午前9時半）
(B) At 10:00 A.M.（午前10時）
(C) At 11 A.M.（午前11時）
(D) At 11:30 A.M.（午前11時半）

40.
At 9:36 A.M., what does Ms. Vuko imply when she writes, "Don't remind me"?（9時36分に、Vukoさんが書いている "Don't remind me" は、何を意図していますか？）
(A) She knows what she has to do.（彼女は自分がしなくてはいけないことを知っている）
(B) Another staff member is responsible.（別のスタッフの責任である）
(C) She is not required to attend an event.（彼女はイベントに出ることを求められていない）
(D) A previous job did not go smoothly.（以前の仕事がうまくいかなかった）

解説

正解：(B)
チャットに散らばる複数のヒントから、書き手たちが働いている会社の業種を考える。①「テントの設営」、②「飲み物の手配で納入業者にいる」、③「料理の保温器が1台壊れたので、その日用に1台借りる」、④「ウエーターの何人かを迎えに行く」というヒントから、書き手たちは仕出し会社で働いていると推測できる。正解は(B)。

正解：(C)
Black氏のこの後の行動を答える問題。答えのヒントは未来を表す表現にあるはずだ。Black氏は3つ目の発言の⑤で、I'll start unpacking the truck（トラックの荷ほどきを始める）と未来形で書いている。トラックの荷ほどきとは、車両から何らかの荷物を下ろすことなので、「機材を車から下ろす」と言い換えた(C)が正解。

正解：(C)
Vuko氏は⑥で、「お客さんたち（Guests）は11時まで到着しない」と述べている。すなわち、11時に到着する予定なので、正解は(C)。guests（客たち）は、設問ではvisitors（訪問者）に言い換えられている。

正解：(D)
ターゲット文の前にある⑦と⑧でBlack氏は、「今はまだ9時半だけど、前回のことがあって、ちょっと心配だ」と述べている。それに対してVuko氏は、「思い出させないでよ」と返している。Vuko氏は、おそらく前回の仕事がうまくいかなかったので、思い出したくないということを示唆している。(D)が正解。

> 問題文と訳

Questions 41-44 refer to the following online chat discussion.

Kamm, Kenny [4:30 P.M.]:
I've invited you all to this chat because ①none of you have any workshops to lead on Thursday afternoon. It turns out that Glen Chang can no longer make it to his Thursday workshop and I was looking for someone to swap with him.

Santiago, Erin [4:31 P.M.]:
You mean that our sessions will be switched to a different day, right?

Spirit, David [4:31 P.M.]:
I might be able to. What time would I finish work?

Kamm, Kenny [4:33 P.M.]:
Erin, yes. David, ②you'd be required at the training center between 1 P.M. and 4 P.M.

Spirit, David [4:35 P.M.]:
③Well, I don't have anything else on, so I'll swap if it helps out.

Nguyen, Juk [4:37 P.M.]:
④I originally wanted to come on Thursday afternoon but I was told there weren't any time slots available. Is it too late?

Kamm, Kenny [4:45 P.M.]:
⑤David, would you mind if I let Juk swap her time with Glen? ⑥I know she wants to attend a panel discussion at the Science Museum on Wednesdays. She was really disappointed ⑦when I told her the schedule.

Spirit, David [4:46 P.M.]:
⑧Of course. I'm glad things worked out, Juk.

Chang, Glen [4:49 P.M.]:
Thanks everyone. I really appreciate this!

問題 41-44 は次のオンライン・チャットでの話し合いによるものです。

Kamm, Kenny ［午後4時30分］：
皆さんは木曜の午後に指導する研修がない方々なので、このチャットに招待しました。Glen Chang が木曜に研修を担当できないことになり、私は彼と代わってくれる人を探していたんです。

Santiago, Erin ［午後4時31分］：
私たちの受け持つ時間が別の日に変わるということですか？

Spirit, David ［午後4時31分］：
僕は可能かもしれません。仕事は何時に終わることになりますか？

Kamm, Kenny ［午後4時33分］：
Erin、その通りです。David、午後1時から4時の間、研修センターにいることが必要になるでしょう。

Spirit, David ［午後4時35分］：
まあ、他に予定はないし、お役に立てるなら僕が代わります。

Nguyen, Juk ［午後4時37分］：
私はもともと木曜の午後に出勤したかったのですが、時間割の空きがないと言われました。もう遅いでしょうか？

Kamm, Kenny ［午後4時45分］：
David、Glen とは Juk に代わってもらっても構わないでしょうか？ 彼女、毎週水曜日にある科学博物館でのパネル討論会に参加したがっているんです。私がスケジュールを伝えたときには、本当にがっかりしていましたから。

Spirit, David ［午後4時46分］：
もちろんどうぞ。希望通りになってよかったですね、Juk。

Chang, Glen ［午後4時49分］：
ありがとう、皆さん。今回のことは本当に感謝しています！

□**swap with** ～：～と交換する　　□**time slot**：時間帯、時間割　　□**panel discussion**：パネル討論会

選択肢と訳

41.
What is Mr. Kamm most likely in charge of?（Kammさんは何を管理していると考えられますか？）
(A) A training program（研修プログラム）
(B) A panel discussion（パネル討論会）
(C) A recruitment event（求人イベント）
(D) A research project（研究プロジェクト）

□ **be in charge of 〜**：〜を管理する、〜を担当する

42.
What does Mr. Spirit say about his Thursday schedule?（Spiritさんは木曜のスケジュールについて何と言っていますか？）
(A) He needs to check with a supervisor.（上司に確認する必要がある）
(B) He is free in the afternoon.（午後は空いている）
(C) He will take time off.（休みを取る）
(D) He cannot change it.（変更できない）

□ **take time off**：休みを取る

43.
Who will most likely take the Thursday time slot?（誰が木曜日の時間割を担当することになると考えられますか？）
(A) Glen Chang
(B) Erin Santiago
(C) David Spirit
(D) Juk Nguyen

44. NEW
At 4:45 P.M., why does Mr. Kamm write, "She was really disappointed when I told her the schedule"?（午後4時45分に、Kammさんはなぜ "She was really disappointed when I told her the schedule" と書いているのですか？）
(A) Ms. Nguyen was forced to change her plans.（Nguyenさんは予定を変えざるを得なかったから）
(B) Ms. Nguyen was asked to work late at night.（Nguyenさんは夜に残業するよう頼まれたから）
(C) Ms. Nguyen's workload was too heavy.（Nguyenさんの仕事量が多過ぎたから）
(D) Ms. Nguyen's travel time was made longer.（Nguyenさんの移動時間が長くなったから）

□ **work late**：残業する　□ **workload**：仕事量、作業量

解説

正解：(A)
Kamm氏は最初の発言の①で、「皆さんは木曜日の午後に指導する研修がない」と述べている。②でSpirit氏に「研修センター」にいることが必要だと答え、⑦ではNguyen氏を指して、「私が彼女にスケジュールを伝えた」と書いている。これらのヒントから、Kamm氏は研修プログラムを管理する立場にあると考えられるので、(A)が正解。

正解：(B)
Kamm氏の発言①から、チャット参加者は全員、木曜日には研修を受け持っていないことが分かる。さらに、Spirit氏自身は③で、「他に予定はないし、お役に立てるなら私が代わる」と言っている。これらのヒントから、正解は(B)。

正解：(D)
Juk Nguyen氏は④で、「木曜日の午後に来たかったのだが、時間割の空きがないと言われた」と述べている。それに対して、Glen Chang氏と木曜日の研修を代わってくれる人を探しているKamm氏はSpirit氏に、「JukにGlenと代わってもらっても構わないか」と⑤で聞いている。Davidは⑧で、「もちろん。希望通りになってよかったですね、Juk」と答えているので、正解は(D)。

正解：(A)
意図を答える問題なので、ターゲット文の前後を読む。該当する文の前⑥で、Kamm氏はNguyen氏について、「彼女は毎週水曜日にある科学博物館でのパネル討論会に参加したがっている」と述べ、その後の⑦で、「私がスケジュールを伝えたときには、本当にがっかりしていた」と言っている。以上から、Nguyen氏は、毎週水曜日のパネル討論会の参加予定を変更せざるを得なかったからがっかりしたと考えられるので、正解は(A)。

Part 7　②チャット系

ひたすら意図問題！
3文トレーニング [Part 7編]

各セット内の下線部①②について最も適切なものを (A) 〜 (C) から選ぼう。
音声を聞く場合はダウンロード・コンテンツの該当するファイル番号を再生してください。

▶▶▶ SET 1 🔊 25

チャット1

Terry Hale 10:20 A.M.: I've decided to apply for the position as store manager.
Joan Spinner 10:23 A.M.: That's the way. ①I'm sure you'll get it.

チャット2

Terry Hale 10:20 A.M.: This instruction manual is really hard to follow.
Joan Spinner 10:23 A.M.: Keep reading. ②I'm sure you'll get it.

At 10:23 A.M., what does Ms. Spinner mean when she writes, "I'm sure you'll get it"?
(A) She thinks Mr. Hale will take a trip.
(B) She thinks Mr. Hale will be promoted.
(C) She believes that Mr. Hale will understand.

①＿＿＿＿ ②＿＿＿＿

▶▶▶ SET 2 🔊 26

チャット1

Lucy Chan 6:16 P.M.: I'm worried about Ms. Hanson because her train has arrived late.
Rusty Cole 6:20 P.M.: ①She'll make it. I spoke to her a moment ago.

チャット2

Lucy Chan 6:16 P.M.: Should Ms. Hanson be in charge of creating the slideshow for the presentation?
Rusty Cole 6:20 P.M.: Yeah. ②She'll make it. I taught her how about a week ago.

At 6:20 P.M., what does Mr. Cole mean when he writes, "She'll make it"?
(A) He trusts Ms. Hanson to prepare.
(B) He believes Ms. Hanson will be on time.
(C) He knows Ms. Hanson is available.

①＿＿＿＿ ②＿＿＿＿

▶▶▶ SET 3 🔊 27

チャット1

Liesel Waters 1:45 P.M.: Do you know much about our arrangement with Wiltshire Industries?
Todd Margaret 1:53 P.M.: ①Not really. That contract was already in place when I started at the company.

チャット2

Liesel Waters 1:45 P.M.: Do you think we should extend our agreement with Wiltshire Industries?
Todd Margaret 1:53 P.M.: ②Not really. It's taking a lot of our resources to serve them and we could be focusing on more profitable activities.

At 1:53 P.M., why does Mr. Margaret write, "Not really"?
(A) He is not familiar with the details of an agreement.
(B) He has not been in touch with a client representative.
(C) He would like to end an arrangement with a client.

①＿＿＿＿ ②＿＿＿＿

※解答・解説は P. 184 〜 187 にあります

▶▶ SET 4 🔊 28

チャット1

Regis Grant 11:56 A.M.: What do you think of the new printing machine?
Heidi Marr 11:59 A.M.: ①Not much. The brand we were using before had a much better design.

チャット2

Regis Grant 11:56 A.M.: How much did we spend to get the printing machine changed?
Heidi Marr 11:59 A.M.: ②Not much. We got a good price for the old one and this new one is the base model so it was a lot cheaper.

At 11:59 A.M., what does Ms. Marr mean when she writes, "Not much"?
(A) There is little time left before a deadline.
(B) She is unimpressed with some equipment.
(C) The cost of replacing some equipment was minimal.

① _____ ② _____

▶▶ SET 5 🔊 29

チャット1

Ireen Wust 8:12 P.M.: Are we going to be able to send the staff on the team building retreat this year?
Meng Wang 8:15 P.M.: ①I'm looking at it. It all depends on our workload in June.

チャット2

Ireen Wust 8:12 P.M.: Have you seen the floor plan for the banquet?
Meng Wang 8:15 P.M.: ②I'm looking at it. I don't think the stage will be big enough.

At 8:15 P.M., what does Ms. Wang mean when she writes, "I'm looking at it"?
(A) She is considering a plan.
(B) She has to accept a decision.
(C) She is viewing a document.

① _____ ② _____

▶▶ SET 6 🔊 30

チャット1

Cal Harris 10:11 A.M.: We'll be moving into our new offices a week early.
Chloe Lahey 10:12 A.M.: ①I can't wait. I hear they look fantastic.

チャット2

Cal Harris 10:11 A.M.: Our technician will be at your office tomorrow at noon to fix the air conditioner.
Chloe Lahey 10:12 A.M.: ②I can't wait. We have some important clients coming in tomorrow morning.

At 10:12 A.M., what does Ms. Lahey mean when she writes, "I can't wait"?
(A) She has an urgent situation.
(B) She is looking forward to a change.
(C) She is about to leave on a trip.

① _____ ② _____

▶▶▶ SET 7 🔊 31

チャット1

Fay Wu 11:03 A.M.: I could get you a ticket on an 8:35 flight to Paris tomorrow evening.
Hannes Mita 11:07 A.M.: ①I'll take it. Can you send me an invoice right away?

チャット2

Fay Wu 11:03 A.M.: The new projector is really small and light, so you should be able to fit it in your bag.
Hannes Mita 11:07 A.M.: ②I'll take it. Otherwise, I'd have to rent one at the venue and they're quite expensive.

At 11:07 A.M., what does Mr. Mita mean when he writes, "I'll take it"?
(A) He will purchase a ticket.
(B) He will use a device.
(C) He will accept some criticism.

①_____ ②_____

▶▶▶ SET 8 🔊 32

チャット1

Boris Saneyev 10:13 A.M.: Do you want me to pick you up at the station?
Clair Fenton 10:27 A.M.: ①If you wouldn't mind. My train will get there at noon.

チャット2

Boris Saneyev 10:13 A.M.: How would you like to get to the apartment today?
Clair Fenton 10:27 A.M.: ②If you wouldn't mind, I'd like to go by car. Is that OK?

At 10:27 A.M., why does Ms. Fenton write, "If you wouldn't mind"?
(A) To ask for permission
(B) To accept an offer
(C) To provide an alternative

①_____ ②_____

▶▶▶ SET 9 🔊 33

チャット1

Paul Dimas 2:41 P.M.: What was the reaction of the people at Sandy College about sharing facilities?
Lance Brown 2:45 P.M.: ①They're positive. Don't worry.

チャット2

Paul Dimas 2:41 P.M.: Are the people at the factory really going to meet their production quota despite the malfunctions?
Lance Brown 2:45 P.M.: ②They're positive. Everything is running smoothly now.

At 2:45 P.M., what does Mr. Brown mean when he writes, "They're positive"?
(A) People are in favor of a plan.
(B) People have passed a test.
(C) People are sure of an outcome.

①_____ ②_____

▶▶▶ SET 10 🔊 34

チャット1

Reginald Sakata 8:10 A.M.: Tony Fisher has been doing an excellent job training the new technicians. They're almost ready to send out in the field.
Laura Stotsky 8:12 A.M.: ①He knows what he's doing.

チャット2

Reginald Sakata 8:10 A.M.: Should I contact Tony Fisher about his role at tomorrow's product demonstration?
Laura Stotsky 8:12 A.M.: ②He knows what he's doing. I contacted him about it last night and he said he understood.

At 8:12 A.M., what does Ms. Stotsky mean when she writes, "He knows what he's doing"?
(A) Tony Fisher is good at his job.
(B) Tony Fisher is aware of his responsibilities.
(C) Tony Fisher has been hired for a task.

① _____ ② _____

▶▶▶ SET 11 🔊 35

チャット1

Gail Gromova 1:20 P.M.: There's some food from the party left in the fridge. Take it if you're hungry.
Vitali Devers 1:23 P.M.: Thanks, ①I'm good.

チャット2

Gail Gromova 1:20 P.M.: I need someone to come into work on the weekend and answer the phones in case there is an emergency.
Vitali Devers 1:23 P.M.: ②I'm good. My weekend plans just got canceled.

At 1:23 P.M., what does Mr. Devers mean when he writes, "I'm good"?
(A) He is satisfied with a product.
(B) He will not take an offer.
(C) He is available to help.

① _____ ② _____

▶▶▶ SET 12 🔊 36

チャット1

Ki-hoon Lee 9:56 A.M.: Have you reserved our accommodation in London yet?
Misty May 10:01 A.M.: ①I'm getting to it. I just have to confirm the dates with the clients first.

チャット2

Ki-hoon Lee 9:56 A.M.: Are you at the front gate yet?
Misty May 10:01 A.M.: ②I'm getting to it. I don't have a key so I'd like you to meet me there in a couple of minutes.

At 10:01 A.M., what does Ms. May mean when she writes, "I'm getting to it"?
(A) She is accustomed to her new position.
(B) She is going to arrive soon.
(C) She is about to make some arrangements.

① _____ ② _____

3文トレーニングの解答・解説

▶▶▶ **SET 1**

チャット1
Terry Hale（午前10時20分）：店長の職に応募することにしたよ。
Joan Spinner（午前10時23分）：いいじゃない。①あなたならきっとなれるわ。

チャット2
Terry Hale（午前10時20分）：この取扱説明書、本当に分かりにくいなあ。
Joan Spinner（午前10時23分）：読み続けなさい。②きっと分かるから。

午前10時23分にSpinner さんが書いている "I'm sure you'll get it" は、何を意図していますか？
(A) 彼女は Hale さんが旅行をすると思っている。
(B) 彼女は Hale さんが昇進すると思っている。
(C) 彼女は Hale さんが理解すると信じている。

【解説】get it の意味がポイント。チャット1では、Hale さん が店長職に応募したと書いている。それを受けてSpinner さんはターゲット文を書いているので、get it は「その役職を得る」という意味。(B) が正解。チャット2では、取扱説明書が分かりにくいと述べた Hale さんに、Spinner さんは読み続けるよう促してから、ターゲット文を続けている。この get it は「理解する」という意味なので、(C) が正解。
正解：①(B)　②(C)

▶▶▶ **SET 2**

チャット1
Lucy Chan（午後6時16分）：電車の到着が遅れたから、Hanson さんのことが心配だわ。
Rusty Cole（午後6時20分）：①間に合うよ。ついさっき彼女と話したから。

チャット2
Lucy Chan（午後6時16分）：Hanson さんがプレゼンのスライドショーを担当しなくちゃいけないの？
Rusty Cole（午後6時20分）：そうだよ。②できるさ。1週間前にやり方を教えたから。

午後6時20分に Cole さんが書いている "She'll make it" は、何を意図していますか？
(A) 彼は Hanson さんに準備を任せている。
(B) 彼は Hanson さんが間に合うと確信している。
(C) 彼は Hanson さんの手が空いていることを知っている。

【解説】make it は基本的に「うまくいく」を意味する表現。チャット1では、Hanson さんが遅刻しないか心配する Chan さんに、Cole さんは She'll make it. と書いている。よって、この make it は「間に合う」という意味。(B) が正解。チャット2で Cole さんが言いたいのは、「大丈夫。Hanson さんはスライドショーを作れるよ」ということ。「彼女に任せて OK だ」というニュアンスなので、(A) が正解。
正解：①(B)　②(A)

▶▶▶ **SET 3**

チャット1
Liesel Waters（午後1時45分）：あなたはわが社の Wiltshire Industries との協定について詳しいですか？
Todd Margaret（午後1時53分）：①そうでもありません。その取り決めは、私がこの会社で働き始めたときにはすでに存在していました。

チャット2
Liesel Waters（午後1時45分）：Wiltshire Industries との契約を延長すべきだと思いますか？
Todd Margaret 1:53 P.M.：②あまり思いませんね。彼らのために働くのは、わが社の多くの資源を要しますが、もっと収益性の高い活動に集中することだってできるわけですから。

午後1時53分に、Margaret さんはなぜ "Not really" と書いているのですか？
(A) 取り決めの詳細をよく知らないから。
(B) クライアントの担当者と連絡を取っていなかったから。
(C) あるクライアントとの契約を終わらせたいから。

【解説】Not really. がどのような情報を否定しているか考える。チャット1では、協定に詳しいかと尋ねられた Margaret さんが Not really. と答えている。つまり、「詳しくない」ことを伝えているので、正解は (A) だ。チャット2では、Waters さんが Do you think we should extend ...? と質問し、Margaret さんは Not really. と否定している。Margaret さんは契約延長に反対なので、正解は (C) だ。
正解：①(A)　②(C)

184

▶▶▶ SET 4

チャット1

Regis Grant（午前11時56分）：新しい印刷機をどう思う？
Heidi Marr（午前11時59分）：①あまり好きじゃないわ。以前使っていたブランドの方がデザインが良かったわ。

チャット2

Regis Grant（午前11時56分）：印刷機を買い替えるのにいくらかかったの？
Heidi Marr（午前11時59分）：②大したことないわ。前のものも手頃な値段で購入したんだけど、今度の新しいのはベースモデルだからそれよりずっと安かったの。

午前11時59分に Marr さんが書いている "Not much" は、何を意図していますか？
(A) 締め切りまでほとんど時間が残っていない。
(B) 新しい機材に心を動かされていない。
(C) 機材を替える費用は最小限だった。

【解説】 Not much. の意味は「多くない」だが、文脈の中でのニュアンスを考える。チャット1では、新しい印刷機への意見を求められた Marr さんが Not much. と答えている。これは I don't think much of the new printing machine. の省略形だ。not think much of 〜 は、「〜を良いと思わない」といった意味なので、(B) が正解。チャット2では、Grant さんが How much ...? と金額について尋ねている。その much を受けて、Marr さんは Not much. と答えているため、正解は (C) だ。
正解：①(B) ②(C)

▶▶▶ SET 5

チャット1

Ireen Wust（午後8時12分）：今年は社員をチーム育成旅行に派遣することができるでしょうか？
Meng Wang（午後8時15分）：①検討中です。全ては6月の仕事量次第ね。

チャット2

Ireen Wust（午後8時12分）：宴会用の見取り図を見た？
Meng Wang（午後8時15分）：②見ているところよ。ステージの広さが十分とは思えないわ。

午前8時15分に Wang さんが書いている "I'm looking at it" は、何を意図していますか？
(A) 彼女は計画を検討している。
(B) 彼女は決定を受け入れなくてはならない。
(C) 彼女は書類を眺めている。

【解説】 チャット1では、社員を派遣する可能性について質問された Wang さんがターゲット文を書いている。ここでの I'm looking at it. は、何かを「目で見ている」という意味ではなく「考えている」という意味なので、正解は (A) だ。一方、チャット2では、Wust さんが「見取り図を見た？」と質問している。よって、ターゲット文は文字通り「見ている」を意味するので、(C) が正解。
正解：①(A) ②(C)

▶▶▶ SET 6

チャット1

Cal Harris（午前10時11分）：僕ら新しいオフィスに1週間早く引っ越すよ。
Chloe Lahey（午前10時12分）：①待ち遠しいわ。すてきなんですってね。

チャット2

Cal Harris（午前10時11分）：うちの技術者が明日の正午、空調設備の修理をしにおたくのオフィスへ伺います。
Chloe Lahey（午前10時12分）：②待てません。重要な顧客が明日の朝来社するんです。

午前10時12分に Lahey さんが書いている "I can't wait" は、何を意図していますか？
(A) 彼女には差し迫った問題がある。
(B) 彼女はある変化を楽しみにしている。
(C) 彼女は旅行に出掛けようとしている。

【解説】 チャット1で、Lahey さんはターゲット文の後に、I hear they look fantastic. と書いている。つまり、引っ越すことに前向きだ。「待ち遠しい」と思ってターゲット文を書いているので、(B) が正解。一方、チャット2では、明日の午前に来客があるのに、エアコンの修理が間に合わないことを知ってターゲット文を書いている。これに合致するのは (A) だ。イントネーションの違いを、ぜひ音声でも確認してみよう。
正解：①(B) ②(A)

▶▶▶ SET 7

チャット1

Fay Wu（午前11時3分）：8時35分発のパリ行きの飛行機をお取りすることができます。
Hannes Mita（午前11時7分）：①<u>それにします。</u>すぐに請求明細を送っていただけますか。

チャット2

Fay Wu（午前11時3分）：新しいプロジェクターはすごく小さくて軽いから、バッグにも入るのよ。
Hannes Mita（午前11時7分）：②<u>それを持っていこう。</u>さもないと会場でレンタルしなくちゃいけないんだけど、すごく高いんだ。

午前11時7分に Mita さんが書いている "I'll take it" は、何を意図していますか？
(A) 彼はチケットを購入するつもりである。
(B) 彼は機材を使うつもりである。
(C) 彼は批判を受け入れるつもりである。

> 【解説】チャット1では、Wu さんが購入可能なチケット情報を提示し、それを受けて Mita さんがターゲット文を書いているので、take it は「それを買う」や「それをもらう」という意味。正解は (A) だ。チャット2では、プロジェクターが小さくて軽いと述べる Wu さんに、Mita さんはターゲット文に加えて、レンタルすると高いと書いている。この take it は「それを持っていく」という意味だ。(B) が正解。
> **正解**：①(A) ②(B)

▶▶▶ SET 8

チャット1

Boris Saneyev（午前10時13分）：駅まで迎えに行こうか？
Clair Fenton（午前10時27分）：①<u>もし構わなければ。</u>列車は正午に到着します。

チャット2

Boris Saneyev（午前10時13分）：今日はアパートまでどのように行かれますか？
Clair Fenton（午前10時27分）：②<u>差し支えなければ車で行きたいのですが。</u>よろしいでしょうか？

午前10時27分に Fenton さんはなぜ "If you wouldn't mind" と書いているのですか？
(A) 許可を求めるため
(B) 申し出を受け入れるため
(C) 代替案を与えるため

> 【解説】チャット1では、Saneyev さんの申し出に対して、Fenton さんは If you wouldn't mind. と応じている。「もし構わなければ」に続く言葉が省略されているが、正午に到着すると補足しているため、「もし構わなければ、お願いします」と伝えようとしている。よって、正解は (B) だ。チャット2では、Is that OK? が大きなヒント。許可を求めているので、(A) が正解。
> **正解**：①(B) ②(A)

▶▶▶ SET 9

チャット1

Paul Dimas（午後2時41分）：設備を共有することについて、Sandy College の人たちの反応はどうだった？
Lance Brown（午後2時45分）：①<u>彼らは前向きだよ。</u>心配いらない。

チャット2

Paul Dimas（午後2時41分）：あの不具合にもかかわらず、工場の人たちは本当に製造ノルマを達成するだろうか？
Lance Brown（午後2時45分）：②<u>彼らは自信を持ってる。</u>今は全て順調に行ってるよ。

午後2時45分、Brown さんが書いている "They're positive" は、何を意図していますか？
(A) 人々は計画を支持している。
(B) 人々は試験に合格した。
(C) 人々は結果を確信している。

> 【解説】チャット1では、まず、Dimas さんが Sandy College の人たちの反応を尋ねている。それに対して、Brownさんはターゲット文を書いている。この positive は、態度や意見が肯定的であることを意味するため、正解は (A) だ。チャット2では、工場の人たちが製造ノルマを達成するかどうかが尋ねられている。ここでの positive は「肯定的」ではなく「確信がある」という意味。(C) が正解だ。
> **正解**：①(A) ②(C)

▶▶▶ SET 10

チャット1

Reginald Sakata（午前8時10分）：Tony Fisher は新人技術者をとてもうまく訓練しているよ。彼らはもう現場に出る準備がほとんどできている。
Laura Stotsky（午前8時12分）：①手慣れたものね。

チャット2

Reginald Sakata（午前8時10分）：明日の製品実演での役割について、Tony Fisher に連絡しましょうか？
Laura Stotsky（午前8時12分）：②彼は分かっているわ。私が昨夜連絡したら、分かっているって言ってたから。

午前8時12分に Stotsky さんが書いている "He knows what he's doing" は何を意図していますか？
(A) Tony Fisher は仕事ができる。
(B) Tony Fisher は自分の職務が何か知っている。
(C) Tony Fisher がある仕事のために雇われた。

【解説】チャット1は、Sakata さんが Fisher さんの仕事ぶりを評価していることから始まっている。ターゲット文は、それに対する Stotsky さんのコメント。He knows what he's doing. は、人を褒めたり、何かが上手であることを評価したりする際に使う表現。よって、(A) が正解だ。チャット2のターゲット文は、文字通り Fisher さんが自分の役割を理解していることを意味しているため、(B) が正解。
正解：①(A) ②(B)

▶▶▶ SET 11

チャット1

Gail Gromova（午後1時20分）：パーティーの料理が冷蔵庫に残っているわ。お腹が空いていたら食べて。
Vitali Devers（午後1時23分）：ありがとう、①私は大丈夫。

チャット2

Gail Gromova（午後1時20分）：週末に出社して、緊急事態が起きたら電話に出てくれる人が必要なんですが。
Vitali Devers（午後1時23分）：②私は大丈夫ですよ。週末の予定が取りやめになったところです。

午後1時23分に Devers さんが書いている "I'm good" は、何を意図していますか？
(A) 製品に満足している。
(B) 申し出を受けるつもりはない。
(C) 助けることができる。

【解説】チャット1では、冷蔵庫に残っている物を食べていいと促されたことを受けて、Devers さんが Thanks, I'm good. と書いている。日本語の「大丈夫」と同じで、この I'm good. は「いいえ、結構です」という意味なので、(B) が正解。チャット2では、人手が必要だと述べる Gromova さんに対して、自分は大丈夫だ（出勤できる）と Devers さんは応じているので、(C) が正解。
正解：①(B) ②(C)

▶▶▶ SET 12

チャット1

Ki-hoon Lee（午前9時56分）：London での宿はもう予約した？
Misty May（午前10時1分）：①やろうとしているところ。まずクライアントに日付を確認しなくちゃいけないの。

チャット2

Ki-hoon Lee（午前9時56分）：もう表門にいる？
Misty May（午前10時1分）：②もう着くわよ。鍵を持っていないから、数分後にそこであなたと待ち合わせしたいんだけど。

午前10時1分に、May さんが書いている "I'm getting to it" は、何を意図していますか？
(A) 彼女は新しい職位になじんでいる。
(B) 彼女はもうすぐ到着するだろう。
(C) 彼女は手配をするところである。

【解説】基本的に get to ~ は「~に到達する」という意味。それぞれの文脈におけるニュアンスを考える。チャット1では、Lee さんの「予約した？」という質問への応答としてターゲット文が書かれている。よって、「やろうとしている」という意味なので、(C) が正解。一方、チャット2では、物理的な意味で「もうすぐ着く」と伝えている。よって、正解は (B) だ。
正解：①(C) ②(B)

「トリプルパッセージ」はこんな形式！

1回のテストに3セット出題される
- 15問（5問×3セット）
- 従来形式のダブルパッセージと合わせて「マルチプルパッセージ（複数の文書問題）」と呼ばれる。Part 7の最後の3セットがトリプルパッセージ

文書が3つある
- 3つの文書＋設問5問がセット
- トリプルパッセージ特有の設問があるわけではない
- 高い確率で同義語問題が1問含まれている

解説 「意外と普通」？！

　新形式によるテストが実施される前に、セミナー等で参加者の方々から得た反応では、最も関心が高かったのがこのトリプルパッセージでした。皆さんが一番ビビっていた変更と言い換えてもいいでしょう。実際に受験した感想を聞くと、「恐れていたほどじゃなかった」「意外に普通だった」と答える人が少なくありません。これから新形式を受験する人の中にも、トリプルパッセージに不安を感じている人はいるかもしれませんが、本書のドリルで形式にしっかり慣れておけば、心配することはありません。

解説 「2文書参照型」問題には段落単位の要約が有効

　トリプルパッセージの文書は、段落単位で、読んだ内容を要約しながら読むことをお勧めします。例えば、「最初の段落で客が先週買った商品について説明し、次の段落でクレームを言っている。最後の段落で返金を要求」のように。なぜなら、「2文書参照型」の設問が確実に、しかも、1セットに2問は出題されるからです。「2文書参照型」とは、2つの文書に分散された情報をつなぐことで初めて解ける設問です。仮に、「文書1」と「文書3」の情報を参照させる問題を解いていて、文書3にヒントを見つけたとします。ここで必要なのは「文書1の前半に関連情報があったな」と思い出し、すぐにそのヒントを見つけることです。これは、段落単位で理解する練習をしていれば難しくありません。段落を意識した読解練習は「文選択問題」と「位置選択問題」にも効きます。ぜひ、普段の学習に取り入れていってください。

「トリプルパッセージ」攻略の基本

　従来のダブルパッセージもそうですが、トリプルパッセージも解きやすいアプローチというのは個人によって違います。ここでは、ボクが実際に問題集や本番のテストで試してみて、個人的に「いいな」と思った解き方を紹介します。

● 2文書を先に読む

設問を読むより先に、3つある文書のうちの1番目と2番目の文書を通しで全部読む
（ここで重要なのは読んでいない文書を1つに限定することです）
↓
2文書を読んだら、設問を1問目から解き始める
↓
設問を読んで「解けない」と感じたら、ヒントは「まだ読んでいない文書にある」と特定できる
↓
3文書目を読んで解答する…

　実際にこの方法で解いたときのことをお話しすると、文書1・2の情報だけで、3問目までは解くことができました。解く瞬間は振り返りのために、文書のどこかをもう一度読みに行くこともありました（段落ごとに要約をしながら、文書全体に目を通しているので、情報を探す時間はそんなにかかっていません）。3・4問目辺りから、まだ登場していない人名が設問に出てくるなど、「ん？　それって何の話？」ということが起き始めました。その情報が3つ目の文書にあることは明らかなので、この「ん？」をきっかけに、3つ目の文書を読みに行きました。

　これは、英文をそこそこ理解できて、読むスピードもそこそこある人にはぜひ試してほしい解き方です。一番重要なのは、虫食い読みをせずに、なるべく多くの情報を頭に入れた状態で解答するということです。理想は「3文書を一気に読んで解く」ですが、それだと最初の方で読んだことを忘れてしまう不安を感じる人もいることでしょう。2文書、それも難しいという人は1文書、とにかく可能な限りの情報を頭に入れましょう。これはトリプルパッセージだけでなく、ダブルパッセージにも有効なアプローチです。

　今は無理だという人も、訓練することでできるようになります。5分～10分連続で英文を読んで、ストーリーを味わう練習をしてください。それがマルチプルパッセージ、そして Part 7 全体に強くなる方法です。

Part 7 ③ トリプルパッセージ｜ドリル

1セット 6分
トータル 54分

文書を読んで問題に答えよう。

Questions 45-49 refer to the following article, order form, and e-mail.

February 1 — Tomorrow, sportswear manufacturer, Running Wilde will release a new line of winter running gear that is sure to sell well in the coming months. They are making use of a new ultra-thin fabric called Freezaway that was developed by their own material design team. The company has been spending more on research and development in recent years, coming up with a number of innovations. Inevitably, competitors imitate their designs to some degree. One such company is Jogalot, which is releasing a new product called Coldpro in the next few days. Of course Running Wilde's loyal customers will most likely ensure that it remains the world's number one sportswear maker.

Major online store, Monte Cristo Online Shopping has been warning customers that because it expects huge demand, delivery of both companies' newest merchandise may be delayed up to a week.

---

http://www.montecristoos.com/orders/

Monte Cristo Online Shopping – Order Form

Customer: Agnes Moore
Address: Unit 7, Belleview Towers, 19 Ocean Road, Florence, Oregon
Date: February 4
Delivered to: Unit 7, Belleview Towers, 19 Ocean Road, Florence, Oregon

Order Number - EM6734836

Item Number	Item Description	Quantity	Price per Item	Total Price
RD7347	Freezaway Compression Pants (Size L)	1	$56	$56.00
RJ8432	Coldpro Thermal Shirt (Size L)	1	$54	$54.00
UY9094	Clodhopper Running Shoes (Size 6)	1	$145	$145.00
HU7348	Softies Runners' Socks (Size 6)	2	$32	$64.00
			Subtotal	$319.00
			Shipping	$8.00
			TOTAL	$327.00

Note: All items will be shipped together to reduce delivery costs.

To: custservice@montecristoos.com
From: Agnes Moore <amoore@whiteswan.com>
Date: February 12
Subject: Order Number - EM6734836

I would like to arrange the return of an item from my recent purchase. The running shoes are a bit too small. I've purchased size six running shoes many times before with no problems, so I am sure there is something wrong with the labeling on these shoes. The Freezaway compression pants are acceptable, but I do not feel that they really have the quality described on the Web site. I'll be leaving a comment to that effect in the customer reviews for that product. On the other hand, the Softies runners' socks were fine. I tried them out at once and was amazed at how well they fit.

45. In the article, the word "line" in paragraph 1, line 1, is closest in meaning to
    (A) selection
    (B) course
    (C) border
    (D) function

46. What is NOT suggested about Running Wilde?
    (A) It has increased spending on research and development.
    (B) It is the best-selling sportswear brand.
    (C) It has developed a new kind of cloth.
    (D) It will sponsor a professional sports team.

47. What is most likely true about Ms. Moore's order?
    (A) It will be shipped free of charge.
    (B) It will be delivered after a delay.
    (C) It was paid for by gift card.
    (D) It is her first purchase from Monte Cristo Online Shopping.

48. Which item does Ms. Moore indicate she was pleased with?
    (A) RD7347
    (B) RJ8432
    (C) UY9094
    (D) HU7348

49. What does Ms. Moore mention that she will do?
    (A) Request a replacement
    (B) Contact a manufacturer
    (C) Write a review of an item
    (D) Pay for express shipping

GO ON TO THE NEXT PAGE

Questions 50-54 refer to the following notice, message, and article.

Baxter Toys

To All Staff,

The Baxter Toys' Research Department needs your help. In recent years, sales have been dropping as we have had to compete more and more with computer game manufacturers. Children seem to prefer to receive software titles as gifts over traditional toys.

The research department has been unable to come up with many exciting new ideas, so we would like other employees to share theirs. As an incentive, the company is offering five percent of the profit generated by any new toy in the form of a bonus to any employee whose idea is adopted. Because I want time to consider each suggestion carefully, each department will be allocated a different submission period.

November 8 ~ 15	Marketing
November 16 ~ 23	Planning
November 24 ~ 29	Customer Service
December 6 ~ 13	General Affairs

I will be placing a suggestion box on a desk by the door of the research department. Please write your suggestions on the message paper supplied and place them in the box.

Thank you,

Takashi Furukawa

New Toy Suggestion

Name: Meredith Birney   **Date:** November 12

Rather than trying to come up with a completely new toy, we should try to improve on a traditional toy. Most parents grew up at a time when computer games were not very advanced, so they played with model train sets or electronic car racing tracks. Parents are the ones who choose and pay for toys, and so they would probably like to introduce their children to a toy similar to what they had when they were young. Baxter Toys used to have the most popular electric toy car racing sets in the country. I suggest we update the designs to incorporate new technology and rerelease them.

Baxter Toys Back on Top

Norma Day, March 3

Baxter Toys has made an amazing recovery from its recent sales slump by appealing to the nostalgia of parents. Toys that were popular 20 or 30 years ago are being rereleased in their original packaging. The company is even running the radio and television advertisements it used when they were first released. The products themselves have received some improvements and upgrades, but children around the country are now getting to experience the toys their parents used to play with. Interestingly, company president Roland Oaks has made good on his pledge to give five percent of the profit to the employee who came up with the idea. As a result, one lucky member of staff has decided to take early retirement at the end of this month.

---

50. What is implied about Baxter Toys?
 (A) It was founded very recently.
 (B) It ships toys to various countries.
 (C) It does not produce game software.
 (D) It is closing its research department.

51. In the notice, the phrase "in the form of" in paragraph 2, line 3, is closest in meaning to
 (A) in place of
 (B) taking the shape of
 (C) close to
 (D) by way of

52. Which department does Ms. Birney most likely work for?
 (A) Marketing
 (B) Planning
 (C) Customer Service
 (D) General Affairs

53. What is indicated about Mr. Furukawa?
 (A) He is a personal friend of Ms. Birney's.
 (B) He accepted an employee's suggestion.
 (C) He was made company president.
 (D) He took a holiday in January.

54. What does the article say about the company's advertising?
 (A) It has won an award.
 (B) It is being shown in the evenings.
 (C) It was produced by a famous firm.
 (D) It is using previously broadcast material.

GO ON TO THE NEXT PAGE

Questions 55-59 refer to the following e-mail, article, and survey.

To:	Silvia Ishikiriyama <sishikiriyama@smalllab.com>
From:	Harper McCann <hmccann@smalllab.com>
Date:	February 16
Subject:	Idea for members
Attachment:	📎 tokyoarticle

Hi Silvia,

I have been reading a magazine article written by one of our members. She is a fairly well-known travel writer, who takes the time to find interesting perspectives on the destinations that are not mentioned in most guidebooks.

After reading about her recent trip to Tokyo, I really started to think that a lot of our members would be interested in taking part in a group tour there. Please take a look at the attached article. If you agree, I'll talk to a travel agent about putting together a tour for us.

Best regards,

Harper McCann

Tokyo's Scattered Oases
By Karla Iversen

I recently took my family on a trip to Japan. We visited two major tourist cities, Tokyo and Kyoto. There were many famous sights to see there and coming from a small Nebraskan farming town, everyone was excited to see the huge buildings and amazing infrastructure of Tokyo, and the historic buildings and cultural traditions of Kyoto. What we were not ready for were the wonderful little gardens built on rooftops and balconies and hanging from the fences in front of people's homes. Tokyo is surprisingly green. The Japanese seem to have found a fun way of enjoying gardening that takes little effort or cost. Yet, it brightens up entire neighborhoods.

BGA Japan Tour — Satisfaction Survey

Name: Laurence David

Comments: Japan was really very different from what I had imagined and I look forward to visiting again sometime. Hiring Karla Iversen as a tour leader was an excellent idea because her wonderful sense of humor and charm made the tour a lot of fun. Nevertheless, it would have been even better if someone with a deeper knowledge of Japanese history and culture had been available to participants.

Overall satisfaction: Unsatisfied 1 — 2 — 3 —(4)— 5 Very Satisfied
Reservation process: Unsatisfied 1 — 2 —(3)— 4 — 5 Very Satisfied
Staff Helpfulness: Unsatisfied 1 — 2 —(3)— 4 — 5 Very Satisfied
Accommodation: Unsatisfied(1)— 2 — 3 — 4 — 5 Very Satisfied

---

55. Why does Mr. McCann write to Ms. Ishikiriyama?
(A) To inform her about an expense report
(B) To suggest that she read an article
(C) To ask for help with some arrangements
(D) To introduce a candidate for a position

56. Who does Mr. McCann indicate that he will contact?
(A) A magazine editor
(B) A travel agency
(C) A sales expert
(D) A family member

57. What kind of organization is Mr. McCann most likely a member of?
(A) A convention steering committee
(B) A city engineering department
(C) A gardening association
(D) A farming industry support group

58. In the survey, the word "available" in paragraph 1, line 4, is closest in meaning to
(A) accessible
(B) responsible
(C) vacant
(D) reliant

59. What is true about the tour?
(A) It featured a lot of information about Japanese culture.
(B) It was more popular than organizers had expected.
(C) It will be held every year.
(D) It was led by a travel writer.

GO ON TO THE NEXT PAGE

Questions 60-64 refer to the following memo, summary, and e-mail.

MEMO

To: All employees
From: Human resources
Re: Employee survey
Date: May 25

On Friday, a survey will be distributed to staff members to help assess employee perceptions of management's strengths and weaknesses. The survey will combine multiple-choice questions with open-ended questions to which you are expected to give full-sentence responses. The surveys are designed to be anonymous. Nevertheless, if you would like to make yourself available for further discussion on any of the topics, you may write your employee number in the box provided at the top right of the page.

Sincerely,

Steve Cameron

Preliminary Summary of Employee Responses to Management Survey

The following points were made by staff members who did not mind being identified and approached for further discussion. Other findings will be published as soon as the data has been analyzed.

Employees are given little opportunity to contribute to decisions before they are made because they are not invited to attend monthly meetings.	Joan Cummings
Staff who wish to acquire new skills should be provided mentorship programs or given time and financial assistance to take courses at local educational institutions.	Peter Gonzalez
More flexible arrangements for time off should be available to allow staff to schedule holidays more freely.	Lucy Wu
Please extend the parking garage to accommodate more staff vehicles. At present, only management-level staff members are able to park on the grounds. Other workers have to walk up to two kilometers to and from their vehicles.	Regis Smith

196

To:	All Staff
From:	Jow Lim
Date:	June 3
Subject:	Policy change

Dear staff:

As a result of the recent employee survey, we have decided to adopt the following change immediately. Other changes may be implemented in coming months after they have been discussed more thoroughly.

Tomorrow's management meeting for April will be held in Conference Room 201 on the second floor. It has seats for up to 60 people, which should be adequate for all interested employees to attend. This does not mean that attendance is mandatory, only that it is open to anyone who would like to be present or express an opinion on the topics tabled for discussion. Unless otherwise notified, you can expect all future monthly meetings to be carried out the same way.

---

60. According to the memo, how can respondents reveal their identities to management?
(A) By supplying their employee number
(B) By handing in their survey in person
(C) By writing their name on a form
(D) By calling a supervisor

61. Who most likely is Steve Cameron?
(A) A job applicant
(B) A client representative
(C) A market researcher
(D) A department director

62. What is implied about the survey data?
(A) It has been sent to a specialist for analysis.
(B) Multiple-choice questions have not been processed.
(C) There were not enough responses.
(D) It will be distributed to all employees.

63. Whose suggestion has been accepted by management?
(A) Joan Cummings
(B) Peter Gonzalez
(C) Lucy Wu
(D) Regis Smith

64. In the e-mail, the word "express" in paragraph 2, line 4, is closest in meaning to
(A) represent
(B) follow
(C) voice
(D) resolve

GO ON TO THE NEXT PAGE

Questions 65-69 refer to the following e-mails and letter.

To:	Joan Carson <jcarson@clarendonhotel.com>
From:	Harold Chang <hchang@peekfishing.com>
Date:	August 9
Subject:	Fishing Tours

Dear Ms. Carson,

My name is Harold Chang and I am the owner of Peek Fishing. We have been running fishing tours on Waring Lake and, as of this month, we are the only fishing company operating on the Hopscotch River. I am writing to request permission to leave our brochures with the staff at your tour desk. In accordance with standard industry practice, we would like to offer you a ten percent commission on bookings made through the hotel.

If you would like to verify the quality of our service before recommending it to your guests, please let me know as I can quickly arrange a complimentary tour for you or any of your staff.

To:	Harold Chang <hchang@peekfishing.com>
From:	Joan Carson <jcarson@clarendonhotel.com>
Date:	August 12
Subject:	RE: Fishing Tours

Dear Mr. Chang,

Thank you for writing regarding your tour offerings and the kind invitation to inspect them. I regret to inform you, however, that we are already providing our guests a fishing tour with Big Catch Fishing Company and it is hotel policy not to list such similar services alongside each other.

We will be reprinting the tour information for distribution in October and we generally negotiate with suppliers wishing to be included on the list in mid-September. I would like to send our tour desk coordinator, Miles Thompson, on one of your fishing tours before we begin any negotiations.

If you choose to submit an application for inclusion at that time, you should keep in mind that the hotel requires a minimum commission of fifteen percent.

November 21

Tour Desk
Clarendon Hotel
25 Valhalla Street
Coopersfield CA 97005

Dear Tour Desk Staff,

My wife and I had the pleasure of staying at your charming hotel on November 17 and 18 this year. I am writing with regard to the fishing tour we booked at the hotel tour desk. The Hopscotch River was an amazing location. The fall colors of the trees were reflected in the water, making a beautiful setting. The tour leader had an excellent knowledge of fishing and local history and we had a fascinating time. Could you please let me know if the tour will be offered during the spring as we are planning on returning with a group of friends at that time?

Sincerely,

Grant Connolly
Grant Connolly

---

65. Who most likely is Ms. Carson?
    (A) A government official
    (B) A sales person
    (C) A hotel manager
    (D) A tour company operator

66. In the first e-mail, the word "practice" in paragraph 1, line 4, is closest in meaning to
    (A) preparation
    (B) convention
    (C) application
    (D) dictation

67. Which offer of Mr. Chang's does Ms. Carson accept?
    (A) A ten percent commission
    (B) A free fishing tour
    (C) Directions to a tourist attraction
    (D) Complimentary accommodation

68. In the letter, what is implied about Clarendon Hotel?
    (A) It has an exclusive arrangement with Peek Fishing.
    (B) It is closed over the winter months.
    (C) It has been operating for many years.
    (D) It offers guests discounts on local tours.

69. What does Mr. Connolly indicate he will do?
    (A) Try Big Catch Fishing Company
    (B) Write a review of his holiday
    (C) Join a nature painting class
    (D) Return to the Clarendon Hotel

GO ON TO THE NEXT PAGE

Questions 70-74 refer to the following e-mails and report.

To: Randy Cole <rcole@simpsonassociates.com>
From: Kalil Mehajer <kmehajer@simpsonassociates.com>
Subject: Tokyo transfer
Date: July 7

Dear Randy,

We discussed the possibility of your transfer to Tokyo for the opening of our first Japanese branch a couple of months ago. I have decided to go ahead with it. The branch is scheduled to open in December, but you ought to be there as early as September to help set up and employ staff.

In preparation for your trip, I'd like you to sign up for a course in Japanese language at the Olivetti School of Business.

You should choose a member of staff to travel with you as an assistant. I will leave the final decision up to you. However, I should mention that Jim Rosen has lived in Tokyo and would be particularly helpful.

To: Kalil Mehajer <kmehajer@simpsonassociates.com>
From: Randy Cole <rcole@simpsonassociates.com>
Subject: RE: Tokyo transfer
Date: July 10

Thank you so much for considering me for this important position. I have been going over the schedule and I think a September start may be problematic. I am obliged to meet with some clients whose investments I am managing at that time. I can certainly manage a departure in early October, however.

I have been in contact with the Olivetti School of Business and it seems that their course does not really suit my work schedule. Instead, I have arranged for a private language tutor by the name of Hisami Tsuchiya to come to the office once a day until my departure. It works out cheaper for the company, so I am sure you will not mind.

Jim Rosen was very receptive to the idea of traveling with me and I have offered him the option of returning after one year.

Yearly Progress Report

The Tokyo branch of Simpson Associates has reached all of its targets with ease. It seems that there are more people than we expected who are looking to invest money in international commerce. Next year's objectives will be more ambitious.

Regrettably, Jim Rosen has decided to return to the United States this month and I am forced to hire a replacement. I have contacted Ms. Tsuchiya, whom you have met on a number of occasions and she has agreed to take over his role here.

---

70. According to the first e-mail, when will the Tokyo branch open?
 (A) In July
 (B) In September
 (C) In October
 (D) In December

71. What kind of business is Simpson Associates?
 (A) An investment firm
 (B) A law office
 (C) A fashion chain
 (D) A construction company

72. What do Mr. Cole and Mr. Mehajer agree about?
 (A) Taking a course at the Olivetti School of Business
 (B) Mr. Cole's leaving in September
 (C) Sending Mr. Rosen as an assistant
 (D) Funding for an advertising campaign

73. In the report, the word "expected" in paragraph 1, line 2, is closest in meaning to
 (A) required
 (B) attracted
 (C) anticipated
 (D) sustained

74. Who will replace Mr. Rosen?
 (A) A director of Simpson Associates
 (B) An applicant from a rival firm in Tokyo
 (C) One of Mr. Mehajer's business contacts
 (D) Mr. Cole's former language teacher

GO ON TO THE NEXT PAGE

Questions 75-79 refer to the following article, Web site, and review.

Pedaling the Globe — Frank Dolby sets himself a seemingly impossible challenge at the start of each book and writes about his adventures trying to achieve it. His previous book was about visiting every state in the United States using less than a dollar a day. It was a bestseller and inspired many young people to try to replicate his journey. For his most recent book, *Pedaling the Globe*, he attempted to travel from South Africa all the way to the southernmost tip of Argentina entirely by bicycle. I would rather not spoil the book by writing too much about whether or not he achieved the feat. It is enough to say that it was an amazing journey filled with humor and excitement.

---

www.frankdolbyadventurer.com

Frank Dolby — Adventurer
Appearances

I have speaking engagements in many parts of the country on the following dates. Check with the venues regarding admission requirements.

June 4 — Brad's Bikes (South Sydney, NSW) **Promotional Event for Sternway Bicycles**
June 6 — Strathpine Library (Strathpine, NSW) **Reading, Question and Answer, Book Signing**
August 10 — Beaumont Conference Hall (Brunswick, VIC) **Presentation on Travel Writing**
August 21 — Harrison's Books and Bikes (Geelong, VIC) **Reading, Question and Answer, Book Signing**

Note to venues: Unless otherwise indicated, a minimum appearance fee of $600 is required. Venues may charge participants to cover any costs incurred in hosting the event.

Customer Views on *Pedaling the Globe*

Reviewer: Jenny Penhall
I met Frank Dolby this August. I purchased a copy of the book at the venue where he was engaged to speak. After reading a section and answering questions from the audience, he was kind enough to sign the book. I suggest that you read the book before listening to him speak. He talks openly about the outcomes of the trip, which ruins much of the suspense. Despite this, I thoroughly enjoyed *Pedaling the Globe* and can recommend it to anyone interested in travel literature.

75. What is the article mainly about?
    (A) A new travel option for tourists
    (B) The latest work of an author
    (C) A money saving system
    (D) Motivating young people

76. What is NOT suggested about Mr. Dolby?
    (A) His previous book was popular.
    (B) He has donated some of his earnings.
    (C) He has visited the United States.
    (D) He is paid for making appearances.

77. On the Web site, the word "cover" in paragraph 2, line 2, is closest in meaning to
    (A) offset
    (B) hide
    (C) distinguish
    (D) include

78. When did Ms. Penhall most likely meet Mr. Dolby?
    (A) On June 4
    (B) On June 6
    (C) On August 10
    (D) On August 21

79. What does Ms. Penhall recommend that readers do?
    (A) Purchase a book at an online store
    (B) Arrive well ahead of the start time
    (C) Contact Mr. Dolby using the details on his Web site
    (D) Read the book before attending Mr. Dolby's talk

Questions 80-84 refer to the following e-mail, Web page, and card.

To:	Toshiki Fujisawa <tfujisawa@whitegoose.com>
From:	Sunil Singh <ssingh@devineair.com>
Date:	May 19
Subject:	Your flight

Dear Mr. Fujisawa,

Please allow me to begin by offering you my sincerest apologies for the overbooking on May 3 this year. Thank you for agreeing to take a later flight at such short notice. Your sacrifice made it possible for another group of passengers to travel to their designation together.

On reviewing the situation, I have come to the decision that the compensation you received for this inconvenience was insufficient. In accordance with company guidelines, I would like to offer you a year of free membership to the Transecutive Club. This will entitle you to use the deluxe airport lounges when traveling with any of our partner airlines based in Europe.

The year of membership starts the first time you use the card to gain entry to a participating airline's lounge or take advantage of a free shuttle bus to a Transecutive Hotel in one of 50 locations.

For more information about the benefits of the club, please visit the following Web site: http://thetransecutiveclub.com/benefits. To take advantage of this offer, please click the button marked "Join" at the top of the page and enter your personal details along with the following coupon code: TYE83K.

Sincerely,

Sunil Singh
Customer Relations Officer
Devine Air

---

http://thetransecutiveclub.com/benefits

The Transecutive Club   JOIN

Membership to the Transecutive Club has been a sign of success among business travelers for more than 40 years. We have facilities in more than 100 airports worldwide, where we offer our cherished members a level of service unmatched by any of our competitors.

Members of the Transecutive Club can take advantage of a wide range of special services at airports around the world. We offer advanced boarding of flights, discounts on hotel accommodation, upgrades to in-flight meals as well as many other benefits that will make your trip much more enjoyable.

The Transecutive Club

Cardholder: **Toshiki Fujisawa**
Membership Number: **7348892**

This card entitles approved passengers on participating airlines to enter The Transecutive Club Lounge at any airport in the world.

Participating Airlines
Sterling Airlines – Flyway Air – Tora Airways – Devine Air

---

80. Why did Mr. Singh write the e-mail?
    (A) To explain the cause of an error
    (B) To request assistance with a problem
    (C) To offer a customer compensation
    (D) To recommend an airline to an employee

81. How can Mr. Fujisawa obtain a membership card?
    (A) By visiting an airline office
    (B) By filling out an online form
    (C) By calling a company representative
    (D) By reserving hotel accommodation

82. What is NOT a benefit of the Transecutive Club?
    (A) Priority boarding of flights
    (B) Access to luxury facilities
    (C) Free hotel transfers
    (D) Discounts on airline tickets

83. On the Web page, the word "sign" in paragraph 1, line 1, is closest in meaning to
    (A) notice
    (B) warning
    (C) symbol
    (D) prediction

84. What is indicated about Sterling Airlines?
    (A) It is based in Europe.
    (B) It rewards frequent fliers.
    (C) It is a domestic airline.
    (D) It specializes in business travel.

GO ON TO THE NEXT PAGE

Questions 85-89 refer to the following e-mail, online review section, and Web page.

To:	Red Stoneway <rstoneway@stoneapps.com>
From:	Megan Korbut <mkorbut@apolonia.com>
Subject:	Runtag
Date:	August 9

Dear Mr. Stoneway,

I am pleased to announce that the software application you submitted to Apolonia for evaluation has been approved. We would like to start offering Runtag among the thousands of other software titles we have in our online store. You may decide to make it available for free or charge customers who purchase a copy of the application. The free version can only generate revenue through advertising, which will appear while people use the application. All software authors who sell through Apolonia are required to pay 20 percent of their sales revenue or 10 percent of their advertising revenue. This is not open for negotiation.

We have created a user account for you so that you can upload the software application to the store. The account page offers many functions to publishers such as uploading software updates, providing customer support, and providing detailed descriptions of your products. Please use the following link to access your account. http://www.apolonia.com/store/stoneapps. You must upload the software to the store by September 9 or you will be required to resubmit it for evaluation.

Sincerely,

Megan Korbut
Apolonia – Sales Department

Reviews of RUNTAG by Stoneapps

Reviewer: Candy Simms (Verified User) ★★★☆☆ (3 stars)
I have been using Runtag for a few months now and I am satisfied with it. I chose this application because I am a long-time user of Stoneapps' bargain hunting software, which is their most popular product. The only shortcoming of the application is that there are still not enough other users. I think more and more people will start using this in future and we should be able to enjoy comparing our fitness statistics with other users'.

Reviewer: Gahl Saag (Verified User) ★★☆☆☆ (2 stars)
I tested this for a month, but decided to go back to the application I had been using before. I might try it again in a few months to see if they've added the features I need.

http://www.apolonia.com/store/stoneapps/statement

Stoneapps' Revenue and Commission Statement for December

	Total Downloads	Total Revenue	Commission Rate	Subtotal
LowPro	321	$3,400	10%	$340
Photogenius	71	$1,065	20%	$213
Traffic Hopper	210	$1,890	20%	$378
Coolways	0	$0	10%	$0
Runtag	190	$2,300	10%	$230
TOTAL		$8,655		$1,161
Total payable to Stoneapps (Total revenue minus commission payable)				$7,494

The total payable amount will be deposited into the stipulated bank account by January 15.

---

85. What kind of company is Apolonia?
(A) An online store
(B) An advertising agency
(C) A software developer
(D) A consulting company

86. What function is NOT available on the Web site?
(A) Uploading software updates
(B) Recruiting temporary staff
(C) Providing customer support
(D) Publishing product descriptions

87. Which Stoneapp product has Ms. Simms purchased in the past?
(A) LowPro
(B) Photogenius
(C) Traffic Hopper
(D) Coolways

88. In the online review section, the word "features" in paragraph 2, line 2, is closest in meaning to
(A) articles
(B) capabilities
(C) conclusions
(D) distributions

89. What is indicated about Runtag?
(A) It is Stoneapps' first release.
(B) It comes in two versions.
(C) It can be downloaded for free.
(D) It will be removed from sale.

Part 7　③トリプルパッセージ　ドリルの解答・解説

Questions 45-49 refer to the following article, order form, and e-mail.
（問題45-49は次の記事、注文フォーム、Eメールに関するものです）

文書1「記事」と訳

February 1 — Tomorrow, sportswear manufacturer, Running Wilde will release ①a new line of winter running gear that is sure to sell well in the coming months. ②They are making use of a new ultra-thin fabric called Freezaway that was developed by their own material design team. ③The company has been spending more on research and development in recent years, coming up with a number of innovations. Inevitably, competitors imitate their designs to some degree. ④One such company is Jogalot, which is releasing a new product called Coldpro in the next few days. ⑤Of course Running Wilde's loyal customers will most likely ensure that it remains the world's number one sportswear maker.

⑥Major online store, Monte Cristo Online Shopping has been warning customers that because it expects huge demand, delivery of both companies' newest merchandise may be delayed up to a week.

2月1日──明日、スポーツウエア製造メーカーの Running Wilde 社は、今後数カ月よく売れるに違いない冬用ランニング用品の新シリーズを発売する。彼らは自社の素材設計チームが開発した Freezaway と呼ばれる極薄手の生地を使用している。同社は近年、研究と開発により多くを費やし、数多くの革新の考案に至っている。必然的に競合相手は彼らのデザインをある程度模倣する。そういった企業の1つが Jogalot 社で、数日後には Coldpro という新製品を発売する。もちろん Running Wilde の忠実な顧客層のおかげで、同社は今後も世界1位のスポーツウエア・メーカーであり続けるだろう。

大手オンライン・ストアの Monte Cristo Online Shopping は、大きな需要が見込まれるため、両社の最新製品の配達は最長1週間遅れそうだと顧客に注意を呼び掛けている。

- □ **gear**：衣服、装備　□ **make use of ～**：～を使用する　□ **ultra-thin**：極薄の　□ **fabric**：生地、繊維
- □ **innovation**：革新　□ **inevitably**：必然的に、不可避的に　□ **to some degree**：ある程度まで

文書2「注文フォーム」と訳

http://www.montecristoos.com/orders/

Monte Cristo Online Shopping – Order Form

Customer: Agnes Moore
Address: Unit 7, Belleview Towers, 19 Ocean Road, Florence, Oregon
Date: February 4
Delivered to: Unit 7, Belleview Towers, 19 Ocean Road, Florence, Oregon

Order Number - EM6734836

Item Number	Item Description	Quantity	Price per Item	Total Price
⑦RD7347	**Freezaway Compression Pants (Size L)**	1	$56	$56.00
⑧RJ8432	**Coldpro Thermal Shirt (Size L)**	1	$54	$54.00
UY9094	**Clodhopper Running Shoes (Size 6)**	1	$145	$145.00
⑨HU7348	**Softies Runners' Socks (Size 6)**	2	$32	$64.00
			Subtotal	$319.00
			Shipping	$8.00
			TOTAL	$327.00

Note: All items will be shipped together to reduce delivery costs.

---

③トリプルパッセージ

http://www.montecristoos.com/orders/

Monte Cristo Online Shopping 注文フォーム

お客さま：Agnes Moore
ご住所：Unit 7, Belleview Towers, 19 Ocean Road, Florence, Oregon
日付：2月4日
お届け先：Unit 7, Belleview Towers, 19 Ocean Road, Florence, Oregon

注文番号 ― EM6734836

商品番号	商品内容	個数	1個当たりの価格	合計金額
RD7347	Freezaway 加圧パンツ（Lサイズ）	1	56ドル	56ドル
RJ8432	Coldpro サーマルシャツ（Lサイズ）	1	54ドル	54ドル
UY9094	Clodhopper ランニングシューズ（サイズ6）	1	145ドル	145ドル
HU7348	Softies ランニング用靴下（サイズ6）	2	32ドル	64ドル
			小計	$319.00
			送料	$8.00
			合計	$327.00

注意：全商品は配送費削減のため、まとめて発送されます。

☐**compression pants**：加圧パンツ ☐**thermal shirt**：サーマルシャツ、保温性シャツ ☐**runners' socks**：ランニング用靴下 ☐**subtotal**：小計

文書3「E メール」と訳

To: custservice@montecristoos.com
From: Agnes Moore <amoore@whiteswan.com>
Date: February 12
Subject: Order Number - EM6734836

I would like to arrange the return of an item from my recent purchase. The running shoes are a bit too small. I've purchased size six running shoes many times before with no problems, so I am sure there is something wrong with the labeling on these shoes. ⑩The Freezaway compression pants are acceptable, but I do not feel that they really have the quality described on the Web site. ⑪I'll be leaving a comment to that effect in the customer reviews for that product. ⑫On the other hand, the Softies runners' socks were fine. I tried them out at once and was amazed at how well they fit.

宛先：custservice@montecristoos.com
送信者：Agnes Moore <amoore@whiteswan.com>
日付：2月12日
件名：注文番号—EM6734836

最近の買い物から1つ、返品の手続きをしたいと思います。ランニングシューズが少し小さ過ぎるのです。私は過去に何度もサイズ6のランニングシューズを問題なく購入しているので、この靴の表示が何かおかしいのだと確信しています。Freezaway 加圧パンツはまあまあですが、ウェブサイトで説明されているほどの品質だとは思いません。その製品のカスタマーレビューに、その趣旨のコメントを残します。一方で、Softies ランナー用靴下は良かったです。すぐにはいてみましたが、ぴったりなじむのに驚きました。

□**labeling**：表示、ラベル付け　□**to that effect**：その趣旨で、この種の　□**try ～ out**：～を実際に使ってみる、～を試しに使ってみる

選択肢と訳

45.
In the article, the word "line" in paragraph 1, line 1, is closest in meaning to（記事の第1段落・1行目の "line" に最も意味が近いのは）
(A) selection（品ぞろえ）
(B) course（コース）
(C) border（境界線）
(D) function（機能）

解説

正解：(A)

同義語問題。line には「線」「行列」「回線」などさまざまな意味があるが、「a line of＋商品」の形で用いられると、「～のシリーズ、～の品ぞろえ」という意味になる。①の a new line of winter running gear は「冬用ランニング用品の新シリーズ」だ。選択肢の (A) がそれに合致する。(C) も「線」という意味では line の同義語だが、ストーリーを理解していれば除外できる。「ストーリーの理解」を試す同義語問題は、まさに新形式の傾向に沿った問題タイプであり、トリプルパッセージの常連だ。

46.
What is NOT suggested about Running Wilde?
(Running Wilde 社について示唆されていないことは何ですか？)
(A) It has increased spending on research and development.（研究開発の支出を増やした）
(B) It is the best-selling sportswear brand.（最もよく売れているスポーツウエアのブランドである）
(C) It has developed a new kind of cloth.（新しい種類の布を開発した）
(D) It will sponsor a professional sports team.
（プロのスポーツ・チームに出資する）

□**sponsor**：～に出資する、～のスポンサーになる

正解：(D)
Running Wilde 社について示唆されていることを除外して解答する。記事の②「自社の素材設計チームが開発した極薄手の生地」は、(C) に該当する。③「同社は近年、研究と開発により多くを費やし」は、(A) に相当する。⑤の「世界第1位のスポーツウエア・メーカーであり続ける」は、(B)「最も売れているスポーツウエアのブランド」の言い換えとしてふさわしい。よって、記述のない (D) が正解。

47.
What is most likely true about Ms. Moore's order?
(Moore さんの注文について、本当である可能性が高いのは何ですか？)
(A) It will be shipped free of charge.（無料で発送される）
(B) It will be delivered after a delay.（遅れて届けられる）
(C) It was paid for by gift card.（ギフト券で支払われた）
(D) It is her first purchase from Monte Cristo Online Shopping.（Monte Cristo Online Shopping での初めての購入である）

□**after a delay**：遅れて

正解：(B)
記事の⑥に「Monte Cristo Online Shopping は、両社の最新シリーズの配達が遅れそうだと顧客に呼び掛けている」とある。「両社の最新シリーズ」とは②と④から、FreezawayとColdproのことである。Moore氏の注文フォームの⑦と⑧から、彼女はそれらの製品を注文していることが分かる。つまり、「配達が遅れそうだ」と言及された製品をMoore氏は注文したことになるので、(B)が正解。記事と申し込みフォームの2文書を参照して解く問題だ。

48.
Which item does Ms. Moore indicate she was pleased with?（Moore さんが満足したと示しているのはどの商品ですか？）
(A) RD 7347
(B) RJ 8432
(C) UY 9094
(D) HU 7348

正解：(D)
これも2文書参照型問題。メールの⑫で Moore氏は、「Softiesのランニング用靴下は良かった」と述べているので、彼女が満足した商品の名称が分かる。選択肢には商品名ではなく商品番号が並んでいる。注文フォームを見ると、商品番号と商品名が併記されているので、⑨からSofties Runners' Socks の商品番号は (D) と判明する。

49.
What does Ms. Moore mention that she will do?
(Moore さんは何をすると述べていますか？)
(A) Request a replacement（交換を依頼する）
(B) Contact a manufacturer（製造元に連絡する）
(C) Write a review of an item（商品に関するレビューを書く）
(D) Pay for express shipping（速達代を払う）

正解：(C)
Moore氏はメールの⑩で「Freezawayの商品がウェブサイトで説明されているような品質ではなかった」と述べている。その直後、彼女は⑪に「その趣旨のコメントをカスタマーレビューに残す」と書いている。よって、(C) が正解だ。Freezaway を用いた製品に満足はしていないようだが、(A)「交換を依頼」、(B)「製造元に連絡」、(D)「速達代を払う」という記述はないので、それぞれ不適切。

Questions 50-54 refer to the following notice, message, and article.
(問題50-54は次のお知らせ、メッセージ、記事に関するものです)

> 文書1 「お知らせ」と訳

Baxter Toys

To All Staff,

The Baxter Toys' Research Department needs your help. ①In recent years, sales have been dropping as we have had to compete more and more with computer game manufacturers. Children seem to prefer to receive software titles as gifts over traditional toys.

The research department has been unable to come up with many exciting new ideas, so we would like other employees to share theirs. ②As an incentive, the company is offering five percent of the profit generated by any new toy in the form of a bonus to any employee whose idea is adopted. Because I want time to consider ③each suggestion carefully, each department will be allocated a different submission period.

④November 8 〜 15	Marketing
November 16 〜 23	Planning
November 24 〜 29	Customer Service
December 6 〜 13	General Affairs

⑤I will be placing a suggestion box on a desk by the door of the research department. Please write your suggestions on the message paper supplied and place them in the box.

Thank you,

⑥Takashi Furukawa

Baxter Toys

スタッフの皆さんへ

Baxter Toysの研究部はあなたの助けを必要としています。近年、コンピューターゲームのメーカーとますます激しく競わなくてはならないために、売り上げが落ちています。子どもたちは昔ながらのおもちゃよりも、ソフトウエアをプレゼントとしてもらうことを好むようです。

研究部では刺激的な新しいアイデアをあまり出せずにいるので、他の従業員の方々のアイデアを共有していただきたいと思います。報奨として、社は新しいおもちゃによって生み出された利益の5パーセントを、ボーナスの形で、アイデアが採用された社員に支給します。それぞれの提案を慎重に検討したいので、部署ごとに異なる提出期間が割り振られます。

11月8日〜15日	営業
11月16日〜23日	企画
11月24日〜29日	顧客サービス
12月6日〜13日	総務

提案箱を研究部のドアのそばのデスク上に設置します。あなたのご提案を備え付けの伝言用紙に記入し、箱に入れてください。

よろしくお願いいたします。

Takashi Furukawa

□**generate**：〜を生み出す　□**be allocated**：割り当てられる、割り振られる　□**supplied**：備え付けられている

文書2「メッセージ」と訳

⑦New Toy Suggestion

⑧**Name:** Meredith Birney	⑨**Date:** November 12

Rather than trying to come up with a completely new toy, we should try to improve on a traditional toy. Most parents grew up at a time when computer games were not very advanced, so they played with model train sets or electronic car racing tracks. Parents are the ones who choose and pay for toys, and so they would probably like to introduce their children to a toy similar to what they had when they were young. ⑩Baxter Toys used to have the most popular electric toy car racing sets in the country. I suggest we update the designs to incorporate new technology and rerelease them.

新しいおもちゃの提案

名前：Meredith Birney	日付：11月12日

まったく新しいおもちゃを考え出すよりも、昔ながらのおもちゃを改良すべきです。大抵の親はコンピューターゲームがあまり発達していない時代に育ったので、鉄道模型のセットや電気自動車のレース場で遊んだのです。おもちゃの代金を払うのは親たちなのですから、彼らはきっと、自身が幼いころに遊んだのと似たおもちゃを自分の子どもたちに紹介したいことでしょう。Baxter Toys にはかつて、国内で最も人気のある電気自動車のレース場セットがありました。新しい技術を組み込むためにデザインを新しくし、再発売することを提案します。

□**improve on ~**：~を改良する、~をもっと良くする　□**incorporate**：~を組み込む　□**rerelease**：~を再発売する、~を再販する

文書3「記事」と訳

Baxter Toys Back on Top

Norma Day, March 3

Baxter Toys has made an amazing recovery from its recent sales slump by appealing to the nostalgia of parents. ⑪Toys that were popular 20 or 30 years ago are being rereleased in their original packaging. ⑫The company is even running the radio and television advertisements it used when they were first released. The products themselves have received some improvements and upgrades, but children around the country are now getting to experience the toys their parents used to play with. Interestingly, company president Roland Oaks has made good on his pledge to give five percent of the profit to the employee who came up with the idea. As a result, one lucky member of staff has decided to take early retirement at the end of this month.

Baxter Toys トップに返り咲き

Norma Day　3月3日

Baxter Toys 社が、親たちの懐古の情に訴えかけることにより、近年の売り上げの落ち込みから驚くべき回復を遂げている。20年や30年前に人気を博したおもちゃが、オリジナルのパッケージに入って再び売られている。同社は、それらが最初に発売された当時に使われていたテレビやラジオ広告まで放送している。商品自体には改良とアップグレードが施されているが、全国の子どもたちは彼らの親たちがかつて遊んだおもちゃを経験している。興味深いことに、同社社長の Roland Oaks は、そのアイデアを思い付いた社員に利益の5パーセントを与えるという自身の誓約を守っている。その結果として、1人の幸運なスタッフが今月末に早期退職することを決めている。

□**slump**：落ち込み、下降　□**nostalgia**：懐古の情、懐かしさ　□**packaging**：梱包、パッケージ　□**run advertisement**：広告を出す　□**make good on** *one's* **pledge**：誓約を守る、公約を守る　□**early retirement**：早期退職

選択肢と訳

50.
What is implied about Baxter Toys?（Baxter Toys について何が示唆されていますか？）
(A) It was founded very recently.（ごく最近設立された）
(B) It ships toys to various countries.（さまざまな国におもちゃを出荷している）
(C) It does not produce game software.（ゲームのソフトウエアを製造していない）
(D) It is closing its research department.（研究部を閉鎖する）

解説

正解：**(C)**

お知らせの①から、Baxter Toys社は昔ながらのおもちゃを販売している会社だと分かる。さらに、「子どもたちがコンピューターゲームを好むせいで売り上げが落ちている」とも書かれている。これらの内容から、同社はコンピューターゲームを製造していないと推測できるので、(C) が正解。記事の⑪から、この会社は30年以上続く会社だと分かるので、(A) は不適切。(B) と (D) に関する記述もないので、それぞれ不適切。

51.
In the notice, the phrase "in the form of" in paragraph 2, line 3, is closest in meaning to（お知らせの第2段落・3行目の "in the form of" に最も意味が近いのは）
(A) in place of（〜の代わりに）
(B) taking the shape of（〜の形をして）
(C) close to（〜の近くに）
(D) by way of（〜として）

正解：(D)

②の文を解釈すると「社は新しいおもちゃによって生み出された利益の5パーセントを、ボーナスの形で、アイデアが採用された社員に支給する」となる。つまり、この文脈では、in the form of 〜 は「手段」を表しており、(D) が最も近い。「丸型」や「四角型」といった、文字通りの「形」を表している場合には、(B) が正解となる。

52.
Which department does Ms. Birney most likely work for?（Birney さんはどの部署で働いていると考えられますか？）
(A) Marketing（営業部）
(B) Planning（企画部）
(C) Customer Service（顧客サービス部）
(D) General Affairs（総務部）

正解：(A)

Birney 氏の氏名は、新しいおもちゃを提案するために使用される用紙⑦の⑧にある。日付欄⑨には「11月12日」とある。お知らせの③に「部署ごとに提出期間が異なる」とあり、⑤から用紙に記載されている日付は、用紙を提出した日と考えるのが妥当である。表④から11月12日は営業部の提出期間だと分かる。よって、Birney 氏は (A)「営業部」で働いていると判断できる。

53.
What is indicated about Mr. Furukawa?（Furukawa さんについて何が示されていますか？）
(A) He is a personal friend of Ms. Birney's.（Birney さんの個人的な友人である）
(B) He accepted an employee's suggestion.（社員の提案を受け入れた）
(C) He was made company president.（会社社長になった）
(D) He took a holiday in January.（1月に休暇を取った）

正解：(B)

設問の Furukawa 氏の氏名はお知らせの⑥にあるので、彼は社員にアイデアを求めている人物の1人である。メッセージの⑩で Birney 氏は、「以前発売していたおもちゃを復刻する」という提案をしている。記事の⑪から、Baxter Toys 社はその提案を受け入れたことが分かる。よって、Furukawa 氏は社員である Birney 氏のアイデアを採用したことになるので、(B) が正解。

54.
What does the article say about the company's advertising?（記事はその企業の広告について何と言っていますか？）
(A) It has won an award.（賞を取った）
(B) It is being shown in the evenings.（夜に放送されている）
(C) It was produced by a famous firm.（有名企業によって制作された）
(D) It is using previously broadcast material.（以前放送されたものを使っている）

正解：(D)

Baxter Toys 社の広告に関しては、記事の⑫に「同社は、それらが最初に発売された当時に使われていたテレビやラジオ広告まで放送している」と書かれている。よって、それを「以前放送されたものを使っている」と表した (D) が正解。その他の選択肢に関する記述はないので、それぞれ不適切。

③トリプルパッセージ

Questions 55-59 refer to the following e-mail, article, and survey.
（問題55-59は次のEメール、記事、調査に関するものです）

> 文書1「Eメール」と訳

To:	Silvia Ishikiriyama <sishikiriyama@smalllab.com>
From:	Harper McCann <hmccann@smalllab.com>
Date:	February 16
Subject:	Idea for members
Attachment:	📎 tokyoarticle

Hi Silvia,

I have been reading a magazine ①article written by one of our members. ②She is a fairly well-known travel writer, who takes the time to find interesting perspectives on the destinations that are not mentioned in most guidebooks.

After reading about her recent trip to Tokyo, I really started to think that ③a lot of our members would be interested in taking part in a group tour there. ④Please take a look at the attached article. ⑤If you agree, I'll talk to a travel agent about putting together a tour for us.

Best regards,

Harper McCann

宛先：Silvia Ishikiriyama <sishikiriyama@smalllab.com>
送信者：Harper McCann <hmccann@smalllab.com>
日付：2月16日
件名：会員のためのアイデア
添付：📎 tokyoarticle

こんにちは、Silvia。

ある会員が書いた素晴らしい記事を読んでいます。彼女はかなり知られている旅行ライターで、各観光地について、大抵のガイドブックが教えてくれない、面白い楽しみ方を、時間をかけて見つけます。

彼女の最近のTokyoへの旅について読んで、私は、多くの会員がそこへのグループツアーに参加することに関心を持つだろうと思うようになりました。添付した記事に目を通してください。もし賛同していただけるのなら、われわれのためにツアーを組んでもらうことを、私から旅行代理店に相談します。

敬具

Harper McCann

□**take the time to ~**：~するのに時間を割く、時間をかけて~する □**perspective**：視点、見方 □**destination**：目的地、行き先

216

文書2「記事」と訳

Tokyo's Scattered Oases

⑥By Karla Iversen

I recently took my family on a trip to Japan. We visited two major tourist cities, Tokyo and Kyoto. There were many famous sights to see there and coming from a small Nebraskan farming town, everyone was excited to see the huge buildings and amazing infrastructure of Tokyo, and the historic buildings and cultural traditions of Kyoto. What we were not ready for ⑦were the wonderful little gardens built on rooftops and balconies and hanging from the fences in front of people's homes. Tokyo is surprisingly green. The Japanese seem to have found a fun way of enjoying gardening that takes little effort or cost. Yet, it brightens up entire neighborhoods.

Tokyo の散らばったオアシス

Karla Iversen

私はつい先日、家族を日本への旅行に連れていった。私たちは2大観光都市である Tokyo と Kyoto を訪れた。そこには見るべき有名な名所があり、Nebraska の小さな農業の町から来ているので、Tokyo の巨大ビルや驚くようなインフラ、Kyoto の歴史的建造物や文化的伝統を目にして、皆興奮していた。私たちが期待していなかったのは、屋上やバルコニーに作られていたり、人々の家の前の塀につり下げられていたりするすてきな小さい庭だった。Tokyo は驚くほど緑が多い。日本人は、労力やお金をほとんどかけないでガーデニングを楽しむ楽しいやり方を見つけているようだ。それでいて、それは近所全体を明るくしている。

□**oases**：オアシス　※oasis の複数形　□**sight**：見どころ、名所　□**rooftop**：屋根の上、屋上　□**brighten up**：〜を明るくする、〜を活気づかせる

文書 3 「調査」と訳

BGA Japan Tour — Satisfaction Survey

Name: Laurence David

Comments: Japan was really very different from what I had imagined and I look forward to visiting again sometime. ⑧Hiring Karla Iversen as a tour leader was an excellent idea because her wonderful sense of humor and charm made the tour a lot of fun. Nevertheless, it would have been even better if ⑨someone with a deeper knowledge of Japanese history and culture had been available to participants.

Overall satisfaction: Unsatisfied 1 — 2 — 3 —④— 5 Very Satisfied
Reservation process: Unsatisfied 1 — 2 —③— 4 — 5 Very Satisfied
Staff Helpfulness: Unsatisfied 1 — 2 —③— 4 — 5 Very Satisfied
Accommodation: Unsatisfied ①— 2 — 3 — 4 — 5 Very Satisfied

BGA Japan ツアー 満足度調査

お名前：Laurence David

コメント：日本は私が想像していたのとまったく違っていて、いつかまた訪れるのを楽しみにしています。Karla Iversen さんをツアーのリーダーに採用したのは優れたアイデアでした。彼女の素晴らしいユーモアのセンスと魅力は、ツアーをとても楽しいものにしてくれました。しかしながら、日本の歴史や文化についてより深い知識を持つ人に参加者が話を聞くことができれば、なお良かったでしょう。

全体的な満足度： 不満である 1 — 2 — 3 —④— 5 とても満足している
予約手続き： 不満である 1 — 2 —③— 4 — 5 とても満足している
スタッフの役立ち度： 不満である 1 — 2 —③— 4 — 5 とても満足している
宿泊施設： 不満である ①— 2 — 3 — 4 — 5 とても満足している

□ overall：全体の、全般的な　□ charm：魅力

選択肢 と 訳

55.
Why does Mr. McCann write to Ms. Ishikiriyama?
（McCann さんはなぜ Ishikiriyama さんにメールを書いていますか？）
(A) To inform her about an expense report （経費報告書について彼女に知らせるため）
(B) To suggest that she read an article （彼女に記事を読むことを提案するため）
(C) To ask for help with some arrangements （手配の助けを求めるため）
(D) To introduce a candidate for a position （ある職の応募者を紹介するため）

解説

正解：(B)

メールの差出人である McCann 氏は④で、添付された記事を読むよう、Ishikiriyama 氏に促している。それを「彼女に記事を読むことを提案するため」と表した (B) が正解。メールや手紙の目的は第1段落に必ずあるとは限らず、この手紙のように今までの経緯や現状を説明した後に、依頼内容や提案を述べるという構成もある。従って、段落を読み終えるごとに「何が書かれていたか」を意識することが大切だ。

56.
Who does Mr. McCann indicate that he will contact?（McCann さんは誰に連絡を取ると示していますか？）
(A) A magazine editor（雑誌編集者）
(B) A travel agency（旅行代理店）
(C) A sales expert（販売の専門家）
(D) A family member（家族）

正解：(B)

メールの最後⑤で「私から旅行代理店に相談します」と McCann 氏は書いているので、(B)「旅行代理店」が正解。本文に magazine という記述はあるが、「雑誌を読んでいる」としか書かれていないので、(A)「雑誌編集者」は不適切。(C)、(D) に関する記述もないので、いずれも不適切。

57.
What kind of organization is Mr. McCann most likely a member of?（McCann さんはどのような団体のメンバーだと考えられますか？）
(A) A convention steering committee（会議運営委員会）
(B) A city engineering department（市の技術部）
(C) A gardening association（園芸協会）
(D) A farming industry support group（農業支援グループ）

正解：(C)

メールの①から McCann 氏は、自身が所属する団体の会員によって書かれた旅行記事を読んだことが分かる。そして、その旅行について、③「他の会員もそのツアーの参加に関心を持つだろう」と書いている。記事の⑦で、Tokyo のガーデニング事情が詳しく述べられている。これらから、McCann 氏はガーデニングに関する団体に所属していると判断できる。よって、(C) が正解。

□**steering**：運営、指揮

58.
In the survey, the word "available" in paragraph 1, line 4, is closest in meaning to（調査の第1段落・4行目の "available" に最も意味が近いのは）
(A) accessible（利用できる）
(B) responsible（責任感のある）
(C) vacant（空いている）
(D) reliant（依存している）

正解：(A)

同義語問題。⑨を見ると、「available to＋人（人が〜を利用できる）」の形で使われている。参加者（participants）が someone with a deeper knowledge of Japanese history and culture（日本の歴史や文化についてより深い知識を持つ人）を「利用できる」という意味で、ここではツアー中にいろいろ話を聞けるということだ。この available と置き換えることができるのは (A)。(C) も部屋などが「空いている（＝利用できる）」という文脈では available の同義語となり得るが、ここでは不適切。

59.
What is true about the tour?（ツアーについて正しいものは何ですか？）
(A) It featured a lot of information about Japanese culture.（日本文化について多くの情報を掲載している）
(B) It was more popular than organizers had expected.（主宰者が予測したよりも人気だった）
(C) It will be held every year.（毎年開催されるだろう）
(D) It was led by a travel writer.（旅行ライターによって引率された）

正解：(D)

調査のコメント⑧から、Karla Iversen 氏がツアーを率いていたことが分かる。彼女の氏名は記事の⑥にもある。McCann 氏はメールの②で、記事を書いた人物のことを「有名な旅行ライター」と述べている。これらから、旅行ライターである Iversen 氏がツアーを引率したことになるので、(D) が正解。

Questions 60-64 refer to the following memo, summary, and e-mail.
（問題60-64は次のメモ、要約、Eメールに関するものです）

文書1「メモ」と訳

MEMO

To: All employees
①From: Human resources
Re: Employee survey
Date: May 25

On Friday, a survey will be distributed to staff members to help assess employee perceptions of management's strengths and weaknesses. ②The survey will combine multiple-choice questions with open-ended questions to which you are expected to give full-sentence responses. The surveys are designed to be anonymous. ③Nevertheless, if you would like to make yourself available for further discussion on any of the topics, you may write your employee number in the box provided at the top right of the page.

Sincerely,

④Steve Cameron

宛先：全社員
発信者：人事部
件名：社員調査
日付：5月25日

金曜日、経営管理側の強みと弱点に対する社員の認識の評価を助けるため、調査書が職員に配布されます。調査は、選択式質問と、完全な文による回答を求められる自由回答式質問が組み合わさっています。調査は無記名となっています。しかしながら、いずれかの問題についてさらなる議論に応じるという場合は、ページの右上にある枠内にあなたの社員番号を記入してください。

敬具

Steve Cameron

□**assess**：～を評価する、～を査定する　　□**perception**：認識、知覚　　□**combine**：～を同時に行う、～を組み合わせる
□**multiple-choice question**：選択式質問　　□**open-ended question**：自由回答式質問　　□**anonymous**：無記名の、匿名の

文書2「要約」と訳

⑤ **Preliminary Summary of Employee Responses to Management Survey**	
The following points were made by staff members who did not mind being identified and approached for further discussion. ⑥Other findings will be published as soon as the data has been analyzed.	

⑦Employees are given little opportunity to contribute to decisions before they are made because they are not invited to attend monthly meetings.	Joan Cummings
Staff who wish to acquire new skills should be provided mentorship programs or given time and financial assistance to take courses at local educational institutions.	Peter Gonzalez
More flexible arrangements for time off should be available to allow staff to schedule holidays more freely.	Lucy Wu
Please extend the parking garage to accommodate more staff vehicles. At present, only management-level staff members are able to park on the grounds. Other workers have to walk up to two kilometers to and from their vehicles.	Regis Smith

経営管理の調査に対する社員回答速報	
以下の提案は、さらなる議論のために個人が特定されたり、連絡を受けても構わないという社員からのものである。その他の調査結果は、データが分析され次第、発表される。	

社員は決定が下される前にそれに貢献する機会をほとんど与えられていません。なぜなら、月例会議に出席するよう招かれていないからです。	Joan Cummings
新しい技術を習得したい社員は、助言プログラムを提供されるか、地元の教育機関で講座を受講するための時間・金銭的支援を提供されるべきです。	Peter Gonzalez
社員がもっと自由に休暇の予定を決められるよう、より柔軟な休日の手続きが利用できるべきです。	Lucy Wu
もっと多くの社員の車を収容できるよう、駐車場ビルを増築してください。現状では、管理職レベルの社員しか止められません。他の社員は、自分の車との行き来に2キロも歩かなくてはなりません。	Regis Smith

□**preliminary summary**：速報　□**finding**：調査結果、研究結果　□**mentorship program**：助言プログラム、指導プログラム　□**parking garage**：駐車場ビル　□**management-level**：管理職レベルの

③ トリプルパッセージ

文書3「E メール」と訳

To:	All Staff
From:	Jow Lim
Date:	June 3
Subject:	Policy change

Dear staff:

As a result of the recent employee survey, we have decided to adopt the following change immediately. Other changes may be implemented in coming months after they have been discussed more thoroughly.

⑧<u>Tomorrow's management meeting for April will be held in Conference Room 201 on the second floor. It has seats for up to 60 people, which should be adequate for all interested employees to attend.</u> This does not mean that attendance is mandatory, only that it is open to anyone who would like to be present or express an opinion on the topics tabled for discussion. Unless otherwise notified, you can expect all future monthly meetings to be carried out the same way.

宛先：全社員
送信者：Jow Lim
日付：6月3日
件名：方針の変更

社員の皆さん

先日の社員調査の結果、われわれは直ちに以下の改革を採用することを決定しました。その他の改革も、さらにじっくり議論された後、今後数カ月の間に実現される可能性があります。

明日の4月度経営会議は、2階の会議室201で開かれます。関心を持つ全ての社員が出席するのに十分であろう、最大60人分の席があります。これは出席が必須であることを意味するものではなく、出席したい人、議論のために提出されている議題について意見を述べたい人は誰でも参加できるということです。通知されない限り、今後全ての月例会議は同様に実施されるとお考えください。

□**be implemented**：実行される、実現される　□**mandatory**：必須の、義務付けられた　□**unless otherwise 〜**：〜でない限り

選択肢と訳

60.
According to the memo, how can respondents reveal their identities to management?（メモによると、回答者たちは自分たちの身元をどうやって経営陣に明かすことができますか？）
(A) By supplying their employee number（社員番号を提供する）
(B) By handing in their survey in person（調査を直接提出する）
(C) By writing their name on a form（名前を用紙に書く）
(D) By calling a supervisor（上司に電話をする）

61.
Who most likely is Steve Cameron?（Steve Cameron とは誰だと考えられますか？）
(A) A job applicant（求職者）
(B) A client representative（クライアントの担当者）
(C) A market researcher（市場調査員）
(D) A department director（部の責任者）

62.
What is implied about the survey data?（調査データについて何が示唆されていますか？）
(A) It has been sent to a specialist for analysis.（分析のため専門家に送られた）
(B) Multiple-choice questions have not been processed.（選択式質問は処理されていない）
(C) There were not enough responses.（十分な回答がなかった）
(D) It will be distributed to all employees.（全社員に配布される）

63.
Whose suggestion has been accepted by management?（経営陣により、誰の提案が採用されましたか？）
(A) Joan Cummings
(B) Peter Gonzalez
(C) Lucy Wu
(D) Regis Smith

64.
In the e-mail, the word "express" in paragraph 2, line 4, is closest in meaning to（E メールの第2段落・4行目の "express" の意味に最も近いのは）
(A) represent（～を象徴する）
(B) follow（～に従う）
(C) voice（～を述べる）
(D) resolve（～を解決する）

解説

正解：(A)
メモの中盤に「調査は無記名」とあるが、逆接を表す③ Nevertheless が続き、「さらなる議論のために、自分を連絡可能な状態にしたい人は、ページの右上にある枠内にあなたの社員番号を記入してください」とある。回答者は「社員番号を提供することによって」身元を明らかにできるので、(A) が正解。逆接を意味する語句の後には重要な情報が述べられがちなので、注意して読むようにしよう。

正解：(D)
Steve Cameron の名はメモの④に記載されているので、このメモを書いた人物だと分かる。さらに、メモ上部の送信者欄①には「人事部」とあるので、彼は人事部に所属していることになる。選択肢の中に「人事部」はないが、(A) は社外の人なので不適切。(B) の「クライアントの担当者」という記述もない。(C) が調査するのは「市場」なので不可。彼は「人事部の責任者」だと思われるので、(D) が正解。

正解：(B)
メモの②から、調査の質問には選択式と自由回答式の2種類があることが分かる。文書2の要約には、寄せられた回答が記載されている（⑤）。内容を見ると、全て自由回答式である。⑥に「その他の調査結果はデータが分析され次第発表」とある。「その他の調査結果」というのは、選択式の回答を指すので、「選択式質問は処理されていない」と考えられる。よって、(B) が正解。

正解：(A)
調査の結果を受け、メールの⑧に「社員が4月度の経営会議に参加できるようにする」と書かれている。文書2の要約を見ると、Joan Cummings 氏がその提案をした人物だと分かる（⑦）。よって、経営陣が採用したのは (A) Joan Cummings 氏の提案である。

正解：(C)
express は、自分の考えや気持ちを「述べる、表す」という意味。ここでは express an opinion だから、「意見を述べる」となる。(C) の voice は、動詞として使われると「～を述べる、～を声に出す」という意味になるので、これが正解。

③ トリプルパッセージ

Questions 65-69 refer to the following e-mails and letter.
（問題65-69は次のEメールと手紙に関するものです）

文書1「Eメール」と訳

①To:	Joan Carson <jcarson@clarendonhotel.com>
From:	Harold Chang <hchang@peekfishing.com>
Date:	August 9
Subject:	Fishing Tours

Dear Ms. Carson,

My name is Harold Chang and I am the owner of Peek Fishing. We have been running fishing tours on Waring Lake and, as of this month, ②we are the only fishing company operating on the Hopscotch River. ③I am writing to request permission to leave our brochures with the staff at your tour desk. In accordance with standard industry practice, ④we would like to offer you a ten percent commission on bookings made through the hotel.

If you would like to verify the quality of our service before recommending it to your guests, please let me know as ⑤I can quickly arrange a complimentary tour for you or any of your staff.

宛先：Joan Carson <jcarson@clarendonhotel.com>
送信者：Harold Chang <hchang@peekfishing.com>
日付：8月9日
件名：釣りツアー

Carson 様

私はHarold Changと申しまして、Peek Fishingのオーナーです。当社はWaring湖で釣りツアーを運営していますが、今月の時点では、Hopscotch川で営業している唯一の釣り会社です。当社のパンフレットをそちらのツアーデスクのスタッフの方にお預けする許可をいただきたくて、メールを書いております。当社は標準的な業界の慣例に従って、ホテルを通しての予約には、10パーセントの手数料をそちらにお支払いしたいと思います。

そちらのお客さまにご推薦いただく前に、当社のサービスの質を検証されたいという場合は、貴殿、あるいはスタッフのどなたかのために無料のツアーをすぐに手配いたしますので、お知らせください。

☐**as of ~**：〜現在 ☐**leave ~ with ...**：〜を…に預ける ☐**in accordance with ~**：〜に従って、〜の通りに
☐**commission**：手数料 ☐**verify**：〜を検証する、〜を立証する

文書2「E メール」と訳

To:	Harold Chang <hchang@peekfishing.com>
From:	Joan Carson <jcarson@clarendonhotel.com>
Date:	August 12
Subject:	RE: Fishing Tours

Dear Mr. Chang,

Thank you for writing regarding your tour offerings and the kind invitation to inspect them. I regret to inform you, however, that ⑥we are already providing our guests a fishing tour with Big Catch Fishing Company and it is hotel policy not to list such similar services alongside each other.

We will be reprinting the tour information for distribution in October and we generally negotiate with suppliers wishing to be included on the list in mid-September. ⑦I would like to send our tour desk coordinator, Miles Thompson, on one of your fishing tours before we begin any negotiations.

If you choose to submit an application for inclusion at that time, you should keep in mind that the hotel requires a minimum commission of fifteen percent.

宛先：Harold Chang <hchang@peekfishing.com>
送信者：Joan Carson <jcarson@clarendonhotel.com>
日付：8月12日
件名：RE: 釣りツアー

Chang 様

ツアーの申し出についてご連絡をいただき、またそれを視察できるという親切なご招待をありがとうございます。申し訳ございませんが、私どもではすでにお客さまに Big Catch Fishing Company の釣りツアーをご提供しており、類似するサービスを並行してリストに載せないことをホテルのポリシーとしています。

10月には配布用のツアー情報を増刷しますが、通常、リストへの掲載を希望する業者とは、9月中旬に交渉します。いかなる交渉を始める前にも、私どものツアーデスクのコーディネーター、Miles Thompson を御社の釣りツアーに派遣したいと思います。

そのときに参入の申し込みをされる場合は、ホテル側は15パーセントの最低手数料を要求するという点にご留意ください。

□**alongside**：〜と一緒に、〜と並行して　□**reprint**：〜を再印刷する、〜を増刷する　□**for distribution**：配布用に
□**inclusion**：参入、含めること

文書3「手紙」と訳

November 21

Tour Desk
⑧Clarendon Hotel
25 Valhalla Street
Coopersfield CA 97005

Dear Tour Desk Staff,

⑨My wife and I had the pleasure of staying at your charming hotel on November 17 and 18 this year. I am writing with regard to the fishing tour we booked at the hotel tour desk. ⑩The Hopscotch River was an amazing location. The fall colors of the trees were reflected in the water, making a beautiful setting. The tour leader had an excellent knowledge of fishing and local history and we had a fascinating time. ⑪Could you please let me know if the tour will be offered during the spring as we are planning on returning with a group of friends at that time?

Sincerely,

Grant Connolly
⑫Grant Connolly

November 21

ツアーデスク
Clarendon Hotel
25 Valhalla Street
Coopersfield CA 97005

ツアーデスクご担当者様

妻と私は、今年の11月17日と18日に、そちらの素晴らしいホテルに滞在させていただきました。ホテルのツアーデスクで予約した釣りツアーのことでお手紙をしました。Hopscotch 川は素晴らしい場所でした。木々の紅葉が水に映り、美しい風景でした。ツアー引率者は釣りや地元の歴史を熟知した方で、私たちは非常に興味深い時を過ごしました。あのツアーは春にも提供されるのか教えてください。そのころに友人のグループと再訪する計画を立てているところです。

敬具
Grant Connolly
Grant Connolly

□**with regard to 〜**：〜に関して

選択肢と訳

65.
Who most likely is Ms. Carson?（Carson さんは誰だと考えられますか？）
(A) A government official（政府関係者）
(B) A sales person（販売員）
(C) A hotel manager（ホテルの支配人）
(D) A tour company operator（ツアー会社の経営者）

66.
In the first e-mail, the word "practice" in paragraph 1, line 4, is closest in meaning to（最初のEメールの第1段落・4行目の"practice"に最も意味が近いのは）
(A) preparation（準備）
(B) convention（慣例）
(C) application（申し込み）
(D) dictation（口述）

67.
Which offer of Mr. Chang's does Ms. Carson accept?（Carson さんは Chang さんのどの提案を受け入れていますか？）
(A) A ten percent commission（10パーセントの手数料）
(B) A free fishing tour（無料の釣りツアー）
(C) Directions to a tourist attraction（観光名所への案内）
(D) Complimentary accommodation（無料の宿泊）

68.
In the letter, what is implied about Clarendon Hotel?（手紙では、Clarendon Hotel について何が示唆されていますか？）
(A) It has an exclusive arrangement with Peek Fishing.（Peek Fishing と独占的な取り決めがある）
(B) It is closed over the winter months.（冬季は閉鎖される）
(C) It has been operating for many years.（長年操業している）
(D) It offers guests discounts on local tours.（客に地元のツアーの割引を提供する）

□**exclusive**：独占的な、排他的な

69.
What does Mr. Connolly indicate he will do?（Connolly さんは何をすると示しているか？）
(A) Try Big Catch Fishing Company（Big Catch Fishing Company を試す）
(B) Write a review of his holiday（自分の休暇のレビューを書く）
(C) Join a nature painting class（自然の絵画講座に参加する）
(D) Return to the Clarendon Hotel（Clarendon Hotel を再訪する）

解説

正解：(C)
設問の Carson 氏は①から、文書1のEメールの読み手だと分かる。③に「パンフレットをそちらのツアーデスクに預けたい」、④に「ホテルを通しての予約には、手数料をそちらに支払いたい」という記述がある。パンフレットを置く許可を求められたり、「ホテルが手数料を受け取れる」という申し出を検討したりする立場にある人物としては、「ホテルの支配人」がふさわしい。よって、(C) が正解。

正解：(B)
practice はいろいろな意味を持つ語だが、industry practice という表現で登場する文書1の該当箇所では、業界の「慣例」という意味。これの同義語となり得るのは (B) の convention だ。この単語は「会議、集会」の意味で用いられることが多いが、「慣例、慣習」という意味もある。なお、「練習」という意味では (A) が同義語となる。

正解：(B)
Chang 氏は、1つ目のメール⑤で「サービスを検証してもらうために、無料のツアーをすぐに手配します」と Carson 氏や他のスタッフを釣りツアーへ招待している。それを受け、Carson 氏は2つ目のメール⑦で、「私どものツアーデスクのコーディネーターを御社の釣りツアーに派遣したい」と返答している。よって、Carson 氏が受け入れた提案は (B)「無料の釣りツアー」である。(A) は提案された条件ではあるが、Carson 氏は15パーセントを要求しているため、不正解。

正解：(A)
2つ目のメール⑥で Carson 氏が「当ホテルではすでに Big Catch Fishing Company の釣りツアーを提供しており、類似するサービスを並行してリストに載せないポリシーだ」と返答していることから、このホテルは1つの会社としか釣りツアーの契約を結ばないことが分かる。手紙の⑨と⑩から、11月の時点で行われている釣りツアーは Hopscotch 川を通ることが分かる。1つ目のメール②に、「Peek Fishing のみが Hopscotch 川でツアーを行っている」とある。これらの記述から、Clarendon Hotel は、取り扱う釣りツアーを Peek Fishing に変更したことが分かる。(A) が正解。

正解：(D)
設問の Connolly 氏の氏名は手紙の最下部⑫に記載されている。つまり、彼はこの手紙を書いた人物である。手紙の冒頭⑧と⑨から、彼は11月に Clarendon Hotel を訪れたことが分かる。その後、⑪で「春に友人と再び訪れる計画がある」と書いている。よって、(D) が正解。

Questions 70-74 refer to the following e-mails and report.
（問題 70-74 は次の E メールと報告書に関するものです）

文書 1「E メール」と訳

①To:	Randy Cole <rcole@simpsonassociates.com>
From:	Kalil Mehajer <kmehajer@simpsonassociates.com>
Subject:	Tokyo transfer
Date:	July 7

Dear Randy,

We discussed the possibility of your transfer to Tokyo for the opening of our first Japanese branch a couple of months ago. I have decided to go ahead with it. ②The branch is scheduled to open in December, but you ought to be there as early as September to help set up and employ staff.

In preparation for your trip, I'd like you to sign up for a course in Japanese language at the Olivetti School of Business.

You should choose a member of staff to travel with you as an assistant. I will leave the final decision up to you. ③However, I should mention that Jim Rosen has lived in Tokyo and would be particularly helpful.

宛先：Randy Cole <rcole@simpsonassociates.com>
送信者：Kalil Mehajer <smehajer@simpsonassociates.com>
件名：東京転勤
日付：7月7日

Randy 様

数カ月前、わが社初の日本支社開設のため、あなたに東京へ転勤してもらう可能性について、話をしましたね。私はそれを進めることを決めました。支社は12月に開く予定ですが、開設とスタッフ採用を支援するため、あなたには早ければ9月にも現地へ行ってもらわなくてはなりません。

旅に備えて、Olivetti School of Business の日本語講座に申し込んでもらいたいと思います。

あなたは補佐として同行するスタッフを1人選ばなくてはなりません。最終決定はあなたに委ねます。しかしながら、Jim Rosen は Tokyo に住んだことがあり、特に頼りになるだろうということは言っておきます。

☐**transfer**：転勤、異動　☐**ought to ~**：~する義務がある　☐**as early as ~**：早ければ~にも　☐**in preparation for ~**：~に備えて

文書2「E メール」と訳

④To:	Kalil Mehajer <kmehajer@simpsonassociates.com>
From:	Randy Cole <rcole@simpsonassociates.com>
Subject:	RE: Tokyo transfer
Date:	July 10

Thank you so much for considering me for this important position. I have been going over the schedule and I think a September start may be problematic. ⑤I am obliged to meet with some clients whose investments I am managing at that time. I can certainly manage a departure in early October, however.

I have been in contact with the Olivetti School of Business and it seems that their course does not really suit my work schedule. ⑥Instead, I have arranged for a private language tutor by the name of Hisami Tsuchiya to come to the office once a day until my departure. It works out cheaper for the company, so I am sure you will not mind.

⑦Jim Rosen was very receptive to the idea of traveling with me and I have offered him the option of returning after one year.

宛先: Kalil Mehajer <smehajer@simpsonassociates.com>
送信者: Randy Cole <rcole@simpsonassociates.com>
件名: RE: Tokyo transfer
日付: July 10

この重要な地位に私をご検討いただき、本当にありがとうございます。スケジュールに目を通しましたが、9月のスタートには問題があるかもしれません。その時期は、私が投資を管理しているクライアントと会わなくてはなりません。10月初旬であれば、間違いなく出発できるのですが。

Olivetti School of Business に連絡をしましたが、彼らの講座は私の仕事のスケジュールにあまり合っていないようです。代わりに、Hisami Tsuchiya という語学の個人指導講師に、出発まで毎日オフィスに来てもらうよう手配しました。その方が会社にとっては安くなるので、差し支えないと思います。

Jim Rosen は私に同行するという提案に非常に理解を示してくれたので、私は彼に1年後に帰国するという選択肢も提示しました。

□**problematic**：問題のある　□**be obliged to 〜**：〜しなければいけない、〜する義務がある　□**tutor**：個人指導講師、家庭教師　□**work out 〜**：結果が〜になる　□**be receptive to 〜**：〜を受け入れようとする、〜に理解を示す

文書3「報告書」と訳

Yearly Progress Report

The Tokyo branch of Simpson Associates has reached all of its targets with ease. ⑧It seems that there are more people than we expected who are looking to invest money in international commerce. Next year's objectives will be more ambitious.

Regrettably, Jim Rosen has decided to return to the United States this month and I am forced to hire a replacement. ⑨I have contacted Ms. Tsuchiya, whom you have met on a number of occasions and she has agreed to take over his role here.

年次進捗報告書

Simpson Associates の Tokyo 支社は、支社の全目標を軽々と達成しました。国際貿易に投資しようという人は、われわれが予想したより多いようです。来年の目標はさらに意欲的なものになるでしょう。

残念ながら、Jim Rosen は今月で the United States に帰国することを決めているため、後任を採用しなくてはなりません。あなたも何度か会っている Tsuchiya さんに連絡を取ったところ、彼女は彼のここでの役割を引き継ぐことに同意してくれています。

☐ **progress report**：進捗報告（書）　☐ **with ease**：容易に、軽々と　☐ **look to ～**：～しようとする、～しようと試みる
☐ **international commerce**：国際通商、国際貿易　☐ **ambitious**：野心的な、意欲的な　☐ **regrettably**：残念ながら

選択肢と訳

70.
According to the first e-mail, when will the Tokyo branch open?（最初の E メールによると、Tokyo 支社はいつ開設しますか？）
(A) In July（7月に）
(B) In September（9月に）
(C) In October（10月に）
(D) In December（12月に）

71.
What kind of business is Simpson Associates?
（Simpson Associates はどのような企業ですか？）
(A) An investment firm（投資会社）
(B) A law office（法律事務所）
(C) A fashion chain（ファッション・チェーン）
(D) A construction company（建設会社）

解説

正解：(D)

According to the first e-mail（最初の E メールによると）で始まるので、ヒントは1つ目のメールにある。②に「支社は12月に開く予定」とあるので、(D) が正解。(A) の「7月」は、このメールが送信された月なので、不適切。(B) の「9月」は、このメールの受取人 Cole 氏が Tokyo に行くべき時期と書かれているだけなので、不可。(C) の「10月」に関する記述もないので、これも不適切。

正解：(A)

1つ目のメールも2つ目のメールも、メールアドレスが @simpsonassociates.com となっているので（①と④）、Simpson Associates の関係者がやりとりしているものだと分かる。2つ目のメール⑤に「私が投資を管理しているクライアントと会う」とあるので、この会社は (A)「投資会社」だと判断できる。報告書の⑧「国際貿易に投資しようとしている人は多いようなので、来年の目標はさらに意欲的なものになる」からも、(A) が正解。

72.

What do Mr. Cole and Mr. Mehajer agree about?
（Cole さんと Mehajer さんは何に同意していますか？）
(A) Taking a course at the Olivetti School of Business（Olivetti School of Business で講座を受けること）
(B) Mr. Cole's leaving in September（Cole さんが9月に出発すること）
(C) Sending Mr. Rosen as an assistant（Rosen さんを補佐として送り込むこと）
(D) Funding for an advertising campaign（広告キャンペーンのために資金調達すること）

正解：(C)

1つ目のメール③で Mehajer 氏は、Rosen 氏を同行スタッフの有力候補であるとほのめかしている。2つ目のメール⑦から、Cole 氏は Rosen 氏を同行スタッフに選んだことが分かる。よって、2人が同意した内容は (C) である。Mehajer 氏は1つ目のメールで「9月に現地に行く必要がある」、「ビジネススクールの日本語講座に申し込んでほしい」と Cole 氏に伝えているが、Cole 氏はそれぞれに対し「できない」と返答しているので、(A) と (B) は不適切。(D) はどの文書も触れていないので不可。

73.

In the report, the word "expected" in paragraph 1, line 2, is closest in meaning to（報告書の第1段落・2行目の "expected" に最も意味が近いのは）
(A) required（～を求めた）
(B) attracted（～を引きつけた）
(C) anticipated（～を予想した）
(D) sustained（～を継続した）

正解：(C)

同義語問題。選択肢の中で 動詞 expected の同義語となりそうなのは、(A) の required（～を要求した）と (C) の anticipated（～を予想した）だ。ターゲットとなる expected がどんな意味で使われているのかを文脈から判断しよう。⑧を読むと、more people than we expected は「われわれが求めたよりも多くの人々」よりも、「われわれが予想したよりも多くの人々」と解釈する方が適切だ。正解は (C)。

74.

Who will replace Mr. Rosen?（誰が Rosen さんの後任になりますか？）
(A) A director of Simpson Associates（Simpson Associates の局長）
(B) An applicant from a rival firm in Tokyo（Tokyo の競合企業からの応募者）
(C) One of Mr. Mehajer's business contacts（Mehajer さんの仕事上のつながりの1人）
(D) Mr. Cole's former language teacher（Cole さんの元語学教師）

正解：(D)

設問にある Rosen 氏は、1年の期間限定で Cole 氏の同行スタッフとして東京に行くことが決まった人物である（⑦）。報告書の⑨から、Tsuchiya 氏が Rosen 氏の後任として選ばれたことが分かる。Tsuchiya 氏に関する情報は、2つ目のメール⑥に書かれている。⑥から、Tsuchiya 氏は以前 Cole 氏に日本語を教えていた人物だと分かる。よって、Rosen 氏の後任となる人物は (D)「Cole さんの元語学教師」である。

Questions 75-79 refer to the following article, Web site, and review.
（問題75-79は次の記事、ウェブサイト、レビューに関するものです）

文書１「記事」と訳

> *Pedaling the Globe* — ①Frank Dolby sets himself a seemingly impossible challenge at the start of each book and writes about his adventures trying to achieve it. ②His previous book was about visiting every state in the United States using less than a dollar a day. ③It was a bestseller and inspired many young people to try to replicate his journey. ④For his most recent book, *Pedaling the Globe*, he attempted to travel from South Africa all the way to the southernmost tip of Argentina entirely by bicycle. I would rather not spoil the book by writing too much about whether or not he achieved the feat. It is enough to say that it was an amazing journey filled with humor and excitement.

> 『Pedaling the Globe』— Frank Dolby は、どの本でも、最初に一見不可能に思える自己目標を設定し、それを達成しようとする自身の冒険について書く。前作は、1日1ドル以下しか使わないで、米国の全ての州を回ることについてだった。それはベストセラーになり、多くの若者を彼の旅路の再現へと駆り立てた。最新作『Pedaling the Globe』では、South Africa からはるばる Argentina の最南端までを自転車だけで旅した。彼がこの偉業を成し遂げたかどうかについて、書き過ぎて、本の楽しみを奪わないでおこう。それがユーモアと興奮に満ちた驚くべき旅だったと言えば十分だ。

☐**pedal**：〜をペダルを踏んで動かす　※*Pedaling the Globe* は「地球をこぐ」ぐらいの意味　☐**set** *oneself* **a challenge**：自分の目標を設定する　☐**seemingly**：一見したところ、見たところ　☐**inspire 〜 to ...**：(人)に…する気を起こさせる　☐**replicate**：〜を複製する、〜を再現する　☐**southernmost**：最南端の　☐**would rather not 〜**：〜しないでおこう、〜したくない　☐**achieve a feat**：偉業を成し遂げる

文書２「ウェブサイト」と訳

www.frankdolbyadventurer.com

⑤Frank Dolby — Adventurer
Appearances

I have speaking engagements in many parts of the country on the following dates. Check with the venues regarding admission requirements.

June 4 — Brad's Bikes (South Sydney, NSW) **Promotional Event for Sternway Bicycles**
June 6 — Strathpine Library (Strathpine, NSW) **Reading, Question and Answer, Book Signing**
August 10 — Beaumont Conference Hall (Brunswick, VIC) **Presentation on Travel Writing**
⑥August 21 — Harrison's Books and Bikes (Geelong, VIC) **Reading, Question and Answer, Book Signing**

Note to venues: Unless otherwise indicated, ⑦a minimum appearance fee of $600 is required. Venues may charge participants to cover any costs incurred in hosting the event.

---

www.frankdolbyadventurer.com

Frank Dolby — 冒険家
出演情報

国内の各地で以下の日に講演をします。入場の要件は会場に確認してください。
6月4日— Brad's Bikes (South Sydney, NSW)　Sternway Bicycles の宣伝イベント
6月6日— Strathpine Library (Strathpine, NSW)　朗読、質疑応答、本のサイン会
8月10日— Beaumont Conference Hall (Brunswick, VIC)　旅行記についてのプレゼンテーション
8月21日— Harrison's Books and Bikes (Geelong, VIC)　朗読、質疑応答、本のサイン会

会場への注意事項：特に指示がない限り、600ドルの最低出演料が必要です。会場側はイベントの主催で発生するあらゆる費用に充てるため、参加者から料金を取ることも可能です。

□**appearance**：出演、登場　□**speaking engagement**：講演の仕事　□**venue**：会場　□**admission requirement**：入場条件、入場の要件　□**travel writing**：旅行記、紀行文　□**unless otherwise 〜**：〜がない限り、〜でない限り　□**incur**：〜を負う

文書3「レビュー」と訳

Customer Views on *Pedaling the Globe*

⑧**Reviewer:** Jenny Penhall
⑨I met Frank Dolby this August. I purchased a copy of the book at the venue where he was engaged to speak. ⑩After reading a section and answering questions from the audience, he was kind enough to sign the book. ⑪I suggest that you read the book before listening to him speak. He talks openly about the outcomes of the trip, which ruins much of the suspense. Despite this, I thoroughly enjoyed *Pedaling the Globe* and can recommend it to anyone interested in travel literature.

『Pedaling the Globe』についての購入者の意見

投稿者：Jenny Penhall
8月に Frank Dolby に会いました。彼が講演をすることになっていた会場で、本を購入しました。朗読と観客からの質問に答えた後、彼は親切にも本にサインをしてくれました。彼の講演を聴く前に本を読んでおくことをお勧めします。彼は旅の結末について率直に話すので、かなりのハラハラ感が損なわれます。このこと以外は、『Pedaling the Globe』をとことん楽しみましたし、旅行記に興味のある方ならどなたにでもお薦めします。

□**suspense**：気掛かり、ハラハラする状態　□**thoroughly**：完全に、とことん

選択肢と訳

75.
What is the article mainly about?（記事は主に何に関するものですか？）
(A) A new travel option for tourists（観光旅行客向けの新しい旅行オプション）
(B) The latest work of an author（ある作家の最新作）
(C) A money saving system（貯蓄システム）
(D) Motivating young people（若者をやる気にさせること）

□**motivate**：〜を刺激する、〜をやる気にさせる

解説

正解：**(B)**

記事の冒頭①の文から Frank Dolby 氏は、自身が経験した冒険を本にしていることが分かる。④には、彼の最新作『Pedaling the Globe』を紹介する記述がある。これらから、この記事は作家の最新作について書かれたものだと判断できる。よって、(B) が正解。本文に young people という記述はあるが、この記事の主題ではないので、(D) は不適切。

76.
What is NOT suggested about Mr. Dolby?（Dolby さんについて示されていないことは何ですか？）
(A) His previous book was popular.（前作が人気を博した）
(B) He has donated some of his earnings.（収入の一部を寄付した）
(C) He has visited the United States.（米国を訪れたことがある）
(D) He is paid for making appearances.（姿を見せることで支払いを受ける）

□**make an appearance**：姿を見せる、登場する

正解：(B)
Dolby 氏について書かれていないものを選んで解答する。記事の③に「前作がベストセラーになった」とあるので、(A) は不可。②に「前作は米国の全ての州を回ったことについて書かれている」とあるので、(C) も不適切。2つ目の文書、ウェブサイトの⑤には Dolby 氏が出演する講演に関する情報が載っている。⑦に「最低600ドルの出演料が必要」とあるので、(D) の記述もある。よって、(B) が正解。

77.
On the Web site, the word "cover" in paragraph 2, line 2, is closest in meaning to（ウェブサイトの第2段落・2行目の "cover" に意味が最も近いのは）
(A) offset（〜を補う）
(B) hide（〜を隠す）
(C) distinguish（〜を区別する）
(D) include（〜を含める）

正解：(A)
ウェブサイトの最終行の cover は、any costs（あらゆる費用）を目的語とする動詞として使われている。「（〜の）費用に充てる、（〜の）費用を賄う」という意味だ。選択肢の中でこの cover に最も近いのが、「〜を補う、〜を相殺する」という意味の offset だ。cover には「〜を覆う」や「〜を（対象に）含める」という意味もあるので、(B) も (D) も cover の同義語だが、この文脈には合わない。

78.
When did Ms. Penhall most likely meet Mr. Dolby?（Penhall さんはいつ Dolby さんに会ったと考えられますか？）
(A) On June 4（6月4日）
(B) On June 6（6月6日）
(C) On August 10（8月10日）
(D) On August 21（8月21日）

正解：(D)
設問の Penhall 氏はレビューを書いた人物である（⑧）。彼女はレビューの⑨に、「8月に Dolby 氏に会った」と書いている。その後の⑩から、彼女が Dolby 氏に会ったときには質疑応答の時間があり、本にサインをしてもらったことが分かる。Dolby 氏の出演情報が載っている2つ目の文書を見ると、この条件に当てはまるのは⑥の8月21日の朗読イベントだと分かる。よって、(D) が正解。

79.
What does Ms. Penhall recommend that readers do?（Penhall さんは読者に何をするよう勧めていますか？）
(A) Purchase a book at an online store（本をオンラインストアで購入する）
(B) Arrive well ahead of the start time（開始時間よりずっと早く到着する）
(C) Contact Mr. Dolby using the details on his Web site（ウェブサイトにある詳細を使って Dolby さんと連絡を取る）
(D) Read the book before attending Mr. Dolby's talk（Dolby さんの講演に参加する前に本を読む）

正解：(D)
Penhall 氏が読者に勧めている内容を問う問題。人に何かを勧めたり、提案したりする表現があるはずと予測しながら本文を読むとヒントが見つかりやすい。レビューの⑪に I suggest that（〜をお勧めします）とある。その後に「講演を聴く前に本を読んでおくこと」と続いている。よって、この内容を「講演に参加する前に本を読む」と表した (D) が正解。

Questions 80-84 refer to the following e-mail, Web page, and card.
(問題80-84は次のEメール、ウェブページ、カードに関する問題です)

文書1「Eメール」と訳

To:	Toshiki Fujisawa <tfujisawa@whitegoose.com>
From:	Sunil Singh <ssingh@devineair.com>
Date:	May 19
Subject:	Your flight

Dear Mr. Fujisawa,

Please allow me to begin by offering you my sincerest apologies for the overbooking on May 3 this year. Thank you for agreeing to take a later flight at such short notice. Your sacrifice made it possible for another group of passengers to travel to their designation together.

①On reviewing the situation, I have come to the decision that the compensation you received for this inconvenience was insufficient. In accordance with company guidelines, ②I would like to offer you a year of free membership to the Transecutive Club. ③This will entitle you to use the deluxe airport lounges when traveling with any of our partner airlines based in Europe.

The year of membership starts the first time you use the card to gain entry to a participating airline's lounge or ④take advantage of a free shuttle bus to a Transecutive Hotel in one of 50 locations.

For more information about the benefits of the club, please visit the following Web site: http://thetransecutiveclub.com/benefits. ⑤To take advantage of this offer, please click the button marked "Join" at the top of the page and enter your personal details along with the following coupon code: TYE83K.

Sincerely,

Sunil Singh
Customer Relations Officer
Devine Air

宛先：Toshiki Fujisawa <tfujisawa@whitegoose.com>
送信者：Sunil Singh <ssingh@devineair.com>
日付：5月19日
件名：お客さまのフライト

Fujisawa様

まずは本年5月3日のオーバーブッキングにつきまして、心よりおわび申し上げます。突然のことにも関わらず、遅い便のご利用に同意していただきありがとうございました。お客さまのご協力のおかげで、別のお客さまの団体が目的地まで一緒に移動することができました。

状況を振り返り、私はお客さまが受け取られた補償は不十分だったという判断に至りました。弊社のガイドラインに従い、Transecutive Clubの1年間の無料会員権を提供したいと存じます。これは、Europeに拠点を置くわれわれの提携航空会社で旅行される際に、豪華な空港ラウンジをご利用いただけるというものです。

会員権の1年は、お客さまが加盟航空会社の空港ラウンジに入るために初めてカードを使うとき、もしくは、50カ所あるTransecutive Hotelの1つに向かうため無料シャトルバスをご利用になったときから始まります。

同クラブの特典に関する詳細は、以下のウェブサイト、http://thetransecutiveclub.com/benefits をご覧ください。このオファーをご利用になるには、ページ上部にある「登録」と表示されたボタンをクリックし、個人情報と次のクーポン・コード「TYE83K」を入力してください。

敬具
Sunil Singh
顧客窓口担当
Devine Air

□**at short notice**：直前の知らせで　□**sacrifice**：犠牲　□**designation**：目的地　□**compensation**：補償、埋め合わせ　□**insufficient**：不十分な、足りない　□**in accordance with ～**：～に従って　□**entitle ～ to ...**：～に…する権利を与える

文書2「ウェブページ」と訳

http://thetransecutiveclub.com/benefits

The Transecutive Club JOIN

Membership to the Transecutive Club has been a sign of success among business travelers for more than 40 years. We have facilities in more than 100 airports worldwide, where we offer our cherished members a level of service unmatched by any of our competitors.

Members of the Transecutive Club can take advantage of a wide range of special services at airports around the world. ⑥We offer advanced boarding of flights, discounts on hotel accommodation, upgrades to in-flight meals as well as many other benefits that will make your trip much more enjoyable.

---

http://thetransecutiveclub.com/benefits

Transecutive Club 登録

Transecutive Club の会員権は、40年以上の間、ビジネス旅行者の間では成功の印となっています。私たちは世界中で100カ所以上の空港に施設を持ち、そこでは、どんな競合相手にも負けないレベルのサービスを大切な会員の皆さまに提供します。

Transecutive Club 会員の皆さまには、世界中の空港で幅広いサービスをご利用いただくことができます。私たちは、優先搭乗、ホテル宿泊の割引、機内食のアップグレードなど、あなたの旅をより楽しめるものにする多数の特典をご提供します。

□**cherished**：大切な　　□**unmatched by ～**：～に負けない　　□**in-flight meal**：機内食

文書 3「カード」と訳

The Transecutive Club

Cardholder: **Toshiki Fujisawa**
Membership Number: **7348892**

This card entitles approved passengers on participating airlines to enter The Transecutive Club Lounge at any airport in the world.

Participating Airlines
⑦**Sterling Airlines – Flyway Air – Tora Airways – Devine Air**

The Transecutive Club

会員証保有者：Toshiki Fujisawa
会員番号：7348892

このカードは加盟航空会社の認められた利用客に、世界のどの空港の Transecutive Club のラウンジにも入る権利を与えるものである。

加盟航空会社
Sterling Airlines、Flyway Air、Tora Airways、Devine Air

選択肢と訳

80.
Why did Mr. Singh write the e-mail?（Singh さんはなぜ E メールを書いたのですか？）
(A) To explain the cause of an error（間違いの理由を説明するため）
(B) To request assistance with a problem（問題について助けを求めるため）
(C) To offer a customer compensation（顧客に埋め合わせを申し出るため）
(D) To recommend an airline to an employee（航空会社を同僚に薦めるため）

解説

正解：(C)

メールの差出人である Singh 氏は、Fujisawa 氏に対し、変更を承諾してくれたことへの感謝の意を第 1 段落で述べている。その後、①「お客さまが受け取られた補償は不十分だったという判断に至った」と述べ、②「1 年間の無料会員権を提供する」と伝えている。よって、このメールの目的は、顧客に感謝の気持ちを伝えると同時に、(C)「埋め合わせを申し出るため」だと判断することができる。

81.
How can Mr. Fujisawa obtain a membership card?
（Fujisawa さんはどうすれば会員証を入手することができますか？）
(A) By visiting an airline office（航空会社のオフィスを訪ねる）
(B) By filling out an online form（オンラインのフォームに記入する）
(C) By calling a company representative（企業の担当者に電話をする）
(D) By reserving hotel accommodation（ホテル宿泊の予約をする）

正解：(B)
メールの第2段落と第3段落で、Transecutive Club の会員証を持っていることで受けられるサービスが述べられている。第4段落⑤で「このオファーを利用するには、ウェブサイトで個人情報とクーポンのコードを入力する必要がある」と説明されている。つまり、会員証を入手するには、まず Transecutive Club に登録する必要があり、そのためにはオンラインのフォームに記入する必要がある。よって、(B) が正解だ。

82.
What is NOT a benefit of the Transecutive Club?
（Transecutive Club のメリットではないのはどれですか？）
(A) Priority boarding of flights（優先搭乗）
(B) Access to luxury facilities（豪華な施設を利用する権利）
(C) Free hotel transfers（ホテル移動）
(D) Discounts on airline tickets（航空券の割引）

正解：(D)
メールの③に「豪華な空港ラウンジを利用できる」とあるので、(B) に関する記述はある。④の「Transecutive Hotel への無料シャトルバス」は (C) に該当する。2つ目の文書のウェブページにも Transecutive Club の特典が書かれている。⑥に「優先搭乗」とあるので、(A) の内容もある。よって、記述のない (D)「航空券の割引」が正解。

83.
On the Web page, the word "sign" in paragraph 1, line 1, is closest in meaning to（ウェブページの第1段落・1行目の "sign" に最も意味が近いのは）
(A) notice（案内）
(B) warning（警告）
(C) symbol（象徴）
(D) prediction（予言）

正解：(C)
本文における sign の意味に最も近い語を問う同義語問題。sign の後に of success（成功の〜）が続いているので、この sign は「印」を意味している。選択肢の中で最も近い意味を持つのは、「象徴」を意味する (C) の symbol だ。同義語問題を解く際には、問われている語句がある位置に選択肢の語句を1つ1つ当てはめて考える。文意がほぼ変わらない選択肢が正解だ。

84.
What is indicated about Sterling Airlines?（Sterling Airlines について、何が示されていますか？）
(A) It is based in Europe.（Europeに拠点を置いている）
(B) It rewards frequent fliers.（頻繁に飛行機に乗る人に見返りを与える）
(C) It is a domestic airline.（国内線である）
(D) It specializes in business travel.（出張に特化している）

正解：(A)
カードの⑦に Transecutive Club に加盟している航空会社が載っている。設問の Sterling Airlines と Singh 氏の所属する Devine Air もあるため、両社は提携関係にあると言える。メールの③で、Singh 氏は「Europeに拠点を置くわれわれの提携航空会社」と書いている。その提携航空会社の中に Sterling Airlines も含まれているので、Sterling Airlinesは (A)「Europeに拠点を置いている」と判断できる。

□**reward**：〜に見返りを与える、〜に報酬を与える
□**frequent flyer**：頻繁に飛行機に乗る人

Questions 85-89 refer to the following e-mail, online review section, and Web page.
(問題85-89は次のEメール、オンラインのレビュー欄、ウェブページに関するものです)

> 文書1「E メール」と訳

To:	Red Stoneway <rstoneway@stoneapps.com>
From:	Megan Korbut <mkorbut@apolonia.com>
Subject:	Runtag
Date:	August 9

Dear Mr. Stoneway,

①I am pleased to announce that the software application you submitted to Apolonia for evaluation has been approved. ②We would like to start offering Runtag among the thousands of other software titles we have in our online store. You may decide to make it available for free or charge customers who purchase a copy of the application. ③The free version can only generate revenue through advertising, which will appear while people use the application. All software authors who sell through Apolonia are required to pay 20 percent of their sales revenue ④or 10 percent of their advertising revenue. This is not open for negotiation.

We have created a user account for you so that you can upload the software application to the store. The account page offers many functions to publishers such ⑤as uploading software updates, ⑥providing customer support, and ⑦providing detailed descriptions of your products. Please use the following link to access your account. http://www.apolonia.com/store/stoneapps. You must upload the software to the store by September 9 or you will be required to resubmit it for evaluation.

Sincerely,

Megan Korbut
⑧Apolonia – Sales Department

宛先：Red Stoneway <rstoneway@stoneapps.com>
送信者：Megan Korbut <mkorbut@apolonia.com>
件名：Runtag
日付：8月9日

Stoneway 様

あなたが Apolonia に審査のために提出したソフトウエア・アプリケーションが承認されたことをお知らせします。弊社オンラインストアの数千タイトルのソフトと一緒に、Runtag の提供を開始したいと思います。無料で使えるようにするのか、アプリを購入する顧客からお金をとるのかを決めてください。無料版は、人々がそのアプリケーションを使う間に表示される広告を通じてしか収益を挙げることができません。Apolonia を通じて販売する全てのソフトの作者には、売上収入の20パーセント、または広告収入の10パーセントを支払うことが求められています。

ソフトウエア・アプリケーションをストアにアップロードできるよう、あなたのアカウントを作成しました。アカウントのページでは、ソフト更新情報のアップロード、顧客サポートの提供、製品の詳細な説明の提供といったたくさんの機能を発行者のために用意しています。あなたのアカウントにアクセスするには、次のリンクを利用してください。http://www.apolonia.com/store/stoneapps ソフトウエアは9月9日までにストアにアップロードしなくてはなりません。そうでなければ、審査に再提出することが必要となります。

敬具

Megan Korbut
Apolonia　販売部

文書２「オンラインのレビュー欄」と訳

Reviews of RUNTAG by Stoneapps

⑨**Reviewer: Candy Simms** (Verified User) ★★★☆☆ (3 stars)
I have been using Runtag for a few months now and I am satisfied with it. ⑩<u>I chose this application because I am a long-time user of Stoneapps' bargain hunting software, which is their most popular product.</u> The only shortcoming of the application is that there are still not enough other users. I think more and more people will start using this in future and we should be able to enjoy comparing our fitness statistics with other users'.

Reviewer: Gahl Saag (Verified User) ★★☆☆☆ (2 stars)
I tested this for a month, but decided to go back to the application I had been using before. ⑪<u>I might try it again in a few months to see if they've added the features I need.</u>

Stoneapps 社 RUNTAG のレビュー

投稿者：Candy Simms（認証済みユーザー）★★★☆☆（星３つ）
Runtag を使って数カ月になりますが、満足しています。私がこのアプリを選んだのは、私が長年、Stoneapps 社の最大の人気製品である、特売品探しソフトウエアのユーザーだからです。このアプリの唯一の欠点は、まだ他のユーザーが十分にいないことです。将来的には、もっと多くの人がこれを使い始めて、自分のフィットネスの数値と他のユーザーの数値との比較を楽しめるようになるでしょう。

投稿者：Gahl Saag（認証済みユーザー）★★☆☆☆（星２つ）
１カ月間試しましたが、以前使っていたアプリに戻ることにしました。私が必要とする機能を追加したかどうかを確かめるため、数カ月後にもう一度試すかもしれません。

☐**verified**：証明された、認証された　☐**bargain hunting**：特売品探し、安値買い　☐**shortcoming**：欠点、至らない点
☐**statistic**：統計値　☐**feature**：特徴、機能

文書3「ウェブページ」と訳

http://www.apolonia.com/store/stoneapps/statement

Stoneapps' Revenue and Commission Statement for December

	Total Downloads	Total Revenue	Commission Rate	Subtotal
⑫LowPro	321	$3,400	10%	$340
Photogenius	71	$1,065	20%	$213
Traffic Hopper	210	$1,890	20%	$378
Coolways	0	$0	10%	$0
⑬Runtag	190	$2,300	10%	$230
TOTAL		$8,655		$1,161
Total payable to Stoneapps (Total revenue minus commission payable)				$7,494

The total payable amount will be deposited into the stipulated bank account by January 15.

---

http://www.apolonia.com/store/stoneapps/statement

Stoneapps 社12月の収益・手数料明細

	総ダウンロード数	総収益	手数料率	小計
LowPro	321	3,400ドル	10パーセント	340ドル
Photogenius	71	1,065ドル	20パーセント	213ドル
Traffic Hopper	210	1,890ドル	20パーセント	378ドル
Coolways	0	0ドル	10パーセント	0ドル
Runtag	190	2,300ドル	10パーセント	230ドル
合計		8,655ドル		1,161ドル
Stoneappsへの合計未払い金（総収益－未払い手数料）				7,494ドル

合計未払い金の金額が1月15日までに規定の銀行口座へ入金されます。

☐**commission**：手数料　☐**statement**：明細書　☐**subtotal**：小計　☐**payable**：未払い金　☐**commission payable**：未払い手数料　☐**be deposited**：入金される　☐**stipulated**：規定の

選択肢と訳

85.
What kind of company is Apolonia?（Apolonia はどんな種類の企業ですか？）
(A) An online store（オンラインストア）
(B) An advertising agency（広告代理店）
(C) A software developer（ソフトウエア開発会社）
(D) A consulting company（コンサルティング会社）

□ **financial analyst**：金融アナリスト、証券アナリスト

86.
What function is NOT available on the Web site?（ウェブサイトで利用できないのはどの機能ですか？）
(A) Uploading software updates（ソフトウエア更新情報をアップロードすること）
(B) Recruiting temporary staff（臨時スタッフを募集すること）
(C) Providing customer support（顧客サポートを提供すること）
(D) Publishing product descriptions（製品の詳細を公開すること）

87.
Which Stoneapp product has Ms. Simms purchased in the past?（Simms さんは過去にどの Stoneapp 社の製品を購入していますか？）
(A) LowPro
(B) Photogenius
(C) Traffic Hopper
(D) Coolways

88.
In the online review section, the word "features" in paragraph 2, line 2, is closest in meaning to（オンラインのレビュー欄の第2段落・2行目の "features" に意味が最も近いのは）
(A) articles（記事）
(B) capabilities（機能）
(C) conclusions（結論）
(D) distributions（分配）

89.
What is indicated about Runtag?（Runtag について何が示されていますか？）
(A) It is Stoneapps' first release.（Stoneapps 社の初めての商品である）
(B) It comes in two versions.（2バージョンある）
(C) It can be downloaded for free.（無料でダウンロードできる）
(D) It will be removed from sale.（販売を取りやめられる）

解説

正解：(A)
Apolonia は Korbut 氏のメールアドレスと最下部⑧にあるので、Korbut 氏が所属する企業であることが分かる。その Korbut 氏がメールの②で「弊社のオンラインストア」と述べていることから、Apolonia は、(A)「オンラインストア」だと判断できる。販売するソフトウエアを採用する旨が①と②で述べられているので、ソフトウエアを開発する側である (C) は不適切。広告の話は③にあるが、Apolonia はソフトウエアの販売サイトであり、(B)「広告代理店」ではない。

正解：(B)
メールの第2段落にアカウントページで利用できる機能が述べられている。1つ目の⑤「ソフト更新のアップロード」は (A) に該当する。2つ目の⑥「顧客サポートの提供」は (C) と合致する。3つ目の⑦「製品の詳細な説明の提供」という記述は (D) に相当する。よって、記述のない (B)「臨時スタッフを募集すること」が正解。

正解：(A)
設問の Simms 氏はオンラインレビューを書いた人物(⑨)。彼女は Runtag を選んだ理由を、⑩「Stoneapps 社最大の人気商品である、特売品探しソフトウエアのユーザーだから」だと述べている。3つ目の文書にある表の⑫から、ダウンロード数も収益も LowPro が最大だと分かる。よって、彼女が購入したことがある製品は (A) である。

正解：(B)
レビュー投稿者は、⑪で「彼らが私の必要とする～を追加したかどうかを確かめるため、数カ月後にもう一度試すかもしれない」と述べている。試すかもしれないのは Runtag（アプリケーション）のことなので、追加されるものとして「～」に入れて文意が通る選択肢は (B)「機能」だ。名詞 feature には、「特集記事」という意味もあるので、ここでは不正解だが、文脈によっては (A) も正解になり得る。ところで英語の paragraph は「文の集まり」なので、「見出し」は含まれない。ここでは、投稿者名や星印がある行を無視するので、features は2行目だ。

正解：(C)
ウェブページの⑬から、Runtag は10パーセントの手数料を払っていることが分かる。メールの③に「無料版は広告を通じて収益を挙げる」とあり、④「広告収入の10パーセントを支払う」と書かれている。これらの情報から、10パーセントの手数料を支払っているRuntagは、広告で収入を挙げる無料版の製品だと分かる。よって、この内容を「無料でダウンロードできる」と表した(C)が正解。

TOEIC® テスト 新形式問題やり込みドリル 解答用紙 [リスニング]

※解答用紙は使用前に複数コピーを取っておくことをお勧めします（原寸B5サイズ）

Part 3 ①

正解： 問／36問

NO.	ANSWER	NO.	ANSWER
1	Ⓐ Ⓑ Ⓒ Ⓓ	11	Ⓐ Ⓑ Ⓒ Ⓓ
2	Ⓐ Ⓑ Ⓒ Ⓓ	12	Ⓐ Ⓑ Ⓒ Ⓓ
3	Ⓐ Ⓑ Ⓒ Ⓓ	13	Ⓐ Ⓑ Ⓒ Ⓓ
4	Ⓐ Ⓑ Ⓒ Ⓓ	14	Ⓐ Ⓑ Ⓒ Ⓓ
5	Ⓐ Ⓑ Ⓒ Ⓓ	15	Ⓐ Ⓑ Ⓒ Ⓓ
6	Ⓐ Ⓑ Ⓒ Ⓓ	16	Ⓐ Ⓑ Ⓒ Ⓓ
7	Ⓐ Ⓑ Ⓒ Ⓓ	17	Ⓐ Ⓑ Ⓒ Ⓓ
8	Ⓐ Ⓑ Ⓒ Ⓓ	18	Ⓐ Ⓑ Ⓒ Ⓓ
9	Ⓐ Ⓑ Ⓒ Ⓓ	19	Ⓐ Ⓑ Ⓒ Ⓓ
10	Ⓐ Ⓑ Ⓒ Ⓓ	20	Ⓐ Ⓑ Ⓒ Ⓓ

NO.	ANSWER	NO.	ANSWER
21	Ⓐ Ⓑ Ⓒ Ⓓ	31	Ⓐ Ⓑ Ⓒ Ⓓ
22	Ⓐ Ⓑ Ⓒ Ⓓ	32	Ⓐ Ⓑ Ⓒ Ⓓ
23	Ⓐ Ⓑ Ⓒ Ⓓ	33	Ⓐ Ⓑ Ⓒ Ⓓ
24	Ⓐ Ⓑ Ⓒ Ⓓ	34	Ⓐ Ⓑ Ⓒ Ⓓ
25	Ⓐ Ⓑ Ⓒ Ⓓ	35	Ⓐ Ⓑ Ⓒ Ⓓ
26	Ⓐ Ⓑ Ⓒ Ⓓ	36	Ⓐ Ⓑ Ⓒ Ⓓ
27	Ⓐ Ⓑ Ⓒ Ⓓ	37	Ⓐ Ⓑ Ⓒ Ⓓ
28	Ⓐ Ⓑ Ⓒ Ⓓ	38	Ⓐ Ⓑ Ⓒ Ⓓ
29	Ⓐ Ⓑ Ⓒ Ⓓ	39	Ⓐ Ⓑ Ⓒ Ⓓ
30	Ⓐ Ⓑ Ⓒ Ⓓ	40	Ⓐ Ⓑ Ⓒ Ⓓ

Part 3 ②

正解： 問／24問

NO.	ANSWER
41	Ⓐ Ⓑ Ⓒ Ⓓ
42	Ⓐ Ⓑ Ⓒ Ⓓ
43	Ⓐ Ⓑ Ⓒ Ⓓ
44	Ⓐ Ⓑ Ⓒ Ⓓ
45	Ⓐ Ⓑ Ⓒ Ⓓ
46	Ⓐ Ⓑ Ⓒ Ⓓ
47	Ⓐ Ⓑ Ⓒ Ⓓ
48	Ⓐ Ⓑ Ⓒ Ⓓ
49	Ⓐ Ⓑ Ⓒ Ⓓ
50	Ⓐ Ⓑ Ⓒ Ⓓ

NO.	ANSWER
51	Ⓐ Ⓑ Ⓒ Ⓓ
52	Ⓐ Ⓑ Ⓒ Ⓓ
53	Ⓐ Ⓑ Ⓒ Ⓓ
54	Ⓐ Ⓑ Ⓒ Ⓓ
55	Ⓐ Ⓑ Ⓒ Ⓓ
56	Ⓐ Ⓑ Ⓒ Ⓓ
57	Ⓐ Ⓑ Ⓒ Ⓓ
58	Ⓐ Ⓑ Ⓒ Ⓓ
59	Ⓐ Ⓑ Ⓒ Ⓓ
60	Ⓐ Ⓑ Ⓒ Ⓓ

LISTENING SECTION

Part 3 ③

正解： 問／30問

NO.	ANSWER	NO.	ANSWER
61	Ⓐ Ⓑ Ⓒ Ⓓ	71	Ⓐ Ⓑ Ⓒ Ⓓ
62	Ⓐ Ⓑ Ⓒ Ⓓ	72	Ⓐ Ⓑ Ⓒ Ⓓ
63	Ⓐ Ⓑ Ⓒ Ⓓ	73	Ⓐ Ⓑ Ⓒ Ⓓ
64	Ⓐ Ⓑ Ⓒ Ⓓ	74	Ⓐ Ⓑ Ⓒ Ⓓ
65	Ⓐ Ⓑ Ⓒ Ⓓ	75	Ⓐ Ⓑ Ⓒ Ⓓ
66	Ⓐ Ⓑ Ⓒ Ⓓ	76	Ⓐ Ⓑ Ⓒ Ⓓ
67	Ⓐ Ⓑ Ⓒ Ⓓ	77	Ⓐ Ⓑ Ⓒ Ⓓ
68	Ⓐ Ⓑ Ⓒ Ⓓ	78	Ⓐ Ⓑ Ⓒ Ⓓ
69	Ⓐ Ⓑ Ⓒ Ⓓ	79	Ⓐ Ⓑ Ⓒ Ⓓ
70	Ⓐ Ⓑ Ⓒ Ⓓ	80	Ⓐ Ⓑ Ⓒ Ⓓ

NO.	ANSWER
81	Ⓐ Ⓑ Ⓒ Ⓓ
82	Ⓐ Ⓑ Ⓒ Ⓓ
83	Ⓐ Ⓑ Ⓒ Ⓓ
84	Ⓐ Ⓑ Ⓒ Ⓓ
85	Ⓐ Ⓑ Ⓒ Ⓓ
86	Ⓐ Ⓑ Ⓒ Ⓓ
87	Ⓐ Ⓑ Ⓒ Ⓓ
88	Ⓐ Ⓑ Ⓒ Ⓓ
89	Ⓐ Ⓑ Ⓒ Ⓓ
90	Ⓐ Ⓑ Ⓒ Ⓓ

Part 4

正解： 問／30問

NO.	ANSWER
1	Ⓐ Ⓑ Ⓒ Ⓓ
2	Ⓐ Ⓑ Ⓒ Ⓓ
3	Ⓐ Ⓑ Ⓒ Ⓓ
4	Ⓐ Ⓑ Ⓒ Ⓓ
5	Ⓐ Ⓑ Ⓒ Ⓓ
6	Ⓐ Ⓑ Ⓒ Ⓓ
7	Ⓐ Ⓑ Ⓒ Ⓓ
8	Ⓐ Ⓑ Ⓒ Ⓓ
9	Ⓐ Ⓑ Ⓒ Ⓓ
10	Ⓐ Ⓑ Ⓒ Ⓓ

NO.	ANSWER
11	Ⓐ Ⓑ Ⓒ Ⓓ
12	Ⓐ Ⓑ Ⓒ Ⓓ
13	Ⓐ Ⓑ Ⓒ Ⓓ
14	Ⓐ Ⓑ Ⓒ Ⓓ
15	Ⓐ Ⓑ Ⓒ Ⓓ
16	Ⓐ Ⓑ Ⓒ Ⓓ
17	Ⓐ Ⓑ Ⓒ Ⓓ
18	Ⓐ Ⓑ Ⓒ Ⓓ
19	Ⓐ Ⓑ Ⓒ Ⓓ
20	Ⓐ Ⓑ Ⓒ Ⓓ

NO.	ANSWER
21	Ⓐ Ⓑ Ⓒ Ⓓ
22	Ⓐ Ⓑ Ⓒ Ⓓ
23	Ⓐ Ⓑ Ⓒ Ⓓ
24	Ⓐ Ⓑ Ⓒ Ⓓ
25	Ⓐ Ⓑ Ⓒ Ⓓ
26	Ⓐ Ⓑ Ⓒ Ⓓ
27	Ⓐ Ⓑ Ⓒ Ⓓ
28	Ⓐ Ⓑ Ⓒ Ⓓ
29	Ⓐ Ⓑ Ⓒ Ⓓ
30	Ⓐ Ⓑ Ⓒ Ⓓ

LISTENING SECTION

TOEIC® テスト 新形式問題やり込みドリル 解答用紙 [リーディング]

READING SECTION

Part 6 正解： 問／40問

NO.	ANSWER
1	A B C D
2	A B C D
3	A B C D
4	A B C D
5	A B C D
6	A B C D
7	A B C D
8	A B C D
9	A B C D
10	A B C D
11	A B C D
12	A B C D
13	A B C D
14	A B C D
15	A B C D
16	A B C D
17	A B C D
18	A B C D
19	A B C D
20	A B C D
21	A B C D
22	A B C D
23	A B C D
24	A B C D
25	A B C D
26	A B C D
27	A B C D
28	A B C D
29	A B C D
30	A B C D
31	A B C D
32	A B C D
33	A B C D
34	A B C D
35	A B C D
36	A B C D
37	A B C D
38	A B C D
39	A B C D
40	A B C D

Part 7 ① 正解： 問／20問

NO.	ANSWER
1	A B C D
2	A B C D
3	A B C D
4	A B C D
5	A B C D
6	A B C D
7	A B C D
8	A B C D
9	A B C D
10	A B C D
11	A B C D
12	A B C D
13	A B C D
14	A B C D
15	A B C D
16	A B C D
17	A B C D
18	A B C D
19	A B C D
20	A B C D

Part 7 ②

NO.	ANSWER
21	A B C D
22	A B C D
23	A B C D
24	A B C D
25	A B C D
26	A B C D
27	A B C D
28	A B C D
29	A B C D
30	A B C D

READING SECTION

(Part 7 ②) 正解： 問／24問

NO.	ANSWER
31	A B C D
32	A B C D
33	A B C D
34	A B C D
35	A B C D
36	A B C D
37	A B C D
38	A B C D
39	A B C D
40	A B C D
41	A B C D
42	A B C D
43	A B C D
44	A B C D
45	A B C D
46	A B C D
47	A B C D
48	A B C D
49	A B C D
50	A B C D

Part 7 ③ 正解： 問／45問

NO.	ANSWER
51	A B C D
52	A B C D
53	A B C D
54	A B C D
55	A B C D
56	A B C D
57	A B C D
58	A B C D
59	A B C D
60	A B C D
61	A B C D
62	A B C D
63	A B C D
64	A B C D
65	A B C D
66	A B C D
67	A B C D
68	A B C D
69	A B C D
70	A B C D
71	A B C D
72	A B C D
73	A B C D
74	A B C D
75	A B C D
76	A B C D
77	A B C D
78	A B C D
79	A B C D
80	A B C D
81	A B C D
82	A B C D
83	A B C D
84	A B C D
85	A B C D
86	A B C D
87	A B C D
88	A B C D
89	A B C D

TOEIC® テスト 新形式問題やり込みドリル

発行日：2016年 9月13日（初版）
　　　　2016年12月20日（第2刷）

著　　　者	ヒロ前田／ロス・タロック
執筆協力	豊馬桃子／玉木史恵
編　　集	英語出版編集部
英文校正	Peter Branscombe
デザイン	茂谷淑恵（朝日メディアインターナショナル株式会社）
イラスト	横須賀麻矢
ナレーション	Josh Keller／Guy Perryman／Sara Greeves／Edith Kayumi／Chris Koprowski／Nadia McKechnie
CD編集・録音	一般財団法人　英語教育協議会（ELEC）
CDプレス	図書印刷株式会社
Ｄ　Ｔ　Ｐ	朝日メディアインターナショナル株式会社
印刷・製本	図書印刷株式会社
発行者	平本照麿
発行所	株式会社アルク 〒102-0073　東京都千代田区九段北4-2-6　市ヶ谷ビル TEL：03-3556-5501　FAX：03-3556-1370 Email：csss@alc.co.jp Website：http://www.alc.co.jp/

落丁本、乱丁本は弊社にてお取り替えいたしております。アルクお客様センター（電話：03-3556-5501　受付時間：平日9時～17時）までご相談ください。
本書の全部または一部の無断転載を禁じます。著作権法上で認められた場合を除いて、本書からのコピーを禁じます。
定価はカバーに表示してあります。

ご購入いただいた書籍の最新サポート情報は、以下の「製品サポート」ページでご提供いたします。
製品サポート：http://www.alc.co.jp/usersupport/

©2016 Hiroyuki Maeda / Ross Tulloch / ALC PRESS INC.
Illustrations ©Maya Yokosuka
PC：7016038
ISBN：978-4-7574-2844-7

地球人ネットワークを創る
アルクのシンボル
「地球人マーク」です。